BEST OF TIMES,
WORST OF TIMES

THE TAUBER INSTITUTE FOR THE STUDY OF EUROPEAN JEWRY SERIES

The Tauber Institute Series is dedicated to publishing compelling and innovative approaches to the study of modern European Jewish history, thought, culture, and society. The series features scholarly works related to the Enlightenment, modern Judaism and the struggle for emancipation, the rise of nationalism and the spread of antisemitism, the Holocaust and its aftermath, as well as the contemporary Jewish experience. The series is published under the auspices of the Tauber Institute for the Study of European Jewry—established by a gift to Brandeis University from Dr. Laszlo N. Tauber—and is supported, in part, by the Tauber Foundation and the Valya and Robert Shapiro Endowment.

For the complete list of books that are available in this series, please see www.upne.com

Eugene M. Avrutin, Valerii Dymshits, Alexander Ivanov, Alexander Lvov, Harriet Murav, and Alla Sokolova, editors *Photographing the Jewish Nation: Pictures from S. An-sky's Ethnographic Expeditions*

Michael Dorland *Cadaverland: Inventing a Pathology of Catastrophe for Holocaust Survival*

Walter Laqueur *Best of Times, Worst of Times: Memoirs of a Political Education*

Berel Lang *Philosophical Witnessing: The Holocaust as Presence*

David N. Myers *Between Jew and Arab: The Lost Voice of Simon Rawidowicz*

Sara Bender *The Jews of Białystock during World War II and the Holocaust*

Nili Scharf Gold *Yehuda Amichai: The Making of Israel's National Poet*

Hans Jonas *Memoirs*

Itamar Rabinovich and Jehuda Reinharz, editors *Israel in the Middle East: Documents and Readings on Society, Politics, and Foreign Relations, Pre-1948 to the Present*

Christian Wiese *The Life and Thought of Hans Jonas: Jewish Dimensions*

Eugene R. Sheppard *Leo Strauss and the Politics of Exile: The Making of a Political Philosopher*

Samuel Moyn *A Holocaust Controversy: The Treblinka Affair in Postwar France*

Margalit Shilo *Princess or Prisoner? Jewish Women in Jerusalem, 1840–1914*

Haim Be'er *Feathers*

Immanuel Etkes *The Besht: Magician, Mystic, and Leader*

Avraham Grossman *Pious and Rebellious: Jewish Women in Medieval Europe*

Ivan Davidson Kalmar and Derek J. Penslar, editors *Orientalism and the Jews*

Iris Parush *Reading Jewish Women: Marginality and Modernization in Nineteenth-Century Eastern European Jewish Society*

Thomas C. Hubka *Resplendent Synagogue: Architecture and Worship in an Eighteenth-Century Polish Community*

BEST OF TIMES, WORST OF TIMES

Memoirs of a Political Education

WALTER LAQUEUR

BRANDEIS UNIVERSITY PRESS
Waltham, Massachusetts

Published by
University Press of New England
Hanover and London

Brandeis University Press
Published by University Press of New England,
One Court Street, Lebanon, NH 03766
www.upne.com

Printed in U.S.A.
5 4 3 2 1

Library of Congress Cataloging-in-Publication Data

Laqueur, Walter, 1921–
Best of times, worst of times : memoirs of a political education / Walter Laqueur.
p. cm. — (The Tauber Institute for the Study of European Jewry series)
ISBN 978-1-58465-798-9 (cloth : alk. paper)
1. Laqueur, Walter, 1921– 2. Laqueur, Walter, 1921—Political and social views. 3. Historians—United States—Biography. I. Title.
D15.L35.A3 2009
973.9092—dc22
[B] 2009015174

University Press of New England is a member of the Green Press Initiative. The paper used in this book meets their minimum requirement for recycled paper.

To the memory of my friend Ruprecht Schulte (1920–2008)

and his father Eduard Schulte (1891–1966)—the man who broke the silence.

CONTENTS

PREFACE

When my grandchildren were growing up I decided to write an autobiography, not because of their insatiable curiosity as far as my early life was concerned; I love them dearly but their interests are quite different from mine, ranging from the theory of probability to issues of social policy such as the adoption of children. I called my autobiography *Thursday's Child Has Far to Go,* which I thought was fairly original, but later I discovered that there were at least half a dozen other books with the same title, including the autobiography of Eartha Kitt. I described my personal experiences and ended my narrative in the early 1950s, for two reasons. Many of those whom I would have had to mention writing about the later years were still alive, and I did not want to have to look over my shoulder when writing about them. But more important, I was not at all sure whether my life during the years after, in America and Europe, was sufficiently remarkable or unusual to be of interest to readers. *Thursday's Child* steered clear of my intellectual interests, of politics, of history.

These are the experiences and interests I have tried to recount in the present volume. I was lucky to have survived, whereas most of those closest to me did not. I have not always fully appreciated my luck, hence the question that often preoccupied me and that I try to answer in the beginning of this book—which historical period, which country, which culture, which profession would have been preferable had there been a choice. There was too much politics, too much history in my time, too little culture, too little entertainment, too little *joie de vivre.* If I could start all over again, I probably would not be dealing with history and politics.

I have been a generalist in an age of specialization, and I deal with a great many topics in this book, beginning with my thoughts on Nazism based (how could it be different) on my own experience growing up and attending school in Nazi Germany. This book is both personal and impersonal; it is based on personal experience but is essentially about what I have learned over the years. However, I also deal with issues for which I did not always find satisfactory answers and explanations—the Soviet Union and the Cold War, the fate of Europe in the twentieth and twenty-first centuries, the Middle East, Israel and Zionism, and the terrorist conundrum and the question of intelligence: Why is it so difficult to anticipate political (and economic) developments even to a modest degree? Writing this book gave me a chance to look back and to reexamine my thoughts of yesteryear in the light of subsequent events and the views of others.

This is not a book of ambitious theoretical breakthroughs or predictions. I have encountered too many of them in my lifetime not to have developed a great deal of skepticism in this respect. It is an attempt to summarize certain experiences gained, certain mistakes made, certain wrong tracks past and present that might have been evaded, certain issues that remain.

The present book was originally conceived as a series of interviews or conversations; I am grateful to Barry Rubin for his help concerning earlier versions of Chapters 2, 3, and 6. And I would like to express deep gratitude to Sylvia Fuks Fried and Ann Hofstra Grogg for their editorial help.

Walter Laqueur
Washington, D.C., 2008

CHAPTER 1

A Surfeit of Politics

or, Why I Would Have Preferred the Nineteenth Century

When Marcel Proust was a boy of thirteen, he was given a questionnaire to fill out. The questions concerned his favorite heroes in literature and real life, his favorite color, his favorite composer, and also some very personal questions, such as, What is your current mood? and, On what occasions do you lie?

This kind of parlor game has been repeated many times since. Years ago I was given such a questionnaire for publication, and I provided answers with some reluctance, for I wondered how interesting these personal details would be to others and how genuine and spontaneous my answers could possibly be, with someone looking over my shoulder. One question asked if writing was my favorite occupation. My first article was published in 1942, my first book in 1947 (I believe it was 1947; I do not now think highly of it and have been reluctant to check it). But writing has certainly not been my favorite occupation at all times. My heroes in history and literature have changed over the years, and even my favorite color has changed from blue to red during the last decade.

The Best of Times

On another occasion I was asked in what period I would have liked to live, if I could have chosen. The period into which I was born, Europe after World War I, was not the best of places. The period after World War II was preferable but in retrospect not ideal either, and I am reluctant to name a distant age for lack of empathy. To have been a contemporary of Pericles or Socrates no doubt has great appeal, provided one did not belong to the *hoi polloi*, the masses, the underclass. But I lack imagination: What would life have been like without so many of the amenities of modern life we now take for granted? It would probably have been short. Pericles and the philosophers such as Socrates, Plato, and Aristotle did live to a ripe old age, but most did not. Alexander the Great was thirty-three years old when he died; today this would be considered too young to be a colonel. Hannibal was twenty-six when he became commander in chief of the army of Carthage.

To be a citizen of Rome must have been a source of much pride—*Civis Romanus sum*—but it was an age of virtue (in theory at least, not always in practice), not of great sweetness, let alone refinement. The transition from the traditional virtues praised by Cato and others to the luxury and decadence of later years was too sudden and too extreme, and virtue, as John Adams once said, is not always amiable. The *saeculum* of Emperor Augustus was thought by most contemporaries to be a Golden Age, but Edward Gibbon had harsh words about Roman decadence in later years. Most have considered it as the main cause of the decline and fall, together with territorial overextension (parallels with America in our time are drawn, and often overdrawn). Yet the Eastern Roman Empire, with all its negative features, lasted for another thousand years after the so-called fall of Rome.

I grew up with romantic fairy tales, full of old castles, fortresses with battlements and drawbridges, young knights and princesses, minnesingers, nightingales and blue flowers, witches and charcoal burners, enchanted evenings in whispering forests, a silvery moon and great solitude. But the Middle Ages were not the best of times to be alive, as always with some notable exceptions such as Spain before the Reconquista or Baghdad or Sicily or Italy during the Renaissance. What Edmund Burke wrote about the unbought grace of life and the age of chivalry under the old regime in France was no doubt correct, but one had to belong to a very small class to enjoy it.

This takes us to the nineteenth century, and with it the appeal is growing. Napoleon III was far from an ideal ruler, and there was of course censorship with Victor Hugo exiled to Guernsey. The years after the French defeat 1870–71 were years of depression, Paul Verlaine's "Je suis l'Empire à la fín de la décadence." But it was also the Paris of the cafés and concerts, a city of great joy of life. Entertainment was by no means the privilege of the rich. There were 150 dancing halls in the working-class quarters of Paris in 1880, and their number was steadily growing; by the end of the century, according to the newspapers, there was a *bal musette* at about every second street corner. In the 1880s about half a million Parisians went to the theater each week. This was the Paris of Baron Georges-Eugène Haussmann, of Camille Pissarro's street scenes of Paris or the parks and fields, of small places like Louveciennes, of municipal gardens and roads in winter, of Claude Monet's Bridge at Argenteuil, which he painted many times. Even London, interesting, impressive, but not the most beautiful of cities, appears almost attractive if we look at Sydenham High Street as painted by Pissarro during his enforced stay in London, after the Paris Commune.

Contemporaries had a chance to visit the first exhibition of the impressionists in Paris, which took place in 1874 in the studio of a photographer. This was also the year of *Anna Karenina* and in which the final story of Ivan Turgenev's *Sport-*

man's Sketches was published. It was the year of Modest Mussorgsky's *Pictures at an Exhibition* and of Pyotr Ilich Tchaikovsky's First Piano Concerto as well as Johannes Brahms's Lieder. It was the year of *Far from the Madding Crowd* and of *Middlemarch.* It was just a year since *Around the World in Eighty Days* had been the bestseller. In 1874 *Die Fledermaus,* the greatest of all operettas, was first performed in Vienna. It would be difficult to think of an equally productive twelve months in the following century.

The general mood in the United States, in Germany, and even in Britain was one of optimism, of enormous progress in almost every respect; there had been no major war for a very long time. In France, too, the mood gradually improved, and after the turn of the century Charles Péguy, not a wild optimist, wrote that the world (and France) had changed less since Jesus Christ than during the last thirty years. Life had become easier; while wages and salaries remained more or less constant, prices had fallen in France by more than a third between 1873 and the early 1890s, and there was a similar trend in the other Europeans countries.

True, Cardinal Segni, the future pope Innocent III, had made it known in *De contemptu mundi* that man is born for work, for sorrow, for fear, and for death. But by the nineteenth century the temptations of the flesh were stronger. As the twentieth century was rung in, the *New York Times,* in a fifteen-part editorial, described the nineteenth century as a glorious century of marvels, the flower of all centuries. Liberal institutions flourished everywhere, scientific progress had been enormous, and there was an unprecedented revolution in medicine. Countless great inventions had been brought forth by Thomas Edison. The theme was taken up by a writer in the *Washington Post* on the same occasion. What was left to discover? During the century, some 700,000 inventions had been patented in the United States alone. In the field of electricity the possibilities for the future were beyond human comprehension. Every department of scientific and intellectual activity had gone far beyond the wildest dreams of the workers and the thinkers of 1800. In all things contributing to human comfort, happiness, and convenience, progress had achieved what would have been unimaginable a century before. Scientific invention had obliterated the limitations of time and space.

Expectations in Paris were not less. "Le dix-neuvième siècle est grand, mais le vingtième sera heureux," according to a prediction by Victor Hugo. And perhaps most surprising was a poem by Algernon Charles Swinburne, the grandfather of the English decadents, the admirer of Charles Baudelaire, entitled "A New Century":

> An age too great for thought of ours to scan
> A wave upon the sleepless sea of time. . . .
> We cry across the veering gale

> Farewell—and midnight answers us Farewell
> Hail—and the heaven of the morning answers Hail.

True, after the turn of the century there was a widespread feeling among artists and poets (more in Germany and Russia, less in France and Britain) that something horrible was about to happen, but this thought was limited to very small groups of people who, albeit wholly apolitical, were correctly reading the signs of the times. Still, the great majority was enjoying itself, dancing in the streets of Paris on July 14, and even the Social Democrats of Berlin and Vienna, marching in their traditional May Day parades, were convinced that the good days were still ahead.

Leon Trotsky wrote that anyone desiring a quiet life did badly to be born in the twentieth century. But the issue is not only that of a quiet life: life in one of the major capitals of Europe in the second half of the nineteenth century seems to have been preferable to present-day life in many other respects, despite the absence of modern dentistry, not to mention all the other technical advances and modern amenities. Mass media predictions in the year 2000 for the twenty-first century were notably less optimistic than a hundred years earlier.

Politics and the Writing of Contemporary History

There is another question that might have been asked in the questionnaire: What profession would you have chosen if the choice had been wide open? What, in an ideal world, would have given you greatest satisfaction? I have been writing mainly on history and politics, and the choice was in some ways obvious for, like most of my contemporaries, I was at the mercy of political forces that we could not possibly influence and the question why this was the case constantly obtruded itself. But I can think of other fields of human endeavor that would have brought greater satisfaction. My generation suffered from a surfeit of politics, and, come to think of it, there was also too much history, not enough culture, not enough entertainment, not enough enjoyment.

I do not believe, as Gibbon wrote, that history is "little more than the register of the crimes, follies, and misfortunes of mankind." But politics and political history, with all their fascinations, deal less with human achievement than human error and failure, perhaps inevitably so in view of the imperfection of the human condition. A wise old man told me many years ago that he looks in the daily newspaper first at the sports pages, which, in contrast, to the rest of the paper, deal principally with human achievements.

It is my impression that the present time is not the most glorious in history. This, like most generalizations, ought to be immediately modified: great works are produced at almost any time, a genius may appear anywhere at almost any time, and while there is much suffering there is also much satisfaction. But there is much less optimism now than a hundred years ago inasmuch as the future is concerned, and with good reason.

Together with my friend, the late George Mosse, I founded the *Journal of Contemporary History* in 1966. His family had owned one of the leading German newspaper empires; he was a very wealthy man, especially during the later part of his life following the restitution of property, but I have not known any person to whom material things meant so little. He owned two suits, and there were occasions when he phoned me that he could not go out because both needed repair. He had studied in Cambridge, where his advisers had told him not to opt for history as a profession, certainly not in Britain. His original field of specialization had been early modern history with special reference to church history; he told me he could celebrate a mass if need be. Later his main interest shifted to nineteenth- and twentieth-century Europe, and fascism in particular.

George was one of the greatest teachers of his generation, very much devoted to his students, and his students were equally devoted to him. He went to many conferences and knew everyone in the field—which I did not. He was as well known in Italy and France as in the United States. In brief, his contribution to the journal was absolutely essential despite the fact that he made his home in Madison, Wisconsin, whereas the journal was published in London—a problem infinitely greater at the time than in our computer days. We did not, of course, always see eye to eye, but our work together over more than thirty years could not have been more harmonious.

Contemporary history meant different things in different countries and still does. In France, for a very long time, it meant everything that happened since Napoleon; in the United States and Russia, since 1917. In most European countries 1918 or 1945 was the starting point; in the Third World it was decolonization. Geoffrey Barraclough, a distinguished British medievalist, wrote a somewhat confused introduction to contemporary history, for he could not make up his mind whether it started in 1890 or 1960.

There had long been considerable resistance against the writing of contemporary history, which was considered just not right for academic study. It was too close to the present, making it difficult if not impossible to write about with the necessary detachment. As George Trevelyan noted, if it is still too early to form a final judgment on the French Revolution, how much more so with regard to more recent events. (And more than a century after Trevelyan's remarks the debate about the French Revolution continues.) Above all, the sources for contemporary history were often not available, and as a classic text of historiography says, "No sources, no history."

Yet many, perhaps most, Greek historians wrote about events that had happened during their own lifetime. Thucydides wrote on the Peloponnesian War; his history ends in its twenty-first year, and the war lasted another six. Xenophon wrote a classic work, *Anabasis,* about a campaign in which he had himself taken part. The same is true with regard to Roman historians, and those who wrote at a later date were not necessarily more reliable. Cassius Dio, for example, maintained that Nero burned Rome, but many modern scholars have their doubts.

Resistance to contemporary history became very much an article of faith for late nineteenth-century academics, as I noted in my preface to the first issue of the *Journal of Contemporary History*. The leading German periodical, *Historische Zeitschrift,* announced when it was founded in 1859 that it would exclude the discussion of unresolved problems of current politics; *Revue Historique,* founded 1876, likewise said it would avoid contemporary controversies. The *English Historical Review,* founded in 1886, did not until after World War I publish an article on British history after 1852 or European history after 1871, wrote Sir Llewelyn Woodward, a contributor to our first issue.

The absence of archival sources during the first two decades after the Second World War was indeed a major problem for contemporary history, for which the many autobiographical sketches could not compensate. For a long time the Nuremberg documents (evidence prepared for the famous trial) were the main, sometimes the only major, source. But this began to change in the 1960s, and contemporary history became respectable.

We had no problem enlisting leading historians to contribute important and well-written articles to our journal. Among the contributors to the first issues of the journal I find the following: Christopher Andrews, Correlli Douglas Barnett, Anthony Burgess, Gordon Craig, Ralf Dahrendorf, Klaus Epstein, J. H. Hexter, James Joll, David Knowles, Adrian Lyttleton, Wolfgang Mommsen, Maurice Nadeau, René Rémond, Fritz Ringer, Norman Stone, Hugh Thomas, Arnold Toynbee, Leo Valiani, Hugh Seton-Watson, Donald Watt, Eugen Weber, and Theodore Zeldin. It would be difficult to enlist today historians of equal stature, for a variety of reasons; most significant, the number of great historians seems to be not that great in our time.

Why this should be the case is not entirely clear to me. There are fat years and lean years in every discipline. One cannot account for the fact that there were many more major figures in German (and French, British, and Russian) literature during the years before and after World War I than there have been since. Today major historians would be far more likely to write books rather than articles. But it is also true that there was more excitement in the field in the early postwar decades than today and that the field as a whole was more attractive. Such fluctuations happen quite frequently in the field of area studies: after the end of the Cold War interest in Russian affairs greatly declined; for some years there was a great influx into Middle Eastern studies; but today the Chinese field is leading.

In the 1960s there was a feeling that we had not yet fully understood the great issues of the recent past, the mainsprings of fascism and communism, the origins and consequences of the Second World War. Today few historians show much interest in Marxism and its political manifestations, while fascism has been discussed from all possible angles. The postwar developments, important as they are, do not exude the same excitement, but there is no doubt that the movement toward European unification, decolonization, and the Cold War will be subject to new interpretations and various forms of revisionism.

If there have been new impulses from psychohistory to the linguistic turn, from poststructuralism to postcolonialism, they have manifested themselves more in the fields of film, comparative literature, or perhaps anthropology than in the writing of history. This point is interesting: neither historical materialism nor psychohistory has produced truly major works, and the more recent fashions have produced even less. Of course, they have provided many polemics, and whatever was valuable in their insights has become part of the knowledge not only of historians but of educated persons in general. But there is a world of difference between a book, say, sympathetic to the Paris Commune or the exploited and oppressed of this world in general, and a study in the spirit of historical materialism, orthodox or more modern. The only truly Marxist-Leninist works of history were those produced by Mikhail Pokrovsky and his school in the Soviet Union in the 1920s, and even they were discarded for being too primitive. They were replaced by works permeated not by a more sophisticated Marxism but by traditional Russian nationalism, with Dmitri Donskoi, Ivan the Terrible, Peter the Great, and military heroes like Alexander Suvorov and Mikhail Kutuzov. Psychohistory has not progressed beyond some biographical essays and I suspect never will. Those who began their work propagating Marxism and psychohistory (or critical theory trying to combine the two) went on to write not social history but biographies of Adolf Hitler and histories of the Holocaust, excellent works unlikely to be surpassed in the foreseeable future but hardly showing much of their original inspiration.

As for subaltern studies and other offsprings of postmodernism, their impact has been in the field of philosophy and the cinema rather than in the writing of history. With the famous linguistic turn new terms entered the language and became very popular—narrative and meta-narrative, discourse and representation, difference and hyperreality as well as archi-writing and many more. But few if any works of history betray their influence, partly no doubt because there were no historians—with the possible exception of Michel Foucault—among the postmodernists, and their *obiter dicta* about contemporary history and political subjects from the Holocaust to the Ayatollah Ruholla Khomeini's revolution in Iran ranged from the strange to the absurd. Perhaps historians are by nature conservative, averse to newfangled and rapidly passing fads and fashions; perhaps their preoccupation with history has made them skeptical. Perhaps they are too pragmatic. Perhaps they thought the advice given by the spokesmen and women of postcolonial studies as to how to prepare a pudding very useful but they still believed that the proof of the pudding was in the eating, and so they questioned whether any important new insights had come from the camp of the subaltern studies preachers. If postmodernism told them that there was no such thing as wholly objective history, this idea had occurred to some of them before. But it did not necessarily mean that a self-respecting historian could in good conscience give free rein to his predilections and prejudices and still expect to be taken seriously; it did not mean that there was no difference between sense and nonsense.

We have seen in recent decades a surfeit of revisionism: all previous history writing is said to be biased, imperialist, racist, sexist, and these charges are usually made by people whose general educational level and knowledge of history are not very impressive. Perhaps this surfeit was also the result of so many main issues having been discussed for so long that not many stones remained unturned, little was left to be discovered, and history had to be rewritten rather than written. This has been the case, of course, since time immemorial, and up to a point it may be useful to be forced to rethink the received wisdom. Some have advised us to provide not radical revision but a "more nuanced" approach. And it is of course true that in human affairs issues are seldom wholly clear-cut; more often than not they are complicated rather than simple. But there is a limit to nuance beyond which only nuances remain and certainties cease to exist.

The Cold War is one example, the Second World War another. Sometimes the danger stems from being overly influenced by hindsight; at other times there is the inclination to attribute too much to planning and too little to accident, in part because of the conspiracy theory thinking embedded in the new ideology. Thus it has become largely the fashion to argue that Hitler really had lost the war even before he started it, because to confront the whole world was a hopeless enterprise and the resources of the Allies were so much greater than those of Germany. True, it was a gamble, but then Hitler was a gambler and it is perfectly possible that his game may have come off. His major weakness was that he did not know when to stop. If Lord Halifax would have succeeded Neville Chamberlain in early summer of 1940—and there were reasonable chances that he might have replaced him—Britain would have reached an accommodation with the Nazis and Hitler would have been the undisputed master of Europe for many years to come. This position would have given him much time to exploit the resources of the continent and to establish a far more efficient and better equipped war machine. Ian Kershaw recently wrote a book about ten fateful decisions that changed the world in 1940–41; details can be disputed but there is no doubt that these were indeed fateful choices and nothing was predetermined.

It has been argued that Hitler had to attack the Soviet Union in June 1941 in order to forestall a Soviet offensive, but the evidence is wholly unconvincing. Hitler's decision to declare war on the United States in December 1941 has been even more of a mystery. Recently it has been maintained that he had to do so to prevent the United States from emerging within five or ten years as the leading world power, but again the evidence is not convincing. The United States rarely figured in the thoughts of Hitler and his followers (no Nazi leader had ever been to the United States), and if they made a mistake, it was not to take America very seriously—like the German command in World War I. The United States went to war only after having been attacked by Japan: it would probably not have gone to war in Europe but for Hitler's declaration of war. Isolationist feeling was strong, and there would have been strategic opposition against conducting a war on two fronts. If Hitler went to war it was not because he feared an attack from either West or East in the foreseeable future, but because he believed that Germany had to expand, it needed more *Lebensraum* and resources, and he felt that only under his leadership could this happen and that as he grew older there was no time to waste.

There were a number of other turning points in the war on which the outcome depended: had Werner Heisenberg not decided that producing a nuclear bomb was too complicated and had Hitler not reached the conclusion that he did not need this weapon to win the war, who knows what the situation would have been in 1945 given the fact that the Germans had a clear superiority as far as missile technique was concerned. Accident plays an underrated role in history, and the temptation of making a judgment based on hindsight should be restrained.

Some of the revisionist impulse has come from inside the profession, but television documentaries, with their built-in tendency toward exaggeration, have also played a role. To give but one example, following a concentration, for years, on German atrocities in World War II, there seems to have been a feeling that something new was needed, hence the sudden discovery that the Allied occupation of Germany had also been brutal. Others discovered religious fundamentalism, but in order not to appear one-sided they would give equal emphasis to fundamentalism in all religions, even though some were much more fundamentalist than others.

I had some experience editing a journal, having been the founding editor ten years earlier of *Survey*, also in London, and I had excellent help as I undertook to edit the *Journal of Contemporary History*. But there were problems. We faced over the years a palpable decline in style; writing well became almost suspect. This decline was particularly obvious in articles that reached us from the United States. There was the most unfortunate emphasis on providing footnotes for every statement, however obvious and uncontroversial. Contributors had to be convinced that readability was an important consideration and that there was a difference between a dissertation in which the author had to enumerate everything he had ever read and an article for a journal of this kind.

Another interesting change that I observed over the years concerned book reviews—not so much in our journal, which for many years did not carry any, but in general. There is a difficult problem inherent in nonfiction reviewing: ideally, it should be done by someone very familiar with the subject, but a fellow specialist is likely to know the author and in the past to have either been on friendly terms with him or to have crossed swords with him. Arthur Schlesinger's father, a professor of history, noted in his autobiography written many years ago that at the age of forty he knew everyone who was someone in his field—and then decided no longer to review books.

I observed that over the years the tenor of reviews became more negative. To be critical was far more in fashion than to give praise, to be generous was often considered a weakness—not doing one's duty as a critic. This tendency may have been connected with the influence of the various "critical" schools in the academic world, "critical" often being interpreted as a synonym for "negative." Book reviewing had probably always been politicized to some extent, but it certainly became more so in our time. In my personal experience I found diplomats and generals the most reliable and sympathetic reviewers. They were cautious in their approach (the idea that they could be wrong must have occurred to them in their careers), and one could be sure that they had read the book in question, not focused only on those issues that struck their fancy. Next most reliable and sympathetic were the very senior figures in the field who could afford to be generous, whereas assistant professors were as a species the most dangerous, for many of them had to prove that they knew more and better than the author of the book in question.

My own interest was less in diplomatic history, more in political and even more in intellectual and cultural history. I preferred to deal with topics that were not too remote because I felt that quite often many of the answers to my questions were not found in the archives. It was equally or more important to have empathy for the mood of a period and its quality of life, something hard to describe and define but of decisive importance for understanding. Too often have I come across academic studies admirably researched, meticulous in every way except that they lacked that deeper understanding for a period that only immediacy can convey or revealed the enormous effort necessary to gain this kind of empathy.

Sir Llewelyn Woodward, a contributor to the first issue of our journal, made the point that the writer of contemporary history has an advantage over scholars investigating earlier periods in being able to remember the impression events made on him at the time. Woodward remembered, for example, the days in London just before and after the outbreak of World War I in August 1914, and his recollections were different from a good many accounts written about half a century later by people who were not there at the time but described excited crowds, bellicose enthusiasm, and demonstrations around the central area of Westminster.

I wrote the history of the German youth movement that came into being around 1900 and ended in 1933. My personal involvement was minimal, but I knew many who had participated and could tell me about aspects that had never been put on paper. I was twelve years of age when the Weimar Republic was liquidated by the Nazis, but I grew up among people who had been intimately involved and could guide my steps. The same was true of the context in which I wrote *A History of Zionism*.

True, for most of history this immediacy does not exist, hence the need for a great effort to gain empathy and an understanding of what it had been like to be alive at periods so distant from our time. When reading Gibbon's autobiography I came across his famous saying that being the captain of the Hampshire grenadiers (which he had been between 1759 and 1762) had not been useless to the historian of the Roman empire. This statement, at first reading, did not make much sense, for the distance in time and everything else seemed to be too great to be of relevance. But on further reflection it did occur to me that the fact that Gibbon had some military experience and had been in command of a body of men, however small compared to the Roman legions, made a difference. In later life I did not regret that I spent years outside the groves of academe; this could have been a serious handicap in the life of a scientist, but not in the fields in which I was interested.

My own life experience, limited as it was, the fact that I had grown up in Nazi Germany and had devoted much of my time in later years to the study of the Soviet Union, seemed to bear out the importance of immediacy and empathy. I realized that people who had never been exposed to life in a totalitarian regime, who had grown up in "normal" conditions, would find it exceedingly difficult to understand a situation so wholly different from what they were accustomed to. I do not mean extreme atrocities, which were not witnessed by many citizens at the time. I have in mind the general, all-pervasive climate prevailing in an unfree society. I also found in later years that most Soviet citizens I encountered believed that foreigners would never understand what life under Joseph Stalin had been like, nor before nor after. They did exaggerate, but not by much.

It was (and is) not easy for citizens of the United States or Britain, who had the good fortune of never having been exposed to life in a dictatorship, or to foreign occupation, to understand what it was like or to understand ideologies the opposite, in many respects, from their own. Having grown up in societies based on toleration and freedom, how could they empathize with fanaticism? The same is true with regard to the generations of Europeans born after the Second World War for whom the age of the dictatorships is almost equally remote and incomprehensible. This kind of inability to understand is perhaps only natural, but it has obvious political consequences. It makes it difficult, for example, to understand the other side during the Cold War, and even more difficult to understand fanatical nationalist and extremist religious movements.

Is it not natural that citizens of the United States and Britain should believe that there are no irreconcilable conflicts and that, given a minimum of goodwill, dialogues will help find a way out of every crisis? I feel uneasy whenever democratic politicians declare that the whole civilized world believes in one thing or another—the abolition of capital punishment, for example. They seem to be unaware of the fact that "the whole civilized world" is at the present time only a small part of all humankind and that of the ten most populous countries only one has abolished the death penalty. A French psychoanalyst once noted that people who lived in the Middle Ages would probably have found it easier than ours to understand the motivation of contemporary suicide bombers, and she may be right.

But the "lessons of history" can sometimes be learned too well. One school of psychoanalysis has pointed to "parataxic distortion," which, put very simply, means that a cat having been burned by a hot stove will in the future shy away from all stoves, even if they have not been heated for years. There has been tendency among some to see in every tin-pot little dictator a new Hitler or new Stalin. Memories of "Munich" are invoked a little too frequently for my taste, and it is of course true that Munich September 1938 was a disaster. I have no quarrel, in principle, with Rudyard Kipling's poem "Danegeld," in which he writes about rich and lazy nations trying to buy off blackmailers:

> For the end of that game is oppression and shame,
> And the nation that plays it is lost.

But it is also true that the Vikings disappeared within a few generations, whereas the descendants of those paying Danegeld still survive. In brief, there are no ironclad rules.

In our age the term "Islamofascism" is used rather indiscriminately. This, I believe, is wrong not because (as some think) the term may offend some Muslims; the term fascism, or Nazism, has never been an opprobrium in Asia or

Africa, let alone in the Arab world. But not every inhuman dictatorship is necessarily fascist—Pol Pot, however murderous his regime, was not fascist, nor was Idi Amin or quite a few others. Fascism and religion are not necessarily incompatible; the Romanian Iron Guard in the 1930s was fascist and religious; so was Ante Pavelić's regime in Croatia in the 1940s, and the roots of Belgian fascism (REX) were in the youth movement of the Catholic church. In the United States Father Charles Coughlin and the Reverend Gerald Smith came fairly close to Nazism and fascism. But in the final analysis, fascism was a European phenomenon. There are parallels between radical Islamism and fascism—their populism, anti-Westernism, antiliberalism, antisemitism; their aggressive, expansionist character; their belief in violence; the interpretation of Islam as both a religion and a totalitarian political-social order that provides answers to all problems. But there are differences between fascism and Islam that should not be overlooked. Dictatorships outside Europe are bound to develop on different lines according to historical tradition and political conditions. Radical Islamism could be interpreted as a postfascist movement, but such a label tends to exaggerate the role of the European predecessors and to downplay the specific homegrown, in other words the Islamic, elements. Hitler did not engage in *jihad*, and he did not want to impose the Sharia.

In brief, the lessons of history can be misunderstood and misapplied. But in our time the greater danger as far as democratic societies are concerned is the lack of memory and understanding of the dynamics of societies and governments that are not like them. And nothing is more difficult than alerting these societies to dangers facing them. Public opinion does not want to be bothered by anything but a clear and present danger, and those who warn are bound to be voices calling in the wilderness. And even farsighted politicians cannot afford to move too far ahead of public opinion. In other words, warnings in democratic societies will usually come late, and sometimes too late.

Predicting from History

As a historian, how do you assess (or what do you expect of) this or that current political development? This is the kind of question historians are often asked to answer, as if historical knowledge offers a magic key for predicting the future. Unfortunately, historians quite often fail to agree about the past, so why do we expect them to play prophets?

Historians tend to believe that each situation is different. Political scientists, on the contrary, believe in commonalities, hoping to discover laws or at least certain patterns that make generalizations possible. Political science is a somewhat pretentious term because it cannot predict; it is therefore at best a very imperfect science. In any case, academic political scientists have no monopoly as far as analysis and comment on current political affairs are concerned. In fact, their influence is probably small compared with their competitors in government, think tanks, and the media who engage in the same craft. Cato (himself an augur) said that he could not understand how two augurs (officials in ancient Rome making predictions on the basis of the flight of birds) or haruspices or other soothsayers, when meeting, could refrain from bursting into laughter, knowing full well the essentially fraudulent character of their enterprise.

Some of the present-day "analysts" (the currently fashionable term) are no doubt more reliable than others, and the wise among them will be reluctant to volunteer predictions. But the field as a whole has been disappointing, and a great deal of charlatanism has been going on. This may have less to do with the politicization and radicalization of the field; there have always been thinkers of the left and the right, revolutionaries and reactionaries, and there has been room for all of them. More important could be the fact that in the past the study of these fields was limited to a much smaller elite; there were far fewer professors and students. A hundred years ago lecturers preaching obvious nonsense would have found it much more difficult to get away with it, let alone find followers and establish a school. It is also true that with so much work having been done, it has become exceedingly difficult to come up with truly novel and important insights; this may explain, at least in part, the ever-growing urge to produce new ideas however far-fetched and foolish.

Philosophers, historians, and politicians have been writing about politics since time immemorial, and some of these writings are studied to this very day. But the idea of treating politics as a science is recent. An association of American political scientists came into being before World War I; in Britain and Germany it became an academic discipline only after World War II. True, LSE, the London School of Economic and Political Science, was founded as early as 1895, but for many years after its foundation the degrees it bestowed were in economics rather than in politics. Columbia University had appointed a professor of political science (Francis Lieber) as far back as 1857, but his real field was international law; in 1880 a school of political science was founded at Columbia. Sciences Po in Paris was established even earlier, in 1872, but in its current form came into being only in 1945.

Max Weber in a famous lecture in 1918 demanded that politics and science be kept apart; politics did not belong to the university as far as students and lecturers were concerned. This point has been disputed, especially after the appearance of the behaviorist school in the United States and Britain in the 1950s. But the status of political science remains somewhat uncertain and controversial despite all attempts to give it a methodological and philosophical underpinning. The respective departments at Harvard, Cornell, and Georgetown, to name but a few, are called department of government rather than political science.

Some self-criticism may be called for prior to criticizing others. If I look back on my thinking and writing on current affairs, I believe I have more often been right than wrong, but I am aware of some basic mistakes and misjudgments. I would like to single out one. When many years ago I received an award from an organization named Inter Nationes for a book I had written, the speaker, Wolf Jobst Siedler, a leading German publisher, made a point that gave me food for thought for a long time. "Unfortunately," he said, "Laqueur's books usually come too early." He was right. Moreover, I was mistaken more than once in ignoring or belittling the retarding factors while analyzing a certain political trend. In other words, it was not enough to have correctly discerned the coming of a crisis and its causes, for in the real world there are almost always other trends that delay its playing out fully. A country may be unstable and everything may point to a further aggravation of the situation. But very often this process takes longer than assumed, for there are always strong vested interests with a stake in preserving the status quo. Nor should one underrate the importance of inertia in societies and the role of accident. Violent, dramatic change may appear just around the corner, but in actual fact it may take years or decades for change to happen. Some societies are more accustomed to accept a miserable state of affairs than others, or the mood may suddenly change for no obvious reason. The economic situation may be dismal but then there might be a temporary recovery. The world situation may change and have an influence on affairs at home.

To give but one example, Russia's attempt to regain superpower status and to recover at least part of its former empire may seem doomed, for it is essentially a colossus on feet of clay, depending entirely on the export of oil and natural gas. Its demographic base is rapidly shrinking, and the non-Russian element is growing quickly. But the outcome depends on various processes that cannot be predicted. It depends, for instance, on the resistance Moscow will encounter in its campaign to regain its former position in the world. If the Kremlin hangs on long enough to its northern and eastern territories despite the constant depopulation, global warming may reduce permafrost and put at the disposal of the rulers in the Kremlin new natural resources that would immensely strengthen its position.

Looking back at my own record over the years I find that my long-term predictions were more often right than those referring to the short term. Perhaps this was inevitable because in the short term almost anything may happen, whereas the long-term possibilities are usually more restricted. But it is certainly true that I did sometimes not pay sufficient attention to unpredictability in the short term, and hence assumed that political processes, correctly analyzed, would take place in only a few years, whereas in fact they took much longer.

A mistake frequently committed by my contemporaries stemmed from Eurocentrism or Americanocentrism, that is to say, the belief that other parts of the world are essentially like ours, are motivated and will react in a similar way. In contrast to many other students of international politics in the West, I had started my career studying parts of what was then called the Third World and was therefore less prone to be misled by these mistaken assumptions and more immune to certain delusions. And yet I find that for a long time I underrated the political importance of nationalism and religion, simply because nationalism in Europe and in America played a less important role after the Second World War than ever before. Because I was not subject to strong nationalist and religious feelings, I tended to underrate their importance in other parts of the world. This is a mistake frequently committed by Western intellectuals on the left, and I was not free from it. True, fascism and the passions underlying it such as extreme nationalism should have been fresh in memory, but after World War II they seemed to have gone forever.

What makes for a more or less reliable assessment, particularly with regard to foreign affairs? In most ways it is stating the obvious: that there are no magic clues goes without saying, but a study of the history and the culture of the country concerned is a precondition. Foreign affairs deal with foreigners, and everyone is of course more familiar with affairs nearer home. Language is of crucial importance: how many Chinese have some knowledge of English, how few Americans master Chinese. The same condition pertains to Arabic, Persian, Urdu, and other Oriental languages. Many years ago I gave up the idea of becoming a Middle Eastern expert because I felt my knowledge of Arabic was insufficient and I was unwilling to undertake the effort to devote years to further study. Today I find that much of the literature on the Middle East is written by authors of fewer scruples. Many present-day misjudgments stem from a lack of linguistic competence. There is the need, more than ever, for a special effort to understand conditions in other parts of the world, not only the languages concerned but the psychology, the beliefs, the manners, and the way of life of others.

At the same time the temptation has to be resisted that because something has happened in the past it is bound to recur ("History always repeats itself"). When communism first appeared on the international scene, it was frequently thought that it had something to do with nihilism (whatever that meant); when fascism emerged, many thought of it as another species of old-fashioned military dictatorship. It would be much easier for the interpreters of history if history did repeat itself, but unfortunately it often does not.

Some of the main sources of error have been mentioned: mirror imaging ("They are people like you and me"); the belief of academics that the main assignment of an intellectual is to be critical; the contention that conflicts can always or almost always be evaded; the idea that in the case of a conflict, truth is more often than not to be found somewhere in the middle and that one's own country is very likely to be in the wrong.

Everyone is sometimes bound to be wrong in his or her judgment; not only political scientists but economists who have engaged in prediction have often erred. Error is inevitable, and it is psychologically notoriously difficult to admit a mistake, but the student of politics and international affairs has to accept failure and revise his or her views or assessments however painful. Political judgment should not be influenced by personal considerations such as the fact that one's advice has been ignored. George Kennan, to give but one example, an excellent student of Soviet politics, erred grievously in his later years when he was out of government and no longer privy to inside information. A frequent source of error is the belief that the less active foreign policy makers are, the fewer the mistakes they are likely to commit. This seems to have been one of the cardinal beliefs of Walter Lippmann in later life; such excessive caution may be commendable in some instances but very wrong in others.

An interesting issue that has been insufficiently studied is that of reputations gained and maintained. Some leading gurus in the field of international affairs have kept their reputation of being wise if not infallible despite a record of profound errors over long periods. This is true with regard to experts in area studies and even more often among generalists, for the likelihood to be mistaken in a wide field is of course even greater. Perhaps the reason was that such gurus expressed a fairly wide consensus; their mistakes reflect those of many others, which gave them long-term immunity. Perhaps those who had helped to build up the reputation of the gurus felt they had a stake in not dropping them even after their errors had become all too obvious. False reputations in this field, in any case, can be maintained longer than in many others, not just the more exact sciences. The issue, as said, certainly deserves further reflection.

The Future Today

Should one encourage, these days, a young man or woman to go into politics, or a related field such a political analysis and comment? I doubt it, and the doubts are especially strong as far as foreign policy is concerned. Hope, of course, springs eternal and miracles do happen, but the prospects are not good. True, it may well be, as the futurists tell us, that this will be an age of great technological breakthroughs and that many people, and not only in China and India, will be materially better off. But being better off is no guarantee of happiness and conflict resolution. The twenty-first century could well be an age of fanaticism, of ecological disasters, of failed countries, and of the spread of the weapons of mass destruction.

True, fanaticism does not last forever, at least not with equal intensity, and it should not be beyond human ingenuity to reduce considerably the ecological threats facing us. Some failed countries may find a way out of their misery. But it is at present very difficult to foresee what political solutions could avert the consequences of the spread of weapons of mass destruction. It is almost impossible to envisage the maintenance of democratic institutions and human freedoms in these circumstances.

There is no superpower able and willing to undertake the assignment of world policeman to safeguard a minimum of international order and safety in what could turn into a political jungle. The trend in Europe and increasingly also in the United States is likely to be toward withdrawal. International conflicts, according to this mood, should be left for the United Nations to solve, and all initiatives should be multilateral, following consultation and agreement with allies. In the 1970s the key words of the neo-isolationist trend were "measured disinvolvement," "partial disengagement," and, at most, "discriminate intervention"; today different terms are used. Perhaps there will be greater readiness toward realism on one hand, and international cooperation on the other, following some major disasters such as nuclear attacks. But there is no certainty, and in any case the learning process is bound to be painful. I must confess to growing pessimism in this respect in the light of the events of my lifetime: there is often great resistance against learning from mistakes that were committed, while the power of ideological preconceptions is great and the power of rational arguments limited. Lessons are learned from blows suffered, from setbacks and disasters. To be prematurely right is quite pointless and to utter warnings is thankless, unless it is done at the right time and unless one moves in the right company.

What solutions have been suggested to deal with the coming perils? They range from the obvious but banal to the ridiculous: there ought to be no new imperialism but the strengthening of the United Nations, no global overstretch but restraint, humility not hubris, smartness not aggression; responsibility should be encouraged; everyone should be treated with equal dignity and respect. After the great Lisbon earthquake of 1755, street vendors appeared in the Portuguese capital selling pills against earthquakes. In Gaetano Donizetti's *Elisir d'Amore*, Dr. Dulcamara ("dottore enciclopedico"), in a famous aria, claims the love potion he sells will also cure all the other diseases in the world and elsewhere. Our present-day Dulcamaras offer their wares free of charge (or almost).

How did we reach this impasse—proceeding from the optimism of Victor Hugo to the dire prospects of the early twenty-first century? Many attribute the fault to recent mistakes that were committed, to imperial overstretch, but this explanation seems a little too easy and it certainly does not apply to Europe. Even if politicians had acted with great wisdom and restraint, few of the dangers confronting us would have been averted. Great powers have always been unpopular and generated fear or at least misgivings among their neighbors, and there is no foolproof way out of this predicament, except by ceasing to be a great power. The United Nations would still be powerless, and there would be no obvious solutions for these problems.

In a search for tragic mistakes and guilty men, one ought to go back to the early twentieth century. The First World War could have been prevented. It was stupid, even frivolous. The conflicting interests of the great powers could have been resolved without a war. It was Europe's misfortune that two of the main players at the time were exceedingly stupid, one (Wilhelm II) stupid and arrogant, the other (Nicholas II) stupid and weak. Without the First World War there would, in all probability, have been no Hitler and no Stalin; the Russian and German autocracies would have disintegrated or been overthrown, even if it had taken a few more years or decades. The First World War made the postwar crises more or less inevitable even if a wiser economic policy could have reduced the effects of the world crisis of the late 1920s and early 1930s. Once the totalitarian movements had seized power, a military conflict became inevitable given German and Italian expansionism. This conflict led to the Cold War, which again could not have been prevented, given Stalin's belief and that of his successors in the inevitable, foreordained course of history—the worldwide victory of communism, Soviet style. In a similar way decolonization after World War II seems inevitable; it is unthinkable that, given political and economic developments, weakening European powers would have been able to hold onto their empires.

Thus the world of the year 2000 was much more complicated, with many more countries (and nationalisms) in existence than in the world of the optimistic year 1900. But the fact that so many national movements had prevailed did not make it a safer and more peaceful place. On the contrary, whereas the conflicts of the late nineteenth century were relatively easy to resolve, many of those of the twenty-first century are unmanageable. There is today no "concert of powers," and the powers that had, in the past, been able to impose international order show little enthusiasm to engage in these ungrateful assignments, unless their own vital interests are involved. The prevailing mood in all major countries is or will be semi-isolationist, with the exception of Russia, but its efforts to reclaim its erstwhile power and influence are not likely to have much success. Europe has steadily become weaker on the international scene, and it will be only natural in the circumstances for European nations to opt for what was once called splendid isolation—trying to stay out of world conflicts. America may face a longish period of retrenchment following its setbacks in Afghanistan and Iraq, the prevailing weakness of political will, and confusion and defeatism among sections of the political elite. China and India will not be ready and willing for a long time to assume responsibilities beyond their immediate vicinity. In Africa and elsewhere, getting access to the raw materials needed for economic growth will be the main endeavor in world affairs.

The lessons of recent years will probably be learned too well: that intervention in foreign affairs is usually wrong and that failed countries cannot be helped from outside except perhaps by economic help and some good advice. These assumptions are sometimes right; it is indeed very difficult to stop ethnic groups killing each other if they feel a desperate urge to do so. But often they are wrong. It is doubtful that the spread of weapons of mass destruction could have been prevented, but it certainly could have been slowed down, made more difficult, and the unacceptable risk of using them could have been made more clear to those playing with the idea.

We have been told that the war on terror will end because all wars eventually end. This idea sounds reassuring, but it rests on the mistaken assumption that the war against terrorism is a war that is somehow comparable to other wars. It is nothing of the sort; it is a condition, a state of affairs, the contemporary manifestation of political conflicts in an age in which regular, traditional wars have become too expensive and modern war too risky and destructive. Terrorism cannot be stamped out altogether unless human conflicts are somehow abolished. With great luck terrorism might be reduced to manageable proportions, and if failed countries cannot be restored to normality their problems might be isolated so that local conflagrations may burn themselves out after a while.

But for this outcome certain preconditions are needed that at present do not exist. They include the realization that intervention within certain limits will succeed only if carried out by massive, overwhelming force; to engage in such ventures in a half-hearted way is dangerous, often doomed to failure. One must proceed with no holds barred, rejecting the rules of asymmetric warfare as established by terrorists and guerrillas. The battlefield, like the playing field, has to be leveled.

Everyone wants both safety and privacy, but the war on terror is, unfortunately, by and large a zero sum game. Some politicians, foreseeing the dangers to come, want to limit some of our traditional liberties, but this is politically unwise. Such an approach is bound to provoke strong opposition in democratic societies, though much less so in countries like Russia or China. And the question will inevitably be asked whether such intervention is really necessary. Are so many cameras in streets and public places, as in Britain, really necessary? Is it the task of a democracy to impose democracy on countries that are not ready for it and do not want it? The answer in the present climate is obvious.

What should be clear is that any such intervention undertaken without the overwhelming support of public opinion, without the resolve to carry it through to the end, and without sufficient power is bound to fail. The need for stringent security measures will gain mass support only after one or more major disasters will have occurred. And who knows, perhaps miraculously they will never occur.

In some respects the strategic debates of our day resemble those between hawks and doves of the Cold War. The doves argue that to gain the moral high ground and to improve relations with allies is the commandment of the hour, and they point out that Western diplomacy (especially American) has missed important opportunities to reduce international tensions. During the Cold War, Stalin's and Lavrentiy Beria's alleged offers of talks concerning the reunification of Germany in 1952–53 were such missed opportunities; now reference is made to alleged Iranian offers in 2003 to make a deal with the United States.

The dangers facing the world in the years and decades to come may have been overdrawn. Not all disasters may come to pass, in which case we shall be, like Candide in Voltaire's famous novel, free to tend to our gardens. But there is little doubt that even if the worst can be avoided, the world will live in the shadow of these dangers, with the possibility of annihilation on an unprecedented scale. Given the present psychological climate, chances that steps will be taken to reduce these dangers are very small. A strategy of fortress America, fortress Europe seems more likely for some time to come; unfortunately the idea of a fortress belongs to bygone ages and offers little safety in the contemporary world. On the other hand, to repeat once again, chances for common action will be far better after the first or second disaster will have occurred. More major shocks might bring about an awakening of public opinion at home and greater readiness to cooperate on an international scale. This is not a pleasant outlook, but probably the most likely one.

The years to come will be difficult for foreign policy makers. There have been few outstanding leaders in the West or indeed anywhere else. What Count Axel Oxenstierna, the seventeenth-century Swedish statesman, told his son is true *a fortiori* for the present and the recent past: "Behold, my son, with how little wisdom the world is governed," he wrote in Latin, as was customary in those faraway days. Oxenstierna junior, representing his country, was going to the negotiations that put an end to the Thirty Years War and feared that he was not the equal of the other, more experienced statesmen.

But it would be a little too easy to put all or most of the blame on the limited mental capacities of some present-day policy makers. It should never be forgotten that very often their freedom of maneuver is quite limited for a great variety of reasons. One could think of many calamities in recent times that could, in all probability, not have been prevented even by the greatest geniuses. In democracies foreign policy strategists and makers can never move too far ahead of the mood of the public; they may be aware of the coming dangers but they still may not be free to act as they would like to. In nondemocratic regimes they may be hampered by other obstacles.

If foreign policy makers in the days to come are not to be envied, it may well be an even more exasperating time for those trying to make sense of the present world situation and the shape of things to come. Oxenstierna's observation applies not only to those who shape foreign policy but also to those trying to interpret it. How much wishful thinking, how much naiveté, how little willingness to learn from past mistakes. How much confusion and intolerance on university campuses (more even in the United States than in Europe). How much exaggeration and sensationalism in the media. They seem to have learned only too well from the popular press that a small earthquake never sold many copies.

True, the situation in these and other respects has never been perfect, but it is becoming more and more difficult to believe that there has been any progress at all. Yet predictions have never been easy. It was not too difficult to anticipate a war in Europe once Hitler had come to power (though, it should be recalled, many dissented at the time). Some still believe that the Cold War could have been prevented if Western statesmen had been less doctrinaire and more farsighted. It was far more difficult to see clearly the coming of World War I, just as it is difficult today to be certain about Iran's nuclear weapons: Will they be used as a political weapon, or will they be used in a war? Above all, it is notoriously difficult to predict internal upheaval. That the Russian autocracy was weak was no secret in 1914; in some ways it was considered a miracle that it could withstand three years of war and countless military setbacks. But the Bolshevik Revolution was still by no means inevitable.

Going back even further, the same was true with regard to the coming of the French Revolution. One of the very best informed observers of France at the time was Arthur Young, a leading English agricultural expert, who visited France in 1787, 1788, and 1789 and in each case wrote detailed reports about his impressions. But with all his knowledge of France and his many meetings with people from all sectors of society, he did not anticipate the revolution any more than others did. True, the government was bankrupt—hence the decision to convoke the three estates—but even then it was next to impossible to predict Maximilien Robespierre and Louis de Saint-Just.

Some of the problems facing political analysts and journalists include the precarious situation of the print media and the dwindling number of foreign correspondents. But there are other, more deep-seated difficulties, including the blurring of the border between editorial and news coverage, between conveying information and purveying entertainment. Newspapers have become viewspapers, personal opinions and ideological views obtrude themselves on news coverage and political comment, and the tone is often very shrill. In recent decades the emphasis has been on critical approach, which is of course legitimate as long as critical is not interpreted as a synonym for negative (as it often is) in the United States and Britain, to a lesser extent in continental Europe. A majority of writers on current affairs belong to the opposition of the government in power. They are the influential but unelected fourth estate.

Many present-day commentators sincerely think of themselves as liberals, but terms like left and right have largely changed their meaning since the nineteenth century. The fortunes of the left in recent history have been mixed, to say the least, and not only as the result of the breakdown of the Soviet empire. Even socialism has frequently become an unacceptable, offensive term for American liberals.

The tragedy of the left is that it was traditionally the party of freedom, of progress, of fighting poverty, obscurantism, repression, but what are its visions, who are its idols now? Today quite often views prevail among the left that would have been derided as immoral, reactionary, and obscurantist in bygone ages. Radical chic, unthinking violence, moral relativism, nonsensical theories taken very seriously, populist slogans, the justification of religious and nationalist repression: What is left of the left? There has been the beginning of self-criticism in the West, much less so elsewhere. Perhaps there will be a second coming, but it could be a long process. Many in the United States, Britain, and France have written about the predicaments of the left in recent decades, so there is little that outsiders can add.

Perhaps the current state of the left is the result of success. Seen in historical perspective, the realization in the Western world of many of the aims of the left over the last generations has been remarkable. There was no revolution, yet the extremes of poverty have disappeared, while education and health services have greatly improved. Was it for these reasons that the left lost its impetus, that the party of freedom and justice has become in our time so often, and not only at its fringes, a movement so different from what it used to be, so distant in its values and aims? I do not believe at all that the left no longer has any historical role to play. On the contrary, there is so much unfinished business to confront: growing income inequality since the 1970s all over the globe (not only in the United States and Europe but even more so in Russia, China, India, and Brazil), well beyond what can be accepted without danger to democratic institutions.

When in London I make my home two minutes from the cemetery where Karl Marx is buried. There are few visitors to his grave compared with thirty years ago. The followers of postcolonial and gender studies have other gurus and other pilgrimages. I grew up belonging to a generation deeply influenced by Marxism and later by the critique of Marxism. I do not think there is much that a nineteenth-century ideology can teach the twenty-first century, but sometimes it occurs to me that perhaps we overdid our denigration of Marxist ideas. They may have been wrong in large part, but they were not nonsensical compared with many fashionable contemporary ideological messages. What a giant Marx was compared with so many of today's thinkers who believe themselves to be in the radical tradition. Should we agree with the British Marxist who wrote that one of the few things that stand between us and an accelerated descent into darkness is the set of values inherited from the Enlightenment, the only foundation for the aspiration to build societies in which all human beings can live? Or should we agree with the Western liberal relativists who rail against "the fundamentalists" of the Enlightenment? Is everything equal—the categorical imperative and cannibalism, tolerance and Hitler, Stalin, stoning women and similar manifestations of barbarism? It is one thing to argue that, once a religion or a secular religion has more than a billion adherents, all public debate about it should cease in order to preserve domestic peace. The belief that Western values should be imposed on the whole world, not by example but by force, has no place in our time. Other nations, other civilizations prefer other values, other human rights (if any) and ways of life. But the abdication of Western values is tantamount to a regression by hundreds of years. Politicians and public figures may have to pretend in the years to come that all beliefs and values are more or less equally justified, and all contain deep spirituality, and we all have to learn from each other. But we should not try to persuade ourselves that this is really true.

I titled the first chapter of my book of reflections on the Soviet Union "The Age of Enthusiasm." And now we are advancing from the age of enthusiasm to the age of humbug, and some even believe in it. It will not be a pleasant age for decent politicians and their Boswells.

La Belle Époque

Which takes me back to the starting point, the fantasies about a more optimistic, more congenial, more enjoyable age in which to have been alive. The more I think about it, the more attractive the last two decades of the nineteenth century appear to be, up to the outbreak of World War I—La Belle Époque.

For this era, Jules Michelet (and many others) called Paris the true center of the world, but it is useful to recall that it became such only during the second half of the nineteenth century. The myth of Paris began in the romantic 1830s, the historians report. Up to that time Paris was considered by many residents and new arrivals to be a dirty, unhealthy, and rather ugly place. It was owing to Baron Haussmann that this old Paris largely disappeared. Not everyone liked these enormous changes. Émile Zola wrote, for instance, "This Paris of

M. Haussmann is an immense hypocrisy, colossal Jesuitism." Zola thought the city deeply corrupt, but his opinion probably had more to do with his hatred of the Second Empire than with the aesthetics of Haussmann. In his later books written in the 1880s about Les Halles (the great food market) and the new enormous department stores (Au Bonheur des Dames), there is much less criticism of this new Paris.

But it is true that earlier on, during the first half of the century, a majority of Parisians were not natives of the capital, and the cultural distance between Paris and the rest of the country was not remotely as great as later on. And it was also only toward the end of the nineteenth century that Paris became the capital of world entertainment and, of course, of the arts.

Historians have called these the banquet years. The plastic arts, above all impressionism, dominated the French cultural scene during the last decades of the nineteenth century. After the turn of the century music became of increasing importance. Composers such as Claude Debussy, Jules Massenet, Gabriel Fauré, Maurice Ravel, Camille Saint-Saëns—not to mention Igor Stravinsky and the Ballets Russes—are not among my favorites, but greater experts than I thought very highly of them and they certainly dominated the cultural life of the *ville lumière.*

In 1900 Émile Loubet, the French president, invited the mayors of France to a luncheon in the Tuileries Gardens (more had actually been invited but only 22,000 came). Many hundred cattle had to be slaughtered to feed these public figures in their repast in a series of tents each 500 meters long. The number of bottles of wine and champagne drunk was astronomical.

It was an age of gigantomania, but also of enterprise and successful improvisation. The Eiffel Tower was constructed in record time, so were the underground railways of London and Berlin, and the new enormous department stores (Wertheim and Tietz—now Hertie—in Berlin; Selfridges in London; Galeries Lafayette, Printemps, and Samaritaine in Paris). The great world exhibition of 1900 attracted 83,000 exhibitors and 50 million visitors.

It was the age of technical breakthroughs, a race between the Wright brothers in the United States and inventors in France such as Alberto Santos-Dumont, Henry Ferman, and Louis Blériot. Blériot was the first to fly over the British Channel, for which Lord Northcliffe gave him a prize of £1,000. Even though the weather was inclement, it took Blériot a mere thirty-seven minutes to accomplish the feat, and he left far behind the destroyer sent by the French government to help him in an emergency. For once many leading politicians, above all David Lloyd George, immediately realized the political, military, and economic implications of the new invention. England was no longer an island. But France was also in the forefront of producing automobiles; up to 1904 it was technologically superior even to the United States, and when World

War I broke out it had more motor cars than any other continental European country.

In this the Germans and the British were lagging a little behind, but not for long. Count Zeppelin was working on a big dirigible, impressive but not that promising for the air traffic of the future. Germans were dreaming about visiting the Moon, and Paul Lincke's musical *Frau Luna* became an all-time favorite. Based on an earlier operetta by Jacques Offenbach, it is the story of Fritz Steppke, a young Berlin engineer who visits the Moon and returns to Earth to realize that all things considered castles on the Moon are not really any more *gemütlich* than his little Berlin apartment.

But La Belle Époque was not only about *flaneurs* on the grand boulevards, the jockey club, and technological breakthroughs. It was also the age of the rediscovery of nature. The Paris aristocracy bought houses out of town, often at the seaside from Deauville to Trouville and beyond; in Britain seaside resorts like Brighton had a second coming. Working-class outings were to Clacton and Blackpool. The Germans and the Viennese went to the countryside and especially to the forests, a little neglected since the days of the romantic school. In the pictures of the French impressionists, seaside scenes figure prominently; so does the Seine nearer Paris. There is a great deal of boating and swimming to be seen, and sometimes the painter is depicted doing his work while on a boat, as in Edouard Manet's picture of Claude Monet's floating studio.

All this enjoyable leisure was by no means the monopoly of the rich. With the spread of the railway network, hundreds of thousands streamed on weekends to the countryside, usually from the Saint-Lazare railway station in Paris, another scene of interest to the impressionists. In Germany the Wandervogel went on hikes far away from the big cities, young people led by leaders only a few years older. It was the age of *Lebensreform*, of all kind of strange prophets preaching healthier food and outlawing alcohol and smoking as well as various other noxious habits that had spread in the big cities.

Those less adventurous or families with small children went to garden restaurants that spread in the suburbs of Berlin and found their painters in August Macke and Max Liebermann. They were located under big trees, often on the shore of a river. Families were permitted to bring their own coffee and heat it provided they bought at least some sandwiches or cake. The choice and quality of coffee and cake was superior in Vienna, which had some 600 *Konditoreien* (pastry shops) in 1900, more than today. The coffeehouses had become the meeting place of artists and intellectuals as well as many others. Viennese literature is unthinkable without these meeting places. And everyone, rich and poor, went to the Prater, the great entertainment center where according to the popular songs the trees were almost always blossoming. They would then proceed to Sievering where the lilac was in full flower or to Grinzing to taste the *Heurigen*, this year's wine harvest. After the second or third glass they would sing, "Wien, Wien nur du allein," announcing that this was the city of their dreams, the only place where true happiness could be found. The composer of this unofficial anthem of Vienna was named Rudolf Siecynski, an indication that acculturation was perhaps working after all.

Yet with all this, Berlin and Vienna—let alone Moscow and St. Petersburg (sometimes called the laboratory of modernism)—could not compete with Paris. Berlin had *savoir faire* but little *savoir vivre*. Even Emperor Wilhelm II admitted as much: What was to be seen in Berlin except a few museums? "Paris is the great whorehouse of the world," he wrote; "therein lies its attraction. . . . There is nothing in Berlin that can captivate the foreigner, except a few museums, castles and soldiers." True, Berlin was the city of *Tempo! Tempo!*, of haste and nervous excitement, but Honoré de Balzac years earlier had complained about Paris suffering from the same afflictions. Berlin high society was the most stratified of all; the landed nobility would not dream of meeting socially the nobility of money. Their children occasionally had to marry these nouveaux riches for all too obvious reasons, but if they could help it they would not be seen with those not belonging to the aristocracy. They were exceedingly arrogant, but this arrogance did not come to them naturally, as it did to the British aristocracy.

With few exceptions Berliners' cultural interests were minimal; a German Proust would not have been able to fill many pages reporting the conversation in their salons, which focused more on horses and dogs than ideas or the arts. When Theodor Fontane, the greatest writer of his time, celebrated his seventy-fifth birthday, not one member of the Prussian nobility—of which he had written so fondly and not without admiration—turned up to congratulate him. In a poem written on this occasion he concluded that the only ones who appreciated him belonged to the oldest aristocracy in the world, the Jews.

True, the number of foreigners visiting Berlin increased with every year, but this was because the German capital was politically important and also an industrial center. The center of Berlin was less and less a place where the wealthy would look for a house and garden; they would move instead to the new expensive suburbs, such as Grunewald. Berlin and Vienna had first-rate theaters, and the musical offerings were second to none; the universities were of the highest quality. And yet there was still something missing: Was it elegance or the night life or the Bois de Boulogne and the Jardin de Luxembourg or the Louvre or simply the pleasure of life, difficult to define but palpably real? There was no one more popular in Vienna than Johann Strauss Jr., *Der Walzer König*. When he died in 1899 Eduard Hanslick, the fiercest music critic of his time, wrote that Vienna's happy years had come to an end. He was not far wrong.

Some Russians thought that Moscow was the most wonderful place on earth—the three sisters in Anton Chekhov's play, for instance— but residents of

St. Petersburg did not share this enthusiasm, and the Russian avant-garde of 1905 was not drawn to Moscow (a big village of a million inhabitants in their view) or to the Russian forest, hunting and collecting mushrooms, but to distant places—Konstantin Balmont to Mexico, New Zealand, and Samoa; Ivan Bunin to India; Nikolai Kondratiev to Palestine; Andrei Bely to Egypt; Nikolay Gumilev (Akhmatova's husband) to Ethiopia; and virtually all of them went to Paris. Some were world weary; Aleksandr Blok called his generation (as well as those slightly older) the children of Russia's dreadful years whose slogan was *tryn trava* (couldn't care lessism). Some thought the smell of burning and blood was in the air; Bely's novel *Petersburg* was the story of a cosmic disaster, the burning of the Russian capital. But others did not share these forebodings; they thought of their generation as enterprising adventurers, conquistadores, in Gumilev's words. And in any case, popular culture in Russia as in other countries was always far more optimistic than the avant-garde.

There was a constant rivalry between Petersburg and Moscow: the former was the bigger city, the seat of the government, and the window to Europe. *Mir Iskusstva* (The World of Art) was published there, the most influential magazine during the early years of the century. Moscow was the more Russian city, but the Petersburg symbolists—the last great moment in Russian literature according to Anna Akhmatova—thought it more decadent. It had the Bolshoi theater; many leading writers and composers lived there and also the wealthy merchants such as Ivan Morozov, who established remarkable collections of French impressionists at a time when few others paid attention. As far as the ballet was concerned, that most Russian of arts at the time (since Tchaikovsky at the latest), the pendulum was swinging to and fro. For a few years Petersburg had the lead, but then the action switched to Moscow as Sergei Diaghilev and the others went to Paris. It has entered the history of Russian literature as the Silver Age. I never quite understood the excitement of Bely about the *ognevaya stikhia* (the fire as a primordial force) that was to engulf his Russia—*Messia gryadushevo dnya* (the messiah of the coming day)—or Blok's fantasies about him and his friends being Skyths and Mongols, which they were clearly not. Perhaps one had to be alive at the time to share such sentiments. But what poetic power, what abundance of talent there was at the time; there has been nothing like it since in Russia and to the best of my knowledge not anywhere else. I do not know anything more moving than Blok's poem (written shortly before his death in 1921) devoted to the Pushkin House in the grounds of the Russian academy of science then in Petrograd—an oasis of peace in a world or war and violence: "Tainuyo svobodu peli mi vosled tebe. . . . Dai nam ruku ve nepogodu, pomogi v nemoi borbe" (Secret freedom we have been singing following you. . . . Give us your hand facing the storms, help us in the mute struggle).

London did not have anything like the Folies Bergère (founded in 1869); the West End Windmill Theatre with its nonmoving nude ladies opened only in 1932. But it did have some 135 theaters, far more than today. In Britain this was the great age of the music hall, such as the Alhambra, with its fire eaters, jugglers, and ventriloquists and above all its performers such as Marie Lloyd or Max Miller singing "Lily of Laguna," "Burlington Bertie from Bow," "Goodbye Dolly Gray," and "Oh, Mr. Porter." Popular above all were the songs about the seaside: "Everyone delights to spend their summer's holiday down beside the side of the silvery sea," with a refrain played by thousands of brass bands, "Oh, I do like to be beside the seaside, I do like to be beside the sea!" Blackpool with its donkey rides, fish and chips and dirty post cards—what a *joie de vivre.*

But if they wanted really to enjoy themselves (and if they could afford it), the British went to Paris ("As I walk along the Bois Boolong with an independent air"). These were the early days of the automobile and of the moving pictures, later to be called cinema. It was the age of the beginning of modern sports; the first Olympic Games took place in Athens in 1896. The beginnings were modest but at the fifth games in Stockholm in 1912 more than 2,500 athletes from twenty-eight countries took part, among them, admittedly, only fifty-seven women.

It was the age of electricity. Lincke's operetta *Lysistrata,* first performed in 1902, included the "Glow Worm Idyll," which has remained part and parcel of light music programs to this day. In some ways it was the hymn of the new age—leading us from darkness to light, from misery to happiness. (Saint-Saëns also composed a hymn celebrating the advent of the age of electricity, but it is forgotten today.) Meanwhile the young people of the Wandervogel were singing their merry songs proclaiming that as they were marching side by side they felt they would prevail because "mit uns zieht die Neue Zeit" (with us the new age, the future). The song was adopted by the left as well as the right, and the name of the theoretical organ of the German Social Democracy also was *Die Neue Zeit.* Hermann Claudius, who wrote the text, was the great-grandson of Matthias Claudius, one of the great and most beloved German eighteenth-century poets. Hermann, who lived to be one month short of 102, was originally a member of the youth movement and a Social Democrat; among his last poems was a prayer to Adolf Hitler. But he was basically a nonpolitical person; Willy Brandt was among those who congratulated him on his ninety-fifth birthday.

But why not opt for the Paris of the 1920s and 1930s, when Josephine Baker was singing about her two loves ("mon pays et Paris"), when Mistinguett compared Paris to a blonde ("qui plait a tout le monde"), when Lys Gauty announced that the sun in every Paris faubourg brought into blossom a dream of love, when Charles Trénet (*La Romance de Paris*) made it known that (following Baudelaire) he loved to walk leisurely along the grand boulevards even though he was only a worker at the Renault plant (the year was 1941 and Paris an occupied city). Why not believe those older and more widely traveled than I telling me with such nostalgia about "the last time they saw Paris, hearing the laughter of her heart in every street café"?

I must have watched René Clair's *Sous les toits de Paris* (1930) half a dozen times, and I was captivated, but when I saw it many years later what struck me above all was the primitive conditions, the poverty in which people lived. When I watched *La Kermesse héroïque* (1935) for the first time I found it very funny. It's the story of how in the sixteenth century the womenfolk of a Flemish town prevent great disaster and suffering by making life as comfortable as possible for the Spanish army occupying the city; twenty years later I found this rationalization of collaboration not funny at all. I felt uneasy watching Jean Gabin in *Le jour se lève, Hôtel du Nord, Quai des Brumes,* and other excellent movies of that period, and I was not surprised when in later years the critics put the stress on the negativism, the pessimism, even fatalism that permeated these films. Marcel Carné, who made these movies, said in his defense that they were only a mirror of the *Zeitgeist*—what Eugen Weber called the hollow years. It seems clear in retrospect that Paris never quite recovered— politically, economically, or above all psychologically—from the consequences of the First World War, the death of so many of the young men. The Great Depression ("Brother can you spare a dime?") was less sharp in France than in the United States or Britain or Germany, but it lasted longer. There was hardly any new building in Paris during that time; the city deteriorated. The *faubourgs* did grow, the Red Belt—politically it became first Communist, later partly fascist (Jacques Doriot the popular mayor of Saint-Denis), and later yet it became African and Muslim.

Sentimental songs about the native city were popular almost everywhere, even in Moscow, as the Soviet Union became patriotic on the eve of the war and in London ("maybe it is because I am a Londoner that I love London so, . . . that I think of her wherever I go"), and young people were dancing even in Lambeth. But there was a dimension of pessimism (more than melancholy) in Paris that to this degree was absent elsewhere. The London unemployed underneath the arches were "dreaming their dreams away," but they were more robust, not in total despair. In brief, Paris in the 1920s and 1930s seemed a good place to visit but not to live.

Optimism and Pessimism

A social psychologist recently complained that there have been about a hundred times as many articles in academic journals on pessimism as on optimism. I do not know whether such statistics can be fully trusted; a search on Google provides different results. But it is certainly true that the political barometer does not now indicate fair weather, and the prophecies about the coming environmental disasters, somewhat exaggerated as they may be, point in the same direction. There were no editorials in 1900 stating that "humanity is more at risk than at any earlier phase in its history," and no scientist went on record saying that the odds were no better than 50:50 that our present civilization on Earth would survive to the end of this century, as Sir Martin Rees did, Baron Rees of Ludlow, the distinguished theoretical physicist and Astronomer Royal of the United Kingdom, in *Our Final Hour* (2003). Perhaps Sir Martin was too pessimistic, and the odds are slightly better, say 60:40, but they are still frightening.

Richard Rorty, one of the most influential American philosophers of his generation, said in his last interview before his death in 2007 that he was not sure America's democratic institutions would survive an attack by a suitcase-size nuclear bomb. He could not quite make up his mind whether this would be the fault of the Republicans eager to impose their total rule or of the terrorists eager to have a repeat performance of 9/11. I had mentioned this danger to the survival of democracy years before 9/11 in my writing and so had a few others, aware of the fact that the danger of traditional terrorism was much smaller than often assumed and that of future threats much larger, but it was reassuring that this fact had eventually percolated to public intellectuals.

Rorty saw some reason for hope because his ideas and those of Jürgen Habermas, the leader of the second generation of the Frankfurt School, had evoked interest among students in Tehran. Perhaps these students would one day constitute a democratic-secular alternative to the present Iranian ideology. Perhaps the effects of global warming and the dangers facing humankind as the result of climate change will induce terrorists to declare an armistice.

Perhaps so—but when? It is quite true that not all the dangers facing humankind originate in Tehran or Pakistan; one could think of many others. It is reassuring to read in the August 2007 issue of the scientific magazine *Discover* that most of the present fears are overhyped, that dirty bombs and biological weapons are not likely to have much life-threatening effect. Many, probably most, such attacks will fail in the early stage, but it will be sufficient for one or two to succeed to cause a great deal of havoc. And it is useful to recall that terrorists of past ages also overcame initial technical difficulties.

It may be wrong to focus one's attention on traditional terrorism only, for, to quote the Astronomer Royal, "We are entering an era when a single person can, by one clandestine act, cause millions of deaths or render a city uninhabitable for years. . . . Indeed disaster could be caused by someone who is merely incompetent." Or, he should have added, by a madman or a fanatic. In brief, it would be unwise to rely too much on the technical difficulties that villains or madmen are bound to face, just as one should not put one's trust in the assumption that all human beings always act rationally. A Nobel Peace Prize has justly been given to those warning about ecological disasters likely to occur. I suspect not many honors are to be earned by those warning of future terrorism.

The generation to which I belong was more or less driven into a preoccupation with politics; there seemed to be no escape. Probably there was none, but if I had a second chance now and if conditions were different, I could think of other subjects to study, promising greater satisfaction. There are more attractive and less tragic historical figures than Cassandra. She had the gift of prescience, but Apollo had put a curse on her that no one should believe her.

CHAPTER 2

Growing Up under the Nazis

or, Why One Had to Be There to Understand It

The first major public event in the outside world I remember must have been the appearance of the dirigible *Graf Zeppelin,* noiselessly gliding over my hometown, light gray in color, nearly 800 feet in length. Flying was still something unusual and fascinating. Families went to the local airport for an outing on warm summer evenings and on weekends to see the small planes take off and land.

The first major political event I remember, much more vividly, was the German general elections of 1930, in which the Nazis emerged as the second strongest political party. How did we hear about it? From the radio, but we had no speaker yet; we had only crystal sets and had to listen to broadcasts with earphones.

The airship and the radio are appropriate first memories, for they signal commercial aviation and commercial broadcasting, two enterprises that shaped the era. They also forecast the style of warfare, propaganda, and mass politics shortly to come into everyone's life. Air travel brought the rapid movement of people; radio brought the rapid movement of information. Adolf Hitler made effective use of both. They knit the world together, yet they also powered totalitarian movements. For the generation after me, the jet plane and television played the same role, and for my grandchildren, it is the computer and all its associated technology. As always, new technologies become weapons in political and military struggles.

Political and Cultural Awakening, from Weimar to the Third Reich

My parents, like most of their class and background, had no interest in politics and thought it an unhealthy and risky occupation. They voted (I think) for the small German Democratic Party. But as this center-left party got smaller and smaller, they shifted to the Social Democrats. They certainly did not encourage any interest on my part in politics. I often heard them say, "Politics spoil the character," echoing a line from Johann Wolfgang von Goethe's *Faust,* written more than a century earlier: "A nasty song, ugh! a political song."

Those about ten years older than I, born just before World War I and growing up in the Weimar Republic, were, most of them, heavily politicized. And to some extent they influenced my generation. But all things considered, I find in retrospect that among my contemporaries there was less interest and involvement in politics than might have been expected. Perhaps there was a feeling that the individual did not really matter, that he (or she) was at the mercy of anonymous powers. One of the Nazi slogans was, "The individual is nothing, the community—everything." This was by no means a purely Nazi belief; it was part of the *Zeitgeist*. But in Germany it was particularly powerful. Individualism had never been considered a virtue in Germany.

Today it is hard not to believe that there must have been a feeling of crisis in the early 1930s, of impending doom, of inevitability about the Nazi takeover. But it wasn't like that really. People were greatly worried by the economic crisis that began with the collapse of big banks in 1929 and sank into the Great Depression, which had such a huge impact on other European countries and in the United States. My most vivid mental pictures are of unemployed people lining up in the streets, of field kitchens to feed the newly poor, of demonstrations.

Politics was in the air, and there was a feeling of great uncertainty. But, after all, this had been the case since the end of World War I. I was an avid newspaper reader from the age of nine even though I cannot possibly have understood much of what I read. Since I could not afford to buy half a dozen papers a day, I went to the newspaper offices and asked for sample copies, which I usually got. On second thought, my political awakening must have begun before the German elections, for I remember that in the winter of 1928–29, the coldest in living memory, my father sent me to the corner shop on a Sunday morning to buy the *Berliner Tageblatt*. I froze horribly, but this did not prevent me standing for minutes in front of the shop studying the headlines of the other papers as well.

People have asked me whether there was fear of war, but I cannot recall anything of the sort, least of all among the veterans of that first war. Virtually every male had been called up. My father, who had been a little too old to serve in a fighting unit, was made temporary head of a big textile factory in Łódź, a part of Poland that was occupied. His brother served on the Russian-Ukrainian front and got the Iron Cross—which did not help him any after Hitler came to power. Two uncles were killed in the war, and this family experience of the war was quite typical.

The veterans were convinced that there would not be another war in their lifetime, and perhaps never. War was not popular except among a few young people such as Ernst Jünger, a writer and a war hero who talked and wrote about fighting as a spiritual experience. But he was the exception. For most, war meant starvation and other deprivations, losing one's dearest friends and closest relations. In Nazi propaganda, war did not figure; the Nazis merely proclaimed that they would not accept the stipulations of the Versailles Treaty, such as the reparations. But Hitler never invoked war; on the contrary, he always claimed that a soldier like him who had been injured (he had been gassed) could not possibly want a war; only the Jews, he said, wanted to unleash a war. Of course the true aims and the consequences of Nazism, mass murder and war, were not known in 1933, when Hitler took over the government.

The Nazis attracted support from all sectors of the population, a little less perhaps in Catholic regions than in Protestant, a bit more among the middle class than among the aristocracy or the working class. Nazi support was a bit above average in Silesia and in Breslau, its capital, a city of about 600,000, where I lived. But the differences between our region and other regions were not large. What went on in Breslau was fairly typical.

Following the Nazi takeover, leaders of the opposition parties in our city were arrested or fled abroad. Nazi flags, the swastika, were displayed all over the place. There was a first concentration camp following a local initiative, quite small and temporary, on the outskirts of the city; the Nazis called them "wild" camps. Then, within a few weeks or months, most non-Nazi political institutions and associations were banned and various institutions were purged of elements the Nazis considered unreliable. This transformation proceeded quite smoothly. There was virtually no resistance. The "bourgeois" parties and the Social Democrats were unprepared for functioning in conditions of illegality. The Communists had made some preparations for operating underground, but the Nazi security services based on the Weimar police were quite effective at infiltrating these illegal cells. After 1934 or 1935, most ceased to function. Illegal pamphlets were smuggled in; I knew some of the young people who did this. A few were caught and paid for it with their lives, including a girl of my acquaintance. Those who wrote these pamphlets were quite out of touch, and this literature was wholly ineffective.

But by and large, after the Nazis took over, life in Breslau went on pretty much as it had during the Weimar years. Our city had never been given to modernism. What we now call Weimar culture was concentrated largely in Berlin or, to be precise, in certain sections of the German capital. Yes, the Bauhaus architectural school was in Dessau, and some avant-garde painters lived in Munich and Dresden. Göttingen, a mecca for physicists and mathematicians, attracted a few American physicists, including Robert Oppenheimer. But by and large, "Weimar" meant Berlin. It was Berlin that attracted French youth and some young Englishmen—notably the writers W. H. Auden, Stephen Spender, and Christopher Isherwood. Berlin's new freedom and modernism are evidence of how easy it is to take some highly publicized or attractive aspect of society and make a minority phenomenon seem like the most important and even familiar aspect of the time. What we now call "Weimar culture" was really only part of the scene, and for most of the time not even the dominant trend. During those years one hardly ever used the term "Weimar." One talked about the "Republik." Even the right preferred terms like "the November republic established by the November criminals," since the monarchy had collapsed in November 1918. Only in the 1960s and 1970s did the term "Weimar" gain wide currency for that interlude between the end of World War I and the rise of the Nazis.

Outside of Berlin, life in Germany was still quite provincial, in a good and a bad sense. Travel abroad was uncommon. Social life, manners, and customs had become somewhat freer since the days of the monarchy. But there had been no cultural or social revolution, only gradual change in some fields.

Schools, for instance, were far less authoritarian than under the empire. I went to a rather exclusive primary school attended by children from rich and aristocratic families as well as from the Jewish upper middle class. It was a bit snobbish, and I often felt out of place. The others had more elaborate and expensive toys than I had. They went with their parents to all kinds of exotic places, such as the Engadine in southern Switzerland or the Adriatic coast, destinations quite rare at the time, whereas we went to the nearby Giant Mountains on the border between Germany and Czechoslovakia (today between Poland and the Czech Republic).

But seen in retrospect, the school was good to me. The administration let me finish four years of primary school in three, and this may have saved my life, for as a result—and also because Hitler introduced obligatory military service—I graduated in February 1938, at age sixteen, and was forced to think about my future. I left Germany just in time—one day before *Kristallnacht*—in November 1938.

Primary schools were coeducational, but the gymnasium—the high school—was not. The high school I attended had a great tradition, and it had had produced three or four Nobel Prize winners. The teachers were excellent, and not authoritarian; they were products of Weimar or had been exposed to it. Many should have become university professors, but there were few such openings at the time. The curriculum had not greatly changed over the years. Recent history was not taught: contemporary history did not exist. We learned about Otto von Bismarck, but not about events thereafter. But I don't think that this was (or is) a specifically German problem. History textbooks in most countries do not cover recent history; it is too controversial.

After 1933, the universities were Nazified very quickly. The Nazis had considerable support among students well before they emerged as a major force in German politics. They were strongest in universities in small towns where there were few Jewish lecturers or students and in faculties and departments such as forestry or veterinary medicine where there were no Jews at all. In fact, pro-Nazi students took the leading part in the famous book burnings of 1933. Political opponents and those considered insufficiently politically reliable were pensioned off. The Jews were thrown out, both lecturers and students. But there were exceptions. Some Jewish professors were permitted to stay on for a year or two, and I knew one Jewish student, Henry Kellermann, who got his doctorate in 1937 and later became an American diplomat and ambassador to UNESCO.

In high schools, Nazification was somewhat more gradual. It took a while for the curriculum and the textbooks to be changed. The teaching of German literature and history was slowly adjusted, and in biology there were some new lessons about race theory. When a teacher entered the classroom the pupils had to stand and return his "Heil Hitler." But on the whole, ideological indoctrination was left to the Hitler Youth. At least, this is how we youngsters saw it. I recently read the diaries of a former teacher of mine, Willy Cohn. He was thrown out of his job overnight. The fact that he had won the Iron Cross, a high military decoration, during World War I did not help him any. Of course, for those of us who had not yet started careers, the impact of the Nazi takeover was, at least at first, less traumatic.

Official policy was to squeeze out the Jews, but apparently they overlooked me and a few others. The Nazi bureaucracy was not always consistent. "Non-Aryans" did not, of course, greet anyone with a "Heil Hitler." And there were certain activities in which we did not participate, such as class excursions or political meetings. But the teachers were, on the whole, fair. Most of my friends were non-Jewish, and there were few provocations by classmates. It may have been different elsewhere; I can report only what I experienced. It may seem surprising, but I was never individually physically molested or attacked, and I do not recall more than three or four occasions of verbal attack, usually directed against a group of us. I have heard from others with similar experiences, but I also know of very different cases.

I was arrested once for a few hours. It was quite harmless. I had taken part in an excursion with a youth group at a time when such excursions were banned. We had made the mistake of cycling in a fairly sizable group instead of traveling in smaller groups. The man who arrested me was a very senior police officer, possibly the head of police in our town, who had by chance come upon our group. I did not ask him for further identification; if I had, he would not have been amused. Afterward I removed all illegal literature from my shelves, but this proved to be unnecessary, as there was no search of our home.

One certainly learned to develop a thick skin in those years, but we did not feel traumatized, perhaps because there was so much emphasis on sport. I was boxing under the guidance of a legendary Jewish trainer named Lachmann. He produced a whole galaxy of amateur German champion boxers, three of whom went on to compete in the Berlin Olympic Games of 1936, and one, Josef Miner, got a bronze medal in the featherweight class. After 1933 German boxers should no longer have trained with him, but they came anyway, under cover of darkness. So I, a mere boy, was training with them, sometimes serving as a sparring partner.

Track and field, soccer, handball: we did it all. My school graduation report says I would probably be a success as a sports teacher. It could be argued that sports provided no more than an illusion of normality. But psychologically it was certainly a good thing, generating much-needed self-confidence. When a grandson of mine got a karate black belt, it impressed me at least as much as his academic achievements.

In any case, school was not the paramount cultural influence. There were books, concerts, museums, art, and cinema. The libraries in the homes of our parents were largely "Weimar" books, that is to say, left-wing, liberal, and in my case to a considerable extent Jewish. Well after the Nazis came to power, I had the good fortune to find, in an uncle's cellar, full sets of the leading journals of Weimar such as *Weltbühne* and *Tagebuch*. My uncle was selling spirits in a provincial town and had an enormous dark cellar in which the barrels and bottles were stored.

Nazi cultural censorship was much less strict than Soviet censorship—unless, of course, Jews were concerned, or well-known opponents of the Nazi regime. Most French, British, and American best sellers appeared in German translation even after 1933. Of course, the Nazis had their foreign favorites such as Céline and Jean Giono in France or Thomas Wolfe, who liked to be in Berlin oblivious of politics. Wolfe was at the time probably more widely read in Germany than in the United States, but that was not unusual. Romain Rolland, for instance, had a greater following in Germany than in France, until he became a Communist sympathizer in the 1930s. But there were also translations of Ernest Hemingway and William Faulkner and, of course, of *Gone with the Wind*.

Erich Kästner, author of the world-famous *Emil and the Detectives*, was one of the most popular authors of the Weimar period. The Nazis intensely disliked him in view of his pacifism and considered him a "degenerate" author; consequently, after 1933 he was forbidden to publish. But he could still write film scripts under another name and did not have to starve. The books of Thomas Mann were sold in Germany up to 1936, when his citizenship was revoked and he published an open letter to the dean of Bonn University dissociating himself from the "New Germany."

Friends in an underground group—the KPO, a Communist right-wing deviationist faction—fed me Marxist literature, which I found a very useful, even essential, part of my political education. I read not only Karl Marx and V. I. Lenin but also their later-day interpreters such as the Dutch school (Herman Gorter and Anton Pannekoek), Fritz Sternberg on imperialism, and Karl Korsch. Friends in the underground also gave me *Fontamara* by Ignazio Silone. Even at the age of fifteen or sixteen I realized that it was a powerful antifascist novel, perhaps the greatest ever written.

The German reading public was absorbed in a very different kind of literature, some of it quite apolitical, some patriotic, praising traditional values and German bravery in World War I. Much later, in the early 1970s, when I gave a paper on best sellers in Germany in the 1920s at a conference on Weimar culture at the New School in New York, Hannah Arendt, who was present, announced with some contempt that "we" never read those books, never even heard of them. But the "we" to whom she referred were a few dozen intellectuals meeting in certain coffeehouses on and off the Kurfürstendamm, mostly left-wing, mostly Jewish. Today histories of Weimar Germany say much about *The Magic Mountain*, expressionism, and atonal music. Sure, all these things were present, and in 1929 Thomas Mann received the Nobel Prize. But they were of passionate interest to only a tiny minority.

In fact, Weimar culture's great success was posthumous, thirty or forty years after it had come to an end. Weimar, or to be precise one strand of Weimar culture, was rediscovered only in the late 1960s and the 1970s—in the United States, in Germany, and other European countries. To a certain extent there were political reasons for its rediscovery. European Marxism had not been well known in the United States (outside New York), and certainly not in the universities. Perhaps the rediscovery had also to do with the fact that there had been a great deal of talent in the 1920s in Germany, whereas the 1960s and 1970s were in the West rather lean years for creative trends of that kind. Hence there was greater readiness to accept the impulses that went back to an earlier generation.

I first saw expressionist and postexpressionist paintings in museums whose directors were more open than others to modern painting and sculpture. There were also substantial private collections of modern paintings. The collectors were not necessarily the superrich. Pictures that now fetch millions in auctions could be purchased at the time for little money. I remember that the waiting room of my eye doctor had a dozen pictures from Die Brücke, a group of pre–World War I modern artists.

But most of all I learned at the cinema. I saw some silent films, usually slapstick comedies, but they did not greatly impress me. All this changed with the advent of sound. Some cinemas, probably the majority, were quite small, while others were enormous and luxurious, with large organs to provide musical accompaniment. They were called "palaces," and like palaces they were. I went to the movies at least once or twice a week, and so did most of my friends. It was high tide in the development of the German cinema, with serious movies, musicals, and comedies. There were real stars such as Emil Jannings or Heinrich George, or Leslie Howard in Britain. Hit songs from the musicals of the 1930s are remembered and played to this day. There was not much specifically Weimar about these films. There were some technical innovations, but, except for Fritz Lang's *M,* the content was conventional. Patriotic movies about Frederick the Great were popular. After the defeat of 1918 many wanted to see Prussia, and Germany, victorious.

There was in later years the temptation to read too many deep motives and symbols into certain movies. For instance, Siegfried Kracauer, a gifted writer on film who migrated to France in 1933 and then to the United States, saw mountain climbing as a precursor of Nazism. There was a grain of truth in this connection, but not much more. Was the cinema a "dream factory," in the phrase of the Soviet writer Ilya Ehrenburg? Perhaps for some. For most it was simply the form of entertainment most easily and cheaply accessible prior to the arrival of television.

Just as a few of the traditions of Wilhelmian Germany lingered on during Weimar, much of Weimar lasted into the Third Reich despite all the efforts of the Nazis to purge what they called the *Kulturbolschewismus,* the "cultural Bolshevism," of the Weimar era. The term "cultural Bolshevism" was, of course, ridiculous, for cultural experimentation in the Soviet Union was limited and of short duration, and most Communists did not approve of it. This is *a fortiori* true with regard to sexual freedom. By the late 1920s Soviet culture had become quite traditional and conservative. Joseph Stalin was no more a modernist than Adolf Hitler.

Following the Nazi takeover, many of the leading actors and actresses continued to perform, and the level of the German cinema was quite respectable even in the late 1930s. There was nationalism, even chauvinism, in some of these films, but also great admiration for France. Britain and the United States were not given much thought by most Germans, however, except perhaps in Hamburg, which always had a weakness for things English. One of the hit songs of 1936 was "Paris, du bist die schoenste Stadt der Welt" (Paris, you are the most beautiful city in the world). Even under Hitler, Germans were willing to admit that Paris was more attractive than Berlin.

Many of the movie producers, too, continued their careers in the Third Reich, unless, of course, they were Jewish. Joseph Goebbels, the Nazi propaganda minister, realizing the importance of the cinema, gave it far more freedom than other arts. Most of the films of the Nazi era—perhaps 90 percent or even more—were nonpolitical. Goebbels understood perfectly well that neither soldiers nor civilians wanted political indoctrination at a time of war.

I loved to see foreign movies: this was the time when great French, British, and American movies were produced, and there was no difficulty seeing them; all the major cities had cinemas specializing in foreign films, and some were even shown for general release. I saw (to give but a few examples) films made by René Clair, Julien Duvivier, Jean Renoir, and others, and I don't think I missed a film in which Jean Gabin performed. The only major movies I missed at the time were Russian films, and I watched them in later years. True, jazz was banned, so its German fans called it "blues" and performed it all the same. Even Benny Goodman and his band performed; apparently those who invited him did not know that he was Jewish.

Nazi policy toward painting and sculpture was not remotely as liberal as it was toward movies, though the famous exhibition of *Degenerate Art* in Munich in 1937 included painters such as Ernst Barlach and Emil Nolde who were ideologically by no means deeply hostile to Nazism. But German expressionists such as Erich Heckel, Karl Schmidt-Rottluff, and Max Pechstein were held up to derision and condemnation. These painters were very poor, surviving only with the support of a few well-to-do art lovers. Ernst Ludwig Kirchner took his own life. His *Berlin Street Scene* was sold for 3,000 Marks (less than $1,000), considered at the time a fair price; in 2006 it went for $36 million at a Christie's auction in New York.

Why Weimar Fell, Why the Nazis Came to Power

I later became a historian of Weimar Germany. Today Weimar is viewed with much nostalgia, as both a golden period of culture and a forerunner of modern society, with all its pluses and minuses, an era in which the idea of freedom was doomed either by its own excesses or by its citizens' carping criticism and refusal to defend their liberties. The Weimar period has been a favorite subject in Western popular culture, particularly in movies. I have found most of them difficult to watch, including the famous *Cabaret*. What bothers me? It is simply not right.

Both politically and culturally, Weimar was an elite phenomenon that never grew deeper roots while alienating those who still preferred the earlier era. It was a democracy with few democrats and a growing number of extremists. This was also true in the cultural field. The Weimar avant-garde represented—in music and the plastic arts even more than in literature—a near total break with the past. This was more than the general public could stomach at the time. Strangely, many of those who belonged to the Weimar cultural avant-garde were not quite aware of their position or tended to forget in later years how isolated they had been. This attitude on the part of the cultural elite is evident in the United States, both politically and culturally, and is, in fact, pretty standard throughout Western culture. The results are most often amusing or at least merely annoying. In Germany, they were tragic.

Given the resurgence of totalitarianism—the attraction of radical, violent, antidemocratic, highly ideological movements—the intellectual Weimar of the

1920s seems today like that fleeting light which is soon extinguished. Why did Germany lack a foundation for democracy? After all, democracy was pretty well-entrenched in Britain and France. What made Germany different, at least at this time? I do not pretend that I can fully account for the fact that democracy was not really deeply rooted in Germany. But there are some events and traditions to take note of. The revolution of 1848 had failed. Defeat in World War I was a shock. Then the inflation of 1922 and 1923 was another shock; many Germans lost their property. At the end of the decade, the world economic crisis, above all the high levels of unemployment, made most people long for stability and reject experimentation, political or cultural. Fear permeated the working class and also the middle class, as academic and white-collar jobs were lost. Everything seemed undermined by the general economic decline. Poverty was a grim reality. Opposition seemed useless, even mad.

There is the temptation with hindsight to regard things as inevitable that could have been prevented at the time. The Social Democrats should have clung to power in 1929 instead of abdicating. But they had no strong leadership and lacked a sense of how to use power, which they did possess to a considerable degree. A number of arrests even up to the last moment would have decapitated the Nazi Party. Or the last German democratic governments could have followed a dynamic economic policy instead of the idiotic restrictions carried out by Heinrich Bruening, head of the Center Party. Bruening's policy response to the depression was similar to that of U.S. President Herbert Hoover. He cut back on government spending, thereby reducing welfare and wages. If the democratic forces had exercised more forceful leadership, they would have gained time. The economic crisis peaked in 1932, and a year or two later, as the situation began to improve, they would have reaped the benefits.

But there was also intellectual opposition to democracy. There was the belief that a country that wanted to be strong could not afford endless parliamentary debates, and the Weimar Constitution, far from perfect, permitted a great number of parties to mushroom. That made the formation of stable governments difficult.

By 1931–32 the antidemocratic parties were stronger than the democratic center, which could no longer hold. Above all, these parties began to rule the street. I remember the big demonstrations, virtually every Sunday, ending in clashes between Nazis and Communists or between Nazis and the police. Every week, people were injured and killed in these demonstrations. Many believed that the country was on the verge of a civil war, hence the call for a government that would restore order.

How important was antisemitism in this process? Was it a relatively minor issue in the Nazis' appeal? Did they need it, at all, to mobilize support? Or was it Hitler's personal fixation?

Antisemitism was certainly more than Hitler's personal obsession. It had deep roots in Germany, and World War I compounded it, as did the political and economic crises that followed. Someone had to be made responsible for these disasters. And yet antisemitism alone would not have attracted the German masses. There was as much, or more, antisemitism elsewhere in Europe. I remember a discussion with my friend George Mosse, one of the great historians of modern Germany and my coeditor on *Journal of Contemporary History*. Both of us were working on nineteenth-century German antisemitism, and I suggested to George an exercise in counterfactual history. If, in 1900, experts had been asked to name the European country in which antisemitism was the greatest danger, what would be the response? Russia, Poland, Romania, perhaps France, but certainly not Germany. George agreed and followed the idea up in his books.

After 1933 there was massive antisemitic indoctrination in the schools, the media, and the party organizations. But I don't think antisemitism ever became the central ideological issue except among a small group of people like Julius Streicher, editor of *Der Stürmer*, a weekly that dealt with little else. But even so, Hitler had the active help of thousands, and the passive support of many millions, in carrying out the murder of European Jewry.

German Romanticism, German Youth

So why did the horrors of the trenches that inspired so much pacifism in England and France—which, after all, won the war—inspire in Germany a romantic attitude toward war and heroism? Perhaps more than anything else, German romanticism explains why Weimar fell and why the Nazis came to power. German youth were not much attracted by modernism, but they were attracted by Nazism. The left was hardly represented in the academic world. There was only a handful of left-wing professors, and none belonged to the extreme left. Those associated with the Frankfurt School had to hide their Marxism carefully, using an esoteric language of their own to present a synthesis of sophisticated Marxism and psychoanalysis. Their influence was limited to a very small circle, and most academics did not even know of the Frankfurt School's existence. Like Weimar culture, they had their blossoming only in America forty or more years later.

The prevailing intellectual trend, if there was such a thing, was neo-romanticism. This was not the apolitical individualistic neo-romanticism of emotional soul searching, not the romanticism of playing the flute or the lute while walking in the forests. It was the patriotic, collectivist kind of romanticism, a spirit that hailed a joining of forces, a strong leader (not necessarily Hitler), and a restoration of the old glory of a powerful country. It was romanticism that beat the drum while marching in step the streets. This was the age of endless, gray, marching columns. It was the age of obeying and marching, not of thinking. This was true also in fascist Italy and the Soviet Union. The marchers, of course, prevailed.

The German youth movement itself was a romantic, or neo-romantic, movement, Germany being the land of classic romanticism, except, of course that in classic romanticism the emphasis had been on the individual, his (or her) moods and sentiments. The new romanticism was that of the campfire and books about World War I, which were very popular among these boys and young men.

When I was young, young people in Germany behaved like children and young adults always behave—exploring city neighborhoods, enjoying birthday parties with chocolate cake, playing soccer and other sports, collecting stamps. All this changed in 1933, but there was by no means a total break. Young people joined the Hitler Youth or the Deutsches Jungvolk, the younger section of the Hitler Youth, most of them not out of deep conviction but because they did what was expected of them. The only ones who did not were some Catholics who belonged to various church groups.

This was not a very intellectual generation, even among the elite. Children were influenced by their elders and the generation of their parents. They were an obedient generation; there was no youth rebellion of the sort there had been around the turn of the century. The earlier Wandervogel was a phenomenon without parallel in other countries. It has been compared with the Boy Scouts, but in essential respects it was quite different. It aimed at developing a specific youth culture that rebelled against school and the parental home. The leaders were not grown-ups but young people, three or four years older than the members. This German youth movement was basically apolitical, or believed that it was so. In fact, it unknowingly accepted much of the patriotic ideology of Wilhelmian Germany; the Weimar Republic had no attraction.

The youth movement was a relatively small elite of perhaps no more than 100,000 members in dozens of groups, each with a different orientation and style. There was a certain cult of militarism, more after the First World War than before, but no feeling of superiority toward other European nations. On the contrary, there were many programs in which German youth could meet the youth of other countries to create ties of friendship or at least understanding. Young people were reading Hermann Hesse, who was anything but a militarist. At the same time there was the belief in the soldier as the ideal—courageous, disciplined, selfless, willing to sacrifice himself on behalf of a higher cause. There was the conviction that the group, the collective, was infinitely more important than the individual. Most of the movement's songs were in praise of soldiers and their commanders, beginning with the medieval mercenaries, the Landsknechte.

I remember classmates with literary ambitions who imitated the immensely popular Werner Beumelburg, a wartime officer and then an anti-Weimar editor who later joined the Nazis and who wrote about the Western Front during the war, or Edwin Erich Dwinger, who wrote about the fate of the German armies in Russia in *Zwischen Weiss und Rot,* with a strong emphasis on the mistreatment of ethnic Germans in Eastern Europe. Some were fascinated by the stories that came out of the former German colonies in Africa—Tanganyika and Southwest Africa. All this was, of course, very much secondhand, as there had been no romanticism in the battles for Verdun, only suffering, mud, and horrible death. But this the young readers did not want to know.

Instead, the youth movement was very interested in examples of heroism. One of the most widely read books in the movement during the late Weimar period was *Heldenfibel* (A Hero's Primer). The author, a charismatic youth leader named Eberhard Koebel, could not make up his mind whether he was closer to Nazism or communism. He died in East Germany after World War II, where the Communists never quite trusted him.

This kind of mentality could be found well beyond the youth movement. Visiting the homes of friends, I often saw crossed swords affixed to the wall, sometimes a memory of World War I, or going further back to the Franco-Prussian War of 1870–71, when the Germans won an overwhelming victory. The cavalry charges at Vionville and Mars-la-Tour: those were the glory days.

For the Weimar Republic, the young had only contempt or at best indifference. I remember one experience, a sunny Sunday afternoon on a little steamer making its way down the Oder River. A few swimmers jumped on the vessel and demonstratively dried their behind with the black-red-gold flag of the republic that flew from the stern. Most of those present applauded. I cannot have been more than twelve years old, but I understood that a political regime not commanding any respect would not last.

In later years, with the general politicization, some in the youth movement went to the right. Eventually the German youth movement was absorbed by the Hitler Youth, albeit without much enthusiasm. Young people had shared with the Nazis the belief in leadership—the need for a Führer—but most initially did not see Hitler as that leader. It occurs to me that the antiauthoritarianism of the 1960s, the generation of Rudi Dutschke and of the Baader-Meinhof terrorist gang, was in many ways a reaction against the obedience of their parents' generation. As so often in recent German history, in both cases they overdid it.

But romanticism was no monopoly of the right, as some in the youth movement turned to the left. In fact those who opted for the far left did so out of romantic notions about the Russian Revolution. The idea of building a new and infinitely better world was not based on reading Karl Marx's *Das Kapital* or

Friedrich Engels's *Anti-Dühring* but because the idea of a revolution exuded such a great fascination.

Ultimately the Communists could not compete with the Nazis because they were not part of the nationalist camp; their dream was of too much change and had too foreign a model. True, around 1930 the Communists made a half-hearted turn toward nationalism, publishing manifestos denouncing the imperialist peace treaty of Versailles as subjugating Germany. But the Nazis easily outflanked them, pointing out that the loyalty of the Communists was to a foreign country ("Heil Moskau" was their slogan for a while) whereas the Nazis were true, unalloyed patriots ("Deutschland Erwache"—Germany Awake!—and "Heil Hitler").

The Communists and the Social Democrats underrated the power of German nationalism, a miscalculation that goes back to an earlier period. True, in the 1920s Goebbels and some other Nazis dreamed of a German-Russian alliance directed against the capitalists in the plutocratic West, but Hitler quickly put them in line. A few dissenters left the party; the others returned to the fold. After the war, I met and interviewed a few of them, such as Otto Strasser, an early Nazi who represented the left wing of the party until expelled by Hitler in 1930. He fled abroad in 1933, when others with such ideas were purged and killed. This group of so-called National Bolsheviks never had a chance of succeeding.

Being internationalist in orientation, the left could not turn chauvinist and compete with the Nazis. But those on the left could have been a bit more realistic. Let me give one obvious example—Rosa Luxemburg, the heroine of the German left to this day. Every January, on the anniversary of her murder in 1919 by proto-Nazi gangs for launching a failed Bolshevik revolution, tens of thousands of sympathizers congregate at her grave in Berlin. Streets, squares, and institutions are named after her not only in Germany but also in France and Italy. She was not only a very courageous woman who became a martyr to her cause but also a sharp intellect and a brilliant orator. But her political judgment, on both tactical and theoretical levels, was mostly wrong. She was wrong in her writings about imperialism, about the collapse of capitalism, about the general strike as a weapon. She was even wrong in her dispute with Lenin, who better understood the importance of nationalism. But she was right in opposing the First World War and predicting in 1918 that the Soviet regime would lead to a dictatorship not of the proletariat but over the proletariat.

In January 1919 Luxemburg supported—not with great enthusiasm, it would appear—a *coup* against the Social Democratic government, an action that was self-defeating. In the course of that *coup* she was killed, together with her colleague Karl Liebknecht, by the proto-Nazis. Did she understand that one does not play with uprisings and revolutions and that the result of profound miscalculation can be deadly? Did she understand that a Jewish woman from Zamość, Galicia, could not be the leader of the German working class? She did not understand because she totally failed to grasp the power of nationalism, and not only in Germany. These errors cost her and many others their lives, though they hardly affected her posthumous reputation.

Luxemburg's fate should be compared with that of Eduard Bernstein, an early Marxist. Born in Berlin in 1850, he was also of Jewish origin. His father was a railroad engineer, one of the first. He joined Marx in his London exile. Bernstein became the father of reformist socialism—or revisionism as its Communist critics called it—believing that the aims of the working class would be achieved gradually, as the result of political pressure. For this and for doubting Marx's predictions concerning the collapse of capitalism, he was virtually excommunicated from the party. In fact, the German Social Democrats, and most other European socialist parties, accepted Bernstein's analysis. His political instincts were usually right—he also opposed World War I—but they were too sober, too unromantic to attract the young generation. With no revolution, no radical, quick solutions, he did not generate enthusiasm, at least among intellectuals. Seen in historical perspective, Bernstein was right but he is forgotten except by the specialists. He died in 1932. No one visits his grave; few even know where it is. You will look in vain for streets commemorating his name except tiny byways in Frankfurt, Bremen, and his native Berlin. When in 2006 a prominent German historian suggested that a major Berlin street be named in his memory, the authorities replied that there was already such a street. But it had nothing to do with the venerable socialist leader, as *Bernstein* is the German equivalent of amber and there is indeed a Berlin neighborhood in which the streets have the names of minerals and semiprecious stones.

So it was not communism but Nazism that had a special appeal for the young generation. The leaders of the Nazi Party were younger than those of other parties, and the same is true with regard to the Fascist Party in Italy, whose anthem was "Giovinezza" (Youth). So the Nazis could easily present themselves as the party of the young, the party of action to whom the future belonged. When the Nazis took over, Hermann Göring was just forty; Goebbels, minister for propaganda, thirty-six; Rudolf Hess, Hitler's deputy, thirty-nine. Heinrich Himmler, the feared leader of the SS and head of all the police and security services, was thirty-three; his deputy, the infamous Reinhard Heydrich, was only twenty-nine years old.

As for the young people in their late teens whom I knew, I would say in hindsight that choosing Hitler was not an act of political decision, not a choice of a political program or ideology; it was simply joining a quasi-religious mass movement as an act of faith. The ideas of democracy and freedom seemed outdated, impotent, and discredited, and there was a readiness to trust the Führer who would know best what to do. As one put it (a quotation I used in *Young Germany*): "National Socialism offered all that a young man in his most secret and proudest imagination would desire—activity, responsibility for his fellows, and work with equally enthusiastic comrades for a greater and stronger fatherland. It held out official recognition, and careers that had been unthinkable before; while on the other side there were only difficulties and dangers, an empty future and doubts in the heart."

In brief, the temptation was irresistible, and not only for the idealists. The majority were *Mitläufer,* fellow travelers who joined because the others did and because it was expected of them, for instance if they wanted to study. They were in broad sympathy with the Nazis and impressed by Hitler, but they were not necessarily fanatics.

Above all there was Hitler's personal role, and the more I think about it, the more decisive it appears in explaining why the Nazis came to power. Just as there would not have been a Bolshevik Revolution in November 1917 but for Lenin, so there would not have been a Nazi takeover in January 1933 but for Hitler. Had Hitler been killed in the attempted *coup* in Munich in 1923—and some of those next to him in the march were hit by bullets—I doubt the Nazis would have come to power. And if they would have come to power, it would not have been the same party and it would not have conducted the same policy. This does not mean, of course, that everything can be explained with reference to Hitler as the great seducer of an innocent people. There was a great readiness to follow him, to believe in a message like the one he offered. But he knew how to use this potential, how to exploit it.

Many have tried to reconstruct Hitler's magic. It is very hard for us to understand today, especially for non-German speakers. How much of it was the content of his talks, and how much his style? Hitler's charisma, his ability to generate enthusiasm, is not easy to explain at a distance of seventy years. When people watch him these days in documentaries, more often than not they are amused (or repelled) by a man rather small of stature with a funny mustache, shouting most of the time, gesticulating wildly: surely this could not have been a serious political figure?

I once watched Hitler for a few minutes at a parade in Breslau. Simplistic or not, I really think he was irreplaceable. Of course, there was Goebbels, a brilliant orator. He would have been a star in the age of television. Göring, a hero of the First World War as a daring fighter pilot, and a dozen other Nazi leaders stood out. But none had the relentless will of Hitler, the fanaticism, single-mindedness, and readiness to gamble.

Consider Göring, Hitler's designated successor in the Third Reich. He was a cruel bully, not lacking in personal courage; he could have been a leading gangster. But being a political leader he would never have gone to war in 1939, as he told interviewers when being held a prisoner after the war had ended. He knew that Germany would be defeated. He mentioned his fears initially to Hitler, but when he realized that Hitler had made up his mind, he did not dare to stand up to him. Nor could a bureaucrat like Himmler have provided the same leadership, nor an ideologue like Alfred Rosenberg. All were devoid of charisma; they were people accustomed to following orders.

Of course the general political climate favored the populist extreme right. It is quite possible that a right-wing authoritarian government would have come to power in Germany based on the right-wing parties, the Nazis, and the armed forces. But it would have been a wholly different proposition. It is probably symptomatic of this fact that today even Marxists or former Marxists write detailed biographies of Hitler rather than social histories of the Third Reich.

Make no mistake, these were different times. A deep crisis prevailed, above all a crisis of confidence, and Hitler promised the Germans exactly what they wanted to hear—work, an end to unemployment, a new order, a new Germany strong in the world. And he did deliver. By 1936 unemployment had been dramatically reduced. There was a new feeling of purpose and achievement. True, there was much less freedom, but the German thirst for freedom was much weaker than the desire for order and prosperity.

And yet Hitler soon traded in the improving material conditions of peace for the risk, and eventually the terrible cost, of war. There was no great enthusiasm to go to war in 1939; too many still remembered the horrors of World War I. Hence Hitler's insistence on *Blitzkrieg*, a quick and decisive victory, and the fear of being bogged down in a war of position rather than movement. World War I had involved years of trench warfare with no big gains despite heavy casualties. Here, too, in the beginning, Hitler seemed to be able to deliver on his promises.

A year after the fighting began, after the victory in France, Hitler was at the height of his glory. Half of Europe had been conquered; most of the rest was under his influence. Internal opposition had been quashed; the doubters had been silenced. Even Hitler's opponents were deeply impressed. In short, the secret of his influence over the masses as well as over those close to him was at that time not so much in his charisma, the quasi-magic he exuded, but in the fact that he made good on his promises. He had restored Germany to a leading position in the world, and he had restored German pride.

How Not to Explain Nazism

Various concepts have been adduced to explain Hitler and the Nazi Party, as the rise of Nazism is among the central issues for understanding of modern politics. But when the Nazi movement is reduced to a cartoon it becomes hard to understand why it was able to mobilize such support. There are those who cannot deal with the fact that an evil ideology can garner so much backing. The *vox populi* cannot be wrong in their eyes. Therefore these foul deeds must have been done by a tiny group of people, or the masses were just fooled (in a version of Marx's concept of "false consciousness"), or it was a conspiracy between Hitler and big business. Many of these misunderstandings prevail to this day.

Much has been written about the power of bureaucracies and institutions, and it has been argued that Hitler (like Stalin) was a prisoner of the bureaucracy and that he did not make the important decisions. But this conclusion is perfect nonsense of the sort that makes one sometimes despair of the uses and value of historiography. Decisions in the Third Reich were never taken by committees. Hitler did not consult others except on matters of detail. The German government was never once convened for a meeting after 1937, and convened only a very few times before. Hitler thought meetings a waste of time and believed that he knew best. The Nazis were the Hitler party.

Of course, Hitler was not omnipresent and omnipotent. But no important decision could be taken without him. It is astonishing, furthermore, to what extent he interfered in small and unimportant matters—for instance, under what conditions fishing licenses should be given to foreigners in Germany or what color the front of certain buildings in Munich should be painted. That he could not follow up on every single order goes without saying. But again, nothing of any importance could be done in Nazi Germany without his permission. He did, of course, delegate, especially regarding the economy, as he was not much interested in the economy so long as it provided what the army needed.

Some thirty years after the war ended, there was a debate among historians and political scientists in Germany and the United States about totalitarianism. One school of thought argued that there was no such thing as "totalitarianism," that the idea was Cold War propaganda, that it had been invented in order to blacken the Soviet system. If there were certain similarities between Nazism and the Soviet system, these were said to be entirely superficial or accidental. But the concept of totalitarianism had been developed well before the outbreak of the Cold War, and who could deny that there was something essentially new in the Nazi system that made it different from earlier dictatorships and also from the regimes established by Francisco Franco in Spain, António Salazar in Portugal, or Juan Perón in Argentina. Benito Mussolini had invented the term "totalitarian," but Italy never quite attained this goal. The monarchy, for instance, was not abolished in Italy even though it was powerless. Denying that there were important differences between totalitarian regimes and old-fashioned authoritarian governments caused a great deal of confusion about the character of Nazism. Unfortunately even now one can find those who, mostly for political reasons, persevere in such views.

For me, the essential point is the structure of the regime. Traditional dictatorships often engage in a philosophy of live-and-let-live. They suppress, perhaps brutally, any outright opposition but are happy to live with indifference. The Nazi regime had an overarching ideology (as did Communist regimes): the demand to control every institution, the insistence on support or terrible punishment. The goal was to mobilize the population. A state that has enthusiastic support is stronger and far better entrenched in power than otherwise. Yet there is a paradox: dictatorships are completely dependent on a single personality. The same was true for Stalin.

Some historians argue that the whole Nazi enterprise was based on feet of clay, that it was bound to fail from the beginning. I know the argument, but I do not share it. The Western powers were willing to appease Hitler in the 1930s right up to the outbreak of the war. They would have given him a great many concessions that they had refused his democratic predecessors. In the midst of the world economic crisis, his economic policy, vaguely similar to Keynesianism, made more sense than that of earlier German governments, which saw their main duty in saving money rather than spending money in order to restart the economy. Such a regime could have lasted for a long time.

Was the Third Reich doomed once it went to war? Again I have my doubts. The problem was that Hitler overreached; he did not know when to stop. The outcome of the war was uncertain for a considerable time. If Hitler had not attacked the Soviet Union and had not declared war on the United States after the Japanese attacked Pearl Harbor, he would have dominated Europe. Neither Stalin nor Franklin Roosevelt would have gone to war against Germany without being forced to do so by Hitler's own actions.

We often see in today's politics how dictators bully and maneuver to get what they want, and how—despite decades of ritual denunciations of appeasement—democratic leaders are willing to make apologies for or concessions to extremist and aggressive regimes, offering explanations for their goals and grievances. Usually such people are—one might say—wise about the past if foolish about the same phenomenon in the present. Yet even with Hitler there was, years after the war, a bitter dispute among German historians. Some tried to downplay, albeit indirectly, the regime's responsibility for war crimes and aggression.

I knew some of the participants in this debate quite well. This was the generation that had been soldiers in the war and/or members of the Nazi Party. It began even earlier with the publications of Fritz Fischer on the First World War. Fischer, who as a young man had been a Nazi sympathizer, reached the conclusion that while Germany was not alone responsible for this war, its responsibility was greater than generally accepted by the German historical profession. Today many, though not all, of Fischer's theses are accepted.

The real *Historikerstreit* (historians' dispute) began some years later and lasted into the 1980s. It was based on the belief among some major historians that there was more to German history than the Holocaust (which is perfectly true) and that a nation could not exist without some pride in its past. Some went beyond this, notably Ernst Nolte, who made absurd claims: that Hitler was compelled to use barbaric (he called them "Asiatic") measures because he faced the Bolshevik (Asiatic) danger; that he simply copied the Soviet Gulag; that Zionist leader Chaim Weizmann's declaration of war against Germany on behalf of the Jewish people apparently justified Hitler's killing the Jews; and so on. This was nonsense, and most German historians, including the nationalists among them, distanced themselves from Nolte. Yet some went further to claim that Auschwitz was used by Germany's enemies as a political weapon to intimidate it and to deprive it of self-confidence.

Others by no means denied the Holocaust but argued that it was not unique in history. By and large, however, the conviction grew, not only among historians, that as so much time had passed since the war and the Holocaust, everything had been said and written about this topic, and that since a new democratic Germany had arisen, the time had come to deal with other aspects of German history and no longer to regard the Holocaust as the beginning and end of it. This process was probably inevitable.

Persecution and Emigration

After 1933, Jews were gradually dismissed from all positions in state administration and from official and semi-official institutions. Jewish enterprises and shops were boycotted, and social relations were cut. Jews were excluded from membership in all associations and banned from many public places, such as swimming pools. They could no longer go to many resorts. The list of places Jews could not go was long and became longer each year.

In the end about half of those Jews who remained in Germany were without income and depended on social assistance. But the younger generation, while well aware that there was no future for them in Germany, suffered less, though we were not oblivious of the impoverishment of our parents. The majority went to Jewish schools and belonged to Jewish youth groups and sport clubs. It was a kind of ghetto existence, but it was not insufferable. One could still travel both inside Germany and abroad—if there was the money to do so.

Gradually, however, the persecution of Jews became more severe, and after *Kristallnacht* (the night of broken glass), tens of thousands of Jews were arrested, and Jews of Polish nationality were deported. By that time, life had indeed become intolerable, and the outbreak of war was only nine months away.

Recent books have argued that German and Austrian Jews were stupid and shortsighted because they did not emigrate in greater numbers and that all who wanted could have found a refuge abroad. I read to my consternation in the Wikipedia article about me that my parents "chose not to leave" the country. (I protested, and the wording has been changed.) In fact, virtually everyone desperately tried to escape, as the letters and stories of many individuals make clear. The question of emigration was the cardinal issue, preoccupying everyone. Willy Cohn's diaries give evidence that whenever Jews met in those years, the issue of leaving was foremost. They exchanged information and read aloud letters from family members about their first experiences abroad. Yet usually these were futile conversations because there were so few ways out of this trap, and each year they became fewer. People desperately awaited the delivery of the mail each day in the hope that there would be some invitation from some place, anything that gave hope. The problem was that other countries did not want to grant entry visas to those applying for shelter, even if only temporary. To read now, sixty or seventy years later, that everyone who wanted to leave could do so and that the Western powers did everything to help is more than annoying. It transfers the responsibility to the victims. It is akin to the desecration of corpses.

It is true that the persecution of Jews in Germany took five years to reach full intensity; in Austria, all this happened within a month or two. As the result of Nazi "gradualism," many thought that after the first Nazi "excesses" of 1933 the policy would moderate. Others thought that Nazi rule would not last long. After all, there had been many governments in Germany after World War I, and few lasted more than a year.

Awareness of the necessity for mass exodus from Germany did not come overnight, and when it came it did not solve the problem, for no one wanted to have the German Jews. In the beginning, 1933, it was relatively easy to enter France and Czechoslovakia. But labor permits were not given, and since money could not be taken out of Germany, such emigration offered no solution. Palestine absorbed more German Jews than any other country until immigration was severely curtailed there by the British Mandatory authorities. It is hard for people today to understand just how difficult it was to get across a border at the time. A Canadian senior official, when asked how many Jews would be permitted to enter Canada, is reputed to have replied, "None is too many," but this was by no means only a Canadian attitude. Emigrants who had actually managed to reach foreign countries were at times sent back—from Switzerland, from the United States, and from the Soviet Union.

Thousands did leave the country, mainly among the younger generation, illegally or semilegally. Consuls of some foreign countries, mainly but not exclusively in Latin America, would give visas in exchange for a few hundred dollars, which was a lot of money at the time. These visas were valid everywhere except in the country that had issued them.

Given the social and age structure of German Jewry, those who remained were in the main elderly people, without means, without the skills needed abroad, without knowledge of foreign languages, often without good health, incapable of manual labor. Such people also tried to emigrate, but, in the face of the totally negative attitude toward immigrants all over the world, they had not the slightest chance.

The idea, indeed the necessity, of leaving first occurred to me around 1935–36. I was fourteen or fifteen at the time. Half of my friends had already left the country. What became of them? Some years ago I tried to prepare a book presenting a collective profile of my generation. It proved to be very difficult because there were too many interesting stories, for our generation did not have a quiet life.

Those who left early, aged fourteen or so, did so together with their families, and had some protection. True, they were quite poor in the country of destination and had to work hard to gain an education. But on the whole they did quite well, producing some five or six Nobel Prize winners. I do not think they were more talented than the generation before or after, but they faced greater challenges, and for them it was a question of swimming or sinking.

But the truly amazing stories were those of the slightly older, say sixteen, seventeen, or eighteen years of age, who went abroad alone, for whom there was no safety net at all. A close friend of mine who was searched, and a revolver found in his apartment, disappeared quickly, crossing the border into Czechoslovakia: we knew where the crossings were that had no frontier control. He went on to South Africa, joined the army when war broke out, was taken hostage by Greek Communists in the early stages of the Greek civil war, returned to South Africa, and was arrested for anti-apartheid activities. He ended up as a distinguished professor of botany in Scotland, a field in which he was responsible for some notable technical innovations.

Another one of this "generation exodus" went to Nigeria and became the world's leading expert on Yoruba art, making it known worldwide; his wife, Vienna born, became something like a goddess of one of the tribes. Another went to Sri Lanka (Ceylon at the time) and by the time he died had become one of the leading monks, a widely respected guru on the island. Yet another had a mystical religious experience, joined a Catholic order (I believe the Benedictines), and later became its representative at the Vatican, the highest position in the order. He died at Beuron monastery in Baden a few years ago. A close friend of mine named Werner Guttentag arrived penniless in Bolivia. He became, among many other things, the founder of the *Encyclopedia Boliviana,* and in recognition of his achievements in the field of Bolivian culture a postage stamp was issued in his honor a few years ago. The legendary chief of East German intelligence Markus Wolf belongs to this generation; so does Henry Kissinger. One of the young women of this generation became America's most famous radio and TV sexologist—"Dr. Ruth."

Some time ago I met the head of a multibillion dollar American corporation; after a few minutes it appeared that we had been in school together. He did not emigrate in time and was sent to Auschwitz. But being very small of stature, he was overlooked at the morning gathering when the candidates for the gas chambers were selected. He did not like to talk about the past.

Another friend named Kurt Reilinger had accompanied a children's transport to Palestine just a week before the outbreak of the war. I was then in Palestine, and I went with him to the ship that was to take him back to Germany, having failed to persuade him not to return. He did great things during the war, helping to organize the underground railway from Holland to Spain by means of which hundreds were saved. Eventually, the Gestapo arrested him, but a few weeks later the British bombed the prison in France in which he was kept and he escaped. Soon after the war he was run over by a car and killed. Among my generation was one—Helmut Hirsch, a member of the youth movement—who volunteered to kill Hitler. Unfortunately his conspiratorial circle was penetrated by Nazi agents and he was arrested and executed, even though he had dual nationality, American and German.

Another young man who also graduated in February 1938, Marcel Reich-Ranicki, a Jew of Polish nationality, was deported to Poland later that year. He escaped from the Warsaw ghetto and later became Germany's leading literary critic. Hilda Monte, a few years older than I and a socialist, was parachuted into Nazi Germany from England during the war. She was later shot while trying to pass the Swiss border. A young left-wing leader whom I knew was arrested by the Gestapo and spent the war years in prison. Normally he should have been sent to Auschwitz and killed, but the bureaucracy had to take its course. And so he was saved, but having rebelled against the Communist Party line in the early 1930s when the Communists declared that the Social Democrats were really fascists, he was unwelcome after the war in East Germany, where the Stalinists ruled. Furthermore his wife had thought him dead and had remarried in England.

My friend Franz escaped to China, which, of course, offered only temporary shelter. I thought he had perished, and great was my joy when suddenly in 1949 he appeared at my apartment in Jerusalem. He had somehow made his way to Israel, found a job as a surveyor, and had recently married. A few weeks later I read in the paper that, working as a surveyor, he had been shot by a Syrian sniper near Lake Tiberias. Quite recently I was told that after his death a daughter was born to his widow. The daughter is now a professor at an Israeli university. I met many other survivors after the war and could continue with their stories, but there is also a danger of forgetting the tens of thousands of my generation who perished.

I also met quite a few of my German classmates after 1945. This was the generation that fought in the war—North Africa, Stalingrad—and more survived than I had thought. As the war ended, they returned. The city of my birth had become Polish in the meantime, so they had to look for a new home, most in West Germany. Nor did they have a profession, and for many years they were very much absorbed in the struggle for survival, with little interest in public affairs. One German classmate, who was half-Jewish and had been persecuted under the Nazis, complained bitterly, in a neo-Nazi periodical, about the injustice that had been done to the fatherland by the victors.

What did I do? Most of my correspondence—and one wrote lots of letters in those days—was related to trying to get out. Most of my pocket money went for postage for letters to faraway countries. My parents encouraged me to look for ways and means to leave the country. In their fifties, they considered themselves elderly and incapable of making a new beginning. They had little money and no contacts with relations or friends abroad. They thought there was no future for them, and unfortunately they were proven right.

I tried to discover relations however remote who had emigrated decades earlier, and indeed I found one in Chile, a "black sheep" who had been sent abroad and made a fortune there. But he or his descendants did not answer. I wrote to Palestine, the United States, Britain, Switzerland, Czechoslovakia, and half a dozen other countries without any success. I went to the various organizations in Germany that provided advice for prospective emigrants—without success.

I did get an offer to study engineering in Czechoslovakia, which, fortunately, I turned down. A protective angel must have guided my steps, for had I accepted this offer I would probably not have survived. It would have meant that in less than a year, with the German takeover, I would again have been trapped.

In the end, owing to a lucky accident and the generosity of an uncle, I was accepted as a student by the Hebrew University in Jerusalem, which overlooked the fact that I was not yet eighteen and, according to regulations, should not have been accepted. Moreover, this uncle was at the time in prison for having defiled the German race; as a bachelor, he had lived with a German woman friend. But since he was a highly decorated World War I officer, he had the privilege of disposing of his income even while in prison. After the outbreak of war he was released and managed to reach Shanghai. At the end of the war, a very sick man, he lived to his death in Oakland, California.

And so on November 8, 1938, just one day before *Kristallnacht*, I boarded the train to Trieste and the ship that was to take me to Palestine. I was lucky. Some of my best friends failed to make it; others survived the war but tragically died soon thereafter. Some members of my own family survived. In the nineteenth century there had been considerable intermarriage and conversion to Christianity, so they were considered half-Jews or quarter-Jews—or even less Jewish. Others lived in so-called privileged mixed marriages. They were persecuted during the Third Reich, but they survived.

Mine is the story of just one individual, but I was an eyewitness. In what way did a youth in Germany shape my historical work and my thinking as a political commentator? I believe it was very important. It was a painful school, but it prevented all kind of delusions in later life, an early antidote or immunization against unrealistic thinking. Exposure to the Nazi experience made some, however, very sensitive to the dangers of dictatorship, and hypersensitivity has thus led them astray. The Nazi phenomenon has today become in itself a political tool. If an individual or a group does not get its way, the opponents or the authorities are labeled Nazi, and their tactics called Gestapo. It is unforgivable that historians and political scientists should engage in such practices.

Of course, it makes a great difference whether one left Nazi Germany (or fascist Italy or the Soviet Union) as a child aged ten or, as in my case, a somewhat precocious seventeen. Growing up in the United States or Britain or belonging to a later generation that did not know that age of violence frequently generates a kind of naive belief that is very attractive but also provincial and misleading. It encourages talking about "the whole civilized world," forgetting that the whole civilized world is so far quite limited and unlikely to expand greatly in the near future.

To what extent were the political lessons of Weimar absorbed in postwar Germany? The Germans certainly learned their lesson, but it took World War II to drive the lesson home. As far as the emigrés are concerned, some learned the lessons too well. In other words, there was among some of them an inclination toward hysteria. In later years they magnified dangers to democracy in America out of all proportion. I remember that in the early 1950s, in New York, Jewish refugees from Germany (including some very distinguished scholars of political philosophy and the social sciences) thought in all seriousness that Senator Joseph McCarthy heralded the triumph of fascism in the United States. This opinion was by no means uncommon.

There was a similar wave of despair some twenty years later in the wake of the Vietnam War, and some made plans to return to Europe, preferably places like Lugano, Ascona, and the vicinity. But in the end only a few left America, and those who did did so mainly because they could not find suitable work or because they were writers and their place was of course in Germany, or at least in a German-speaking country.

Recently I read that a prominent historian of the erstwhile younger generation has warned that the rise of Christian fundamentalism may lead to America becoming fascist, pointing out that Nazism, too, was a mixture of racial dogma and "German Christianity." This is a total misreading of Germany in 1933 and of the United States in 2007. Hitler did not want an open conflict with the churches, certainly not while preparing for or conducting war. But he said quite clearly in a speech at the annual party convention in Nuremberg that the age of Christianity was over and that it had been replaced by National Socialism.

So how can we explain this kind of crying wolf at the wrong time and in the wrong place? The reason must be psychological. For someone who has grown up in a free society, it takes a major leap of imagination to understand unfree societies, and these are unfortunately in the majority for the time being.

Of course, there are dangers growing up in a dictatorship of the kind in which I grew up, an inclination toward pessimism, worst-case assumptions, even cynicism. I was aware of this liability and had to make a major effort to overcome it.

CHAPTER 3

Marxism, the Soviet Union, and the Cold War

or, The Dream That Failed

For many of my generation of young German Jews—and even more for that before us—Marxism and the Soviet Union were the dream that failed. It is not easy to understand at a distance of so many years their attraction and the enthusiasm they generated. But given the weakness of liberal democracy in Germany, the main alternative to Nazism, in both political and ideological terms, seemed to be the radicalism of the left.

Marxism in the 1930s

By the 1930s, the Social Democrats were not a radical party. They certainly did not invoke the class struggle and other elements of Marxist ideology. Indeed, in the Weimar Republic, the Social Democrats were an establishment party. Adolf Hitler used the term "Marxist" to refer to both the Socialists and the Communists, but this was a propaganda maneuver designed to discredit the moderate as well as the extreme left.

For many of those who experienced firsthand, even as children, the horrors of World War I, the collapse of the monarchy, the ruthless suppression of the postwar uprisings, the Russian Revolution, and the financial collapse in Germany, communism was bound to have a real attraction. These young people became the activists of the Communist Party—and also of the socialist parties and the splinter groups in between. They took part in the street demonstrations that often ended in bloody clashes.

My generation had missed many of these earlier events. For us, the environment was the late Weimar Republic, with all its problems. Moreover, after 1933 access to Marxist literature and left-wing groups was limited. It had become dangerous to hold such ideas or be engaged in such activities, the merest hint of which led straight to a concentration camp. Contacts and activities went underground or had to be camouflaged. At the very moment, then, when young people in other countries were becoming mobilized around movements that worked for a united front against fascism, viewing Marxism as the great alternative to Nazism, this was not happening—for obvious reasons—in Germany itself.

Young people tend to sympathize with revolutionary ideas and movements of the left or the right, at least in our modern era. The political situation in Europe in the late 1920s and early 1930s was not just bad; it seemed hopeless. The economic situation was the same. The depth and breadth of the depression meant that recovery could not be taken for granted. And what would replace the existing system? There was no confidence that capitalism and democracy could solve the problems; the concept of the welfare state did not exist. The available choices seemed quite stark.

I remember masses of unemployed aimlessly roaming the streets. The middle class was to a considerable extent impoverished. At the same time there were glaring extremes between the very rich and the destitute. There was something radically wrong with this kind of society. People were starving. When I now think back it occurs to me that the superrich of 1930 were not really that rich—at least not in Europe—compared with the state of affairs today. The middle class still had domestics and servants, which today not even the rich can afford. But the poor were certainly much worse off than today. There were real slums such as do not exist anymore except in the Third World.

How did the radicalization of young people proceed at the time? Usually there was an older person, a relation or acquaintance who recommended a pamphlet such as the *Communist Manifesto.* And from this one advanced to more substantial fare, say Karl Marx's historical writings about the civil war in France, well written though not really relevant to the situation almost a hundred years later. Very enterprising spirits went on to read Friedrich Engels about the origins of the family and private property, Marx's early essays, or even the three-volume analysis of capitalism, *Das Kapital.* This work was heavy going; I do not know anyone among my generation who finished even one volume of *Das Kapital,* let alone understood what he was reading. Still, the basic issues were not difficult to grasp: that there was something like the class struggle and that the present society was unjust and had to be destroyed and replaced by a more just one.

Marxism had suffered heavy setbacks in Germany. The German Communist Party had been considered the best disciple in the Communist school and also the strongest force outside the Soviet Union. Everyone looked up to it as exemplary. Yet when Hitler came to power it collapsed like a house of cards. Elsewhere in Europe, however, the left had made great progress. In France, a Popular Front came to power in 1936. Furthermore, there was the Soviet Union itself, which, we were told, was going from strength to strength with its five-year plans. According to the Soviets and their supporters, the country had stamped out unemployment. There was equality. There was a plan, and there was a feeling of purpose, absent in other countries. Above all, there was the issue of fascism—the great danger to civilization. And was it not true that the Communists were the staunchest, the most militant antifascists? And so if one had to chose between Adolf Hitler and Joseph Stalin—and that is often the way things seemed in those days—was it not clear what the choice should be? Actually, the Communists were not as consistently antifascist as we had believed in our naiveté, but this became clear only toward the end of the 1930s.

I was certainly strongly influenced by the ideas of the radical left, but I never belonged to any organized group. I had, however, close friends who did and supplied me with literature, including the older brother of a friend who before 1933 had been a militant. But I had some doubts right from the beginning. Growing up in Nazi Germany I could not fail to realize that Marxism underrated the power of nationalism. People did not act solely in accordance with their economic interests. To explain such "irrational behavior" (as the Frankfurt School did) with reference to "false consciousness" seemed to me patronizing and unconvincing, even at an early age.

After Hitler took power, we listened to Radio Moscow broadcasts in German fairly regularly. The theme song played before and after each broadcast was the "Internationale." Later, when the Soviets began to stress antifascism rather than revolution, Radio Moscow dropped it. On the other hand, Soviet propaganda was not at all tailored to the audience. There was a terrible boredom about it. Announcers rhapsodized about the number of tractors operating in Uzbekistan and the fact that the output of nickel in Siberia had risen by an amazing 17 percent over the previous year. It was scanty fare. Still, whatever doubts we had were outweighed by the attractions of a revolutionary ideology and a movement that promised a better world order. We had not the slightest idea what really went on in the Soviet Union, and when we were told that the Soviet regime had eradicated not only illiteracy but also mental disease, who were we to doubt it?

Our texts were the books published by the Communist Malik publishing house before 1933. These covered the early heroic period of the Russian Revolution: how the brave soldiers of the Red Army had prevailed over reactionary czarism, the landlords, and the obscurantist church. The American journalist John Reed's *Ten Days That Shook the World* was very popular at the time. These books told us about the enthusiasm of the young generation building a new society, about their spirit of sacrifice. The fact that there had also been social democrats and liberals in Russia before November 1917 was not widely known and did not evoke much interest. There were also books about our contemporaries in the Soviet Union, such as *The Diary of Kostya Ryabtsev* or *The First Girl*: how we envied them. Sergei Tretyakov wrote about the Chinese revolutionaries: how exciting it was; we had apparently been born too late. Little did we know that by the late 1930s the authors of all these books had been arrested and most of them executed on trumped-up, ridiculous charges.

Malik also published Ilya Ehrenburg, a gifted Soviet writer who specialized in the decadent West and was given far more freedom than his contemporaries. Malik brought out Upton Sinclair, who was very popular at the time, as well as other writers of the far left such as the Danish author Martin Andersen-Nexø and the French author Henri Barbusse, who wrote on the horrors of World War I and later about Stalin, the great leader who had arisen. The French fellow traveler Romain Rolland was also very influential. Here was a highly idealistic writer whose main interest earlier on had been classical music, especially German music, who had written with great admiration about Mahatma Gandhi and Sri Aurobindo, an Indian professor and nationalist who had become a master of yoga. But Rolland in the early 1930s (and following a marriage to a Soviet citizen) had embraced Stalin as the only hope for progressive mankind.

It should be stressed, though, that only a very few German intellectuals became Marxists or Communists. Even among those young Jews in Germany belonging to political youth groups, not more than perhaps 5–10 percent became Communists. Democratic socialism eventually had a much wider appeal. It also offered an infinite variety, rather than a single party line. Almost everyone seemed to be a socialist of some sort, since that was such a vague label.

Of those who became Communists in their late teens, some stuck with the party through thick and thin. During World War II, a few survived in concentration camps or abroad. Those who went to England retained a sentimental attachment to communism. Although they were eager to become English, the English did not really welcome them. Several hundred German Jewish physicians, for example, were not permitted to practice medicine in Britain until the war broke out. Communists were very active among the German refugees in England, and the Communist organization called Free German Youth indoctrinated them quite effectively. On the other hand, those who went to the United States, a nation of immigrants, were more easily integrated.

Most of these young Communists went to East Germany after the war, where they had modest careers. But in 1949, when Stalin launched his campaign against the Rootless Cosmopolitans, with its not-so-thinly disguised antisemitism, they became suspect for having spent the war years in the imperialist world. After Stalin's death in 1953 they were rehabilitated.

The really unfortunate ones were those who went to the Soviet Union. They were suspected of being spies or enemy agents and arrested. Some were executed during the Soviet purges of 1936–39; of those who were merely arrested and sent to the Gulag concentration camps some survived, but many did not. These were very sad, heartbreaking stories. After the war I interviewed about a dozen of these survivors of Vorkuta and other camps. A few had kept their political convictions, but they were broken people.

The lucky ones were those who had immigrated with their parents and been too young to be arrested at the time of the purges. Even in the Soviet Union there were certain limits: a boy aged fourteen could not be put to trial as a Japanese spy. But very often these young people saw their parents arrested, to return only after many years, or not at all. And it was no fun to be at school as the son or daughter of a so-called Enemy of the People. Some of them, however, remained faithful Communists who returned to East Germany after the war, where a few had spectacular careers. Some defected to the West.

In general, everyone who could escape from Nazi Germany did so. But I have heard of at least a few cases in which young Jews were told by their Communist gurus that they had a duty to stay in Germany and help the German working class overthrow Nazism. If this is true, and I suspect it is, it was of course the height of folly because there was nothing a young Jew could do politically at the time in the prevailing conditions. The German Communists did not want "non-Aryans" in their underground cells. They told them to have their own groups.

I refer above all to the group headed by Herbert and Marianne Baum in Berlin. This was a loose group of young people headed by a Jewish Communist. Virtually all of them were arrested after an abortive attempt in early 1942 to set fire to a Nazi anti-Soviet exhibition in Berlin. It failed because the group had been penetrated by Gestapo agents, and more than twenty were executed. It could be argued that since these young people were doomed anyway, it did not really matter whether they died in 1942 or only a year later. But this argument does not hold, because if they had gone underground or crossed the border into a neutral country, as a few hundred others did, they would have had a certain chance to survive. In other words, those who persuaded these young people to stay behind and help the German working class—a hopeless endeavor—bear a heavy responsibility. Moreover, their actions allowed Nazi propaganda to argue that only "Jewish Communists" were trying to sabotage the Nazi crusade to liberate Europe from the Bolshevik specter.

Confronting the Marxist School, Studying Russia and Soviet Affairs

The 1930s were the decade of the Stalin cult and of the Moscow trials in which most of the Bolshevik old guard was accused of having been enemy agents all along. These trials should have raised questions about the validity and the truthfulness of the Soviet cause, but they apparently did not undermine the belief of many true believers, at least not immediately. There were several reasons why this was so. The Soviet arguments about the guilt of the Bolshevik old guard were unconvincing. And the "cult of the individual" as it was called after Stalin's death, was indeed nauseating. But both were new to people at the time, who did not have the knowledge of previous examples or skepticism that later generations would develop toward such arguments. At the time, no argument, however far-fetched, could simply be rejected. Perhaps there was, after all, a grain of truth in the accusations against the old Bolsheviks; perhaps they were "subjectively innocent" but "objectively guilty" by undermining Stalin's rule.

Gradually, I began to understand that "real existing Marxism," with all its claims to be a rational and even scientific worldview, was a belief based on faith. It was a secular religion. It gave its believers the security they craved for, just as a believing Christian or Jew was certain that God knew best. Marxists had faith that the ways of providence (meaning, in this case, the leader or the Politburo) were unfathomable for ordinary mortals and were not to be questioned. There is a famous short poem by Fyodor Ivanovich Tyutchev, a nineteenth-century Russian poet and diplomat, "Umom Rossii ne ponyat": Russia cannot be rationally understood, one has to believe in it.

The community of the faithful encompassed the whole life of the movement's followers. If they defected they would lose not just this feeling of security but also all their friends and those close to them. I met some who had been many years in the Gulag, who had lost their best friends, their family, their husbands or wives in the "purges," and yet were not shaken in their belief in the party and its leader. This allegiance was clearly not an ideological but a psychological and religious phenomenon. Some of the writers of the 1930s and 1940s, such as Arthur Koestler, later described it in a book entitled *The God That Failed* (1951).

As time went by, the indications that the religion of Marxism was imperfect became stronger and stronger. An ever-greater effort was needed to believe in what otherwise seemed to be absurd. And furthermore, after 1945 Hitler and fascism—the overriding peril—had disappeared. Indeed, the fact that the Soviet Union was now in confrontation with the United States and Western Europe brought the gap between loyalty to one's own government or to Moscow into stark contrast. It was also harder for the Soviet Union to disguise its own relative backwardness and shortcomings, revealed all the more by the Soviet leaders' criticism of Stalin after his death.

This situation, of course, undermined Marxism and communism in the long run. But I still think there was something positive in having to confront the Marxist school in one's study and thinking. I don't mean the Stalin cult and the blind obedience to the changing party line; I mean Marx. Marx was wrong in most of his predictions concerning capitalism and socialism. And he overemphasized not just the importance of the class struggle in history but also exaggerated the importance of economic factors in general. Still, people who went through the Marxist school also acquired a certain sense of realism and understanding of political power. They were less prone to be taken in by some of the later absurdities, for instance that China or North Korea or Osama bin Laden was pointing the way for progressive humankind. In my experience few intelligent people were not affected to some extent by Marxism at the age of twenty, and very few had not put this behind them by age thirty or thirty-five.

In addition, one should remember that people's attitude toward Marxism as an ideology, quite influential at the time, did not always correlate with their attitude toward the Soviet Union. Many who had no sympathy for Marxism and communism—and certainly would never have favored that system in their own countries—had considerable respect for, and even an excessively positive view of, the Soviet Union itself. The great struggle of the 1930s and into the 1940s conditioned this fact. The policy of the Western powers vis-à-vis the Axis was one of appeasement right up to the outbreak of World War II. America was isolationist. Only the Kremlin seemed to be consistently anti-Nazi—at least up to its nonaggression pact with Germany of August 1939. To be critical of the Soviet Union could be credibly portrayed as weakening the strongest force in the fight against Nazism.

The August 1939 pact between Stalin and Hitler came as a great shock, but with an effort it could be explained as a necessary stratagem, though only the faithful fully accepted this notion. The Soviet Union, it was said, had been betrayed by the Western democracies, Britain and France, which were trying to maneuver Hitler into attacking it. In these circumstances, Stalin had no alternative. This justification was lame; would Hitler have gone to war at all but for the assurance given him as the result of the pact? Some old Communists never got over the shock. But the pact lasted for less than two years, and after that Stalinism was again politically correct on the left.

More than that, after June 22, 1941, when an overconfident Hitler attacked, the Soviet Union became quite popular in almost every respect— our great, virtually our only hope of survival. Up to that time the war had gone badly. Western and northern Europe had been overrun by the Germans. France had surrendered. The invasion of Britain had been postponed but was not inconceivable. Perhaps England under Prime Minister Winston Churchill would hold out, but how could it defeat Nazi Germany single-handedly? Anyone who wished for the survival of democracy had to hope for the victory of the Soviet Union in the war.

Still, 1941 was a year of Soviet defeats. In parts of the Soviet Union the Germans were received as liberators, often by members of discontented non-Russian ethnic groups. The German attack during summer and autumn was very successful. Millions of Soviet soldiers were killed or taken prisoner. This outcome shows how unprepared the Soviets were. Stalin gave more credibility to Hitler's professions of peacefulness than he did to Western statesmen, who had warned him.

The Soviet leader had received intelligence information from a hundred sources, including the famous Soviet agent Richard Sorge in Japan and the Czech underground, but he dismissed it merely as disinformation intended to provoke the Soviet Union into a war with Germany. There is something exquisitely ironic in Stalin's behavior: this man who did not trust anyone (least of all faithful old Bolsheviks) and who suspected everyone of treason and betrayal swallowed the lies of Hitler and his foreign minister, Joachim von Ribbentrop.

But it was not only Stalin's credulity that explained the Soviet setbacks in 1941. He had decapitated the military leadership of the Red Army, and the new commanders were as yet inexperienced. Furthermore, Stalin constantly meddled in military decision making. Only after the great setbacks was a freer hand given to experts like Marshal Georgy Zhukov.

And Stalin had an even more powerful ally—the Soviet Union's size and climate. Like Napoleon, the German generals found out that Russia was a big country, the roads were inferior, and once winter set in the offensive came to a halt. The Germans did not capture Leningrad and then suffered a major setback in front of Moscow in December 1941 and had to retreat.

This retreat was really the beginning of the end—even if we could not know it at the time. Britain and later also the United States were helping the Soviet Union in every possible way, delivering planes, tanks, jeeps, and food through the Lend-Lease program. In later years, the Soviets tried to play down this help, but it was really decisive. However, without the soldiers of the Red Army fighting bravely and suffering tremendous losses, nothing much would have been achieved. This is not to say that Hitler would have won the war, but there could have been a stalemate, and the first atom bomb could have been used against Germany rather than Japan.

Still, the effectiveness of Soviet resistance compared to the French and Polish collapse greatly influenced Western public opinion, and it was at this time that Uncle Joe and the Soviet system became tremendously popular. Joseph E. Davies, a former U.S. ambassador to Moscow, when asked why a fifth column did not exist in the Soviet Union, replied that Stalin took care of that; he shot them in the 1930s. And there were many ill-informed people who were impressed by this kind of talk. Hollywood produced movies in this vein. People were saying that obviously there must be something very positive in the Soviet system that makes it superior to the decadent, weak Western democracies. There was a tremendous interest in things Russian, and almost everyone was affected.

Fascinated by this country, I started to study the language. Sometime in late 1941, I broke my leg. I was a member of a kibbutz at the time, and when such a misfortune befell our women comrades they had to darn socks, but there was little for young men to do while the bones were healing. I had a neighbor, an elderly Russian lady, born in Nikolayev near the shores of the Black Sea, the area Leon Trotsky also came from. She had been a teacher and was quite happy to find an eager student.

And so I studied Russian eight hours a day and at the end of a month I could read *Pravda* with the help of a dictionary. This is not such a great achievement, because the editors of *Pravda* did not use more than a thousand words, perhaps even less, so that everyone could understand them. From *Pravda* I progressed to Aleksandr Pushkin's *Kapitanskaya Dochka* (The Captain's Daughter), a well-known historical novel with the eighteenth-century Pugachev peasant rebellion as the background. It was a standard text for Russian schoolchildren. I next read some of the wartime Soviet literature brought out in tiny format by *Ogonyok*, the illustrated weekly newspaper.

Even with all my enthusiasm, I could not fail to understand that *Pravda* and *Izvestia* were newspapers of infinite boredom. In 1943, however, a new periodical began to appear, *Voina i Rabochi Klass* (War and the Working Class), which was more attractive in design and a little more interesting in content. I began to read this regularly, but also the more famous of the wartime writers, Ilya Ehrenburg, Alexei Tolstoy, Vasili Grossman, Konstantin Simonov (*Wait for Me*), and so on. Little did I anticipate that many years later *Izvestia* and *Novoe Vremya* (*Voina i Rabochi Klass* had changed its name) would ask me to write for them, which I gladly did (albeit not in Russian) out of a feeling of—what to call it? Perhaps it was nostalgia.

My language teacher was not, however, my only source of inspiration and information as far as things Russian were concerned. I worked at the time as a mounted guard in the fields of northern Israel. Most of my colleagues were Jews from Russia, a few from Siberia. They taught me songs and curses in their native language and, generally speaking, that part of the vocabulary not found in the dictionaries. This was a romantic atmosphere. Standing guard at night, there was not much else to do but sing and keep the campfire burning. While my spoken Russian remained less than wonderful, I acquired a good knowledge of Russian prerevolutionary and Soviet songs, and it is interesting how they have stuck in my memory.

More than ten years were to pass before I first visited the Soviet Union, but during that time Russia became my main field of interest. I had to make up my mind between Arabic and Russian—not just the language but culture and politics in general. I had at the time a reasonable knowledge of spoken Arabic, much less of the literary language. I was not a gifted linguist, and I knew that I could not master both languages and fields. Russian, and with it the whole world of Russian culture that opened up once one could read the language, seemed so much more interesting.

And so I immersed myself in things Russian. I was more or less familiar with Soviet politics and the history of the Communist Party, but the history of Russia in the nineteenth and early twentieth century I found immensely interesting—in contrast to current affairs. If one knew the members of the Politburo and other leading organs and a bit about their career and background, that was about all one could know. For what really went on in these circles was totally unknown, censorship being complete. Those who tried to make sense of Soviet decision making on the highest level (later this profession was called Kremlinology) had their work cut out for them. Kremlinology was uninspiring. It had to rely on how often certain leaders were mentioned in the leading newspapers, in what order their names were mentioned, and so on. And even if one knew what leader was rising and who was on the way out, temporarily or permanently, this was not really very important, for one did not know what these leaders stood for, whether there were important policy differences. Soviet policy was important but to follow it was exceedingly boring; Russian cultural history, on the other hand, was very rich and stimulating.

There was, of course, yet another source of information—recent arrivals from the Soviet Union. At the end of the war and in the chaotic postwar months of 1945–46 many hundreds of thousands either chose to remain in the West (prisoners of war, for instance) or defected, an action not too difficult at the time, borders being more or less open. In addition there were the many Poles and Czech soldiers who had been stationed in the Soviet Union during the war and were permitted to leave as the war ended, political émigrés from more than a dozen countries who had found a refuge in Moscow, and so on. Although there were no leading figures among the defectors, they had been eyewitnesses and could tell a lot about how the system worked. Few of them wrote books at the time, as there was no demand for critical literature as yet. Furthermore, many were afraid to draw attention to themselves, fearing that if they did they would not be given asylum in the West.

It would be wrong to think that most of them were Nazi collaborators (even though some of them were). Many thousands were Jews who had served in the Polish army commanded by General Władysław Anders, a non-Communist force that fought the Nazis under British patronage, or from the Baltic countries, recently annexed by Moscow, who had no wish to spend the rest of their lives in the Soviet Union. I met many of them in later years.

The picture that emerged from their stories was very different from the official accounts emanating from the Soviet media, and also from Western correspondents in Moscow who were operating in conditions of the strictest censorship. Some of the leading correspondents were married to Soviet women who would not have been permitted to leave the country if their husbands had been expelled for writing anything critical. This situation, too, was an important consideration influencing the coverage of Soviet affairs from Moscow. Henry Schapiro of United Press belonged to this category, as did Louis Fischer, whom I came to know quite well, a sympathizer with communism who was later disillusioned and became famous for his biography of Gandhi; Edmund Stevens, author of *Russia Is No Riddle* was another; and there were several others.

Pressures like these on correspondents are a problem that in one way or another continues to exist in various parts of the world. I recently followed the reports of a leading Western correspondent in Iran. He was obviously very well-informed and knew the language. Yet I felt a certain reticence in his writing. In Russian this was called *perestrakhovka*, an overcautiousness or extra insurance, a looking over one's shoulder, the making of gestures that would be pleasing to the regime. What could be the reasons? I later found out that the correspondent was married to an Iranian citizen and that her family was living in Tehran. I do not blame him, except for the fact that in these circumstances he should perhaps have looked for another country to cover.

I faced for a while a similar problem when in the late 1950s and early 1960s I went each year for extended visits to Russia on behalf of a leading newspaper, the Swiss *Neue Zürcher Zeitung*. The parents and family of Naomi, my wife, since deceased, were living in the Caucasus, and I felt uneasy in my reporting. I tried to resolve the problem by not covering Soviet politics but only other aspects of Soviet life. But such self-restriction would hardly have been a solution for a permanent correspondent.

Well before this, in the 1940s, I had become increasingly skeptical toward the Soviet Union. My view had less to do with current affairs, more with history. I had read the standard textbook on the Communist Party's history, the famous *Kratkii Kurs* (History of the Communist Party of the Soviet Union [Bolsheviks]: Short Course) composed on Stalin's orders and allegedly partly written by himself in 1938. Every Communist had to read it at the time; it was quoted in every article, translated into every language; the total circulation was in the tens of millions. But I also read a lot of other books on the history of the party, and it soon appeared that there were glaring discrepancies and contradictions between the authentic, contemporary documents and the *Short Course*. In other words, the official history had been fabricated.

It was not hard for me to find all this literature. The Hebrew University in Jerusalem had an excellent collection of Russian and Soviet periodicals, prerevolutionary and from the 1920s. Many mornings I sat in the campus library at Mount Scopus working my way through dusty journals that clearly no one had looked at for years. My appetite was insatiable; the librarians cursed me for all the work I made for them. One was the father of Amos Oz, the famous Israeli writer.

Many of these items had apparently been donated by Max Eitingon, a well-known psychoanalyst who belonged to Sigmund Freud's inner circle. Years after Eitingon's death I bought some of the remaining material. Eitingon himself was to become the center of a curious story, alas all too typical of how history is often written, that would marginally involve me.

Eitingon came from a Russian Jewish family that had settled in Leipzig and made a fortune trading in fur, a business for which Leipzig was the center at the time, so he was independently wealthy. In his younger years he had been involved in, or at least had been interested in, the Russian radical movement, and he collected its publications. Many years after his death, the *New York Times Book Review* published a sensational article by a man named Stephen Schwartz, a Trotskyist who later became a Muslim. He claimed that Eitingon had been a KGB general (and Freud an agent?) and had organized Trotsky's murder in Mexico City. This notion was breathtakingly ridiculous. The murder of Trotsky had indeed been coordinated by a high NKVD officer named Eitingon, but this Eitingon—whose first name was Naum-Leonid—was neither the psychoanalyst nor his brother, as was later argued. The whole affair has been investigated in detail by Theodore Draper and by me, and the truth is beyond doubt. A leading French psychoanalyst, Michelle Moreau Ricaud, went over the same ground and reached the same conclusion. But once such a conspiracy theory has been set out in the world it refuses to die, and I was not surprised to find a rehash in a more recently published book that had Max Eitingon as the "resident manager" of the KGB in Vienna.

Much writing about politics is tendentious. But there was something different in the Communist literature, a systematic disregard for truth that undermined the claims of the movement itself. But there was also much more. Reading the Russian émigré literature I found that some was raving mad: I refer to the writings about *The Protocols of the Elders of Zion*, of giant conspiracy theories involving Jews, Freemasons, and what not. But I also found that some of the critics of Bolshevism were far more astute in their political analysis and prediction than others.

Let me give two examples—the Mensheviks and Smena Vekh (Change of Landmarks). The Mensheviks were social democrats. They had taken part in the struggle against czarism but believed in social reform and gradual change once democracy prevailed in Russia. They were convinced that establishing the dictatorship of one party would eventually lead to the dictatorship of a small group of people, or indeed of a single dictator, as it indeed did later on. Such a system was not what true socialists wanted, they said. It would be inhuman, cause much death and destruction, and most probably not achieve the promised economic and social progress.

In their periodical *Sotsialisticheski Vestnik* and in their books during the 1920s and 1930s, the social democrats provided a running commentary on developments in the Soviet Union that proved to be amazingly astute. In later years, in the 1960s in the United States, I met some of the surviving Mensheviks, such as Boris Nikolaevsky, Solomon Schwarz and his wife Vera Alexandrova, and others—

nice people, probably too nice for politics. But there is no denying that they saw it coming.

Smena Vekh was a group of a very different character. Russian émigrés in Central Europe and the Far East, they like millions of others had left Russia after the revolution in protest against Bolshevism. Their foremost thinker was a Moscow professor named Nikolai Ustryalov. But in the years that followed they concluded that emigration had been a mistake and gradually most of them returned to the Soviet Union. Why? They thought they had taken communism too seriously and now believed it to be a passing phenomenon, perhaps the only way to restore power to a country defeated in World War I. The enduring factor was nationalism and great power status. Bolshevism, they expected, was likely to restore Russia as a superpower.

Smena Vekh was right, but not in the short run. Ustryalov and his comrades were arrested in the 1930s and not heard of again, almost certainly executed by the secret police; Ustryalov was shot in 1937. But in the longer run their predictions were borne out by events. Nationalism proved to be much stronger than communism. If Vladimir Putin had read Ustryalov, he would have built statues for him in every major Russian city.

Somehow, instinctively, I realized that Smena Vekh had been unjustly forgotten. I was not surprised, therefore, when Soviet patriotism emerged first under Stalin, then under his successors, and in the 1970s and 1980s more and more strongly as National Bolshevism, on the margins of the Russian literary scene, in journals such as *Nash Sovremennik* and *Molodaya Gvardiya*. After the breakup of the Soviet Union, National Bolshevism became part of the new Russian ideology and in its extreme form it appeared as neo-Nazism. Ironically, there is not now much difference ideologically and in other ways between the present-day Russian Communist Party and the Russian extreme right.

I should perhaps mention two more people whose writings I found stimulating and who are now forgotten even by the experts. One was Marc Vishniak, a right-wing social revolutionary and law professor who had been arrested repeatedly under the czarist regime. He served in the first elected parliament (quickly dissolved by the Bolsheviks) and then fled first to Paris and then to the United States, where he worked for *Time* magazine. He wrote at the end of the war (as I reported in *Fin de Siècle)* that Bolshevism would one day disappear but its legacy of unfreedom was pernicious and profound and would not easily vanish. While the thousands of kilometers that separated Russian Bolshevism from the West had given it "features of sublimity and grandeur," he saw no reason for optimism as far as the future of freedom in Russia was concerned.

The other thinker was Georgi Fedotov, a theologian and liberal anti-Communist who emigrated to the United States. His essays were published both in the United States and in Russia by admirers after his death. He also feared that Russia might be crushed by its history of unfreedom. But I doubt whether he had many readers. All this was as yet light-years away in 1945 when I worked my way through this literature on Mount Scopus. But it certainly helped to shape my outlook on things Russian and my general understanding of politics.

In my intellectual odyssey I was also bound to encounter Trotskyism, and I even read the whole of that movement's *Biulleten Oppositsii* from beginning to end. This was the organ of the Russian Trotskyites, and I found it very interesting as an antidote to the Stalinist party line. I later met Max Schachtman, head of one of the two main American Trotskyite groups, and also Tony Cliff, an Israeli (or, rather, a Palestinian, for he left the country before the establishment of the state) who became the guru of International Socialism, the more enlightened wing at the time of Trotskyism in Britain.

But I cannot honestly say that I was very impressed. Of course Leon Trotsky wrote much better than Stalin, was more educated, and was a far more accomplished orator. Under Trotsky there would not have been a "cult of the individual" (even though he was quite vain) and certainly no bloody mass purges affecting people wholly innocent. But as a politician he was, of course, a failure. And as a political thinker he is of no great interest because he never succeeded in developing Marxism any further even though it had clearly become outdated. Trotskyite attempts to present a Marxist appraisal of the Soviet Union as an example of state capitalism or a case of bureaucratic degeneration were not convincing.

The story of Trotskyism is a tragic one. So many of its leading figures were killed, but how much sympathy could one muster for a movement constantly splitting and engaged in infighting? Trotskyism was a major intellectual influence among postwar French intellectuals and also to a lesser degree among some Americans during the years before World War II. In Germany it hardly existed, and in Britain it has a certain influence but not among intellectual circles. The British Trotskyites in their eagerness to acquire a mass basis by trying to infiltrate and take over groups with vastly different agendas (called "entryism" in leftist parlance) have today became an ally of the radical Islamists. Is this a tragedy, or perhaps a comedy, of history? At any rate, while many intelligent young people passed through Trotskyism, very few stayed with it.

If Marxism was a disappointment, what replaced it? I thought of myself as a person of the center-left, and in most ways I continue to do so. (Culturally I am a conservative. I have no feeling for ultramodern arts, music, literature.) The problem is, of course, What is left? And what can be said to be of the left? I did not believe that Stalin was a left-winger, nor his followers, nor the various postmodernist schools such as postcolonialism, nor the German or the Italian terrorists of the 1970s, nor North Korea, nor the Albania of Enver Hoxha or the Cambodia of Pol Pot, nor the Islamists whether following Osama bin Laden or other versions of that ideology.

This is a list that could be much prolonged. A "leftist" in Israel is a person striving, against all odds, for an understanding with the Arabs, but he is by no means necessarily a socialist in the traditional or any other sense. If one looks at election results one finds that the rich neighborhoods in Israel (say Kfar Shmaryahu) vote "left," whereas the poor development towns vote "right." In the U.S. elections of 2008, a greater percentage of high income earners opted for Barack Obama (considered the left-wing candidate) than for his rivals.

There have been profound changes in the meaning of these terms all over the world. In Europe and the United States, the left was traditionally the party of the ideals of the French Revolution, of social progress, of freedom, while the conservative right stood for traditional values and for the preservation of the status quo. Is the traditional definition with the emphasis on freedom still applicable to the present-day left? The term "populism" has increasingly been used to describe this new left, but populism can with equal ease turn left or right.

Explaining the Cold War

The Second World War ended in Europe in May 1945. Expectations were, of course, very high after six years of fighting and destruction. So many people dear to me had been killed. My generation had to start from scratch, to study, to work, to get married, to have children. Millions returned from military service. At the same time, the enormity of the crimes committed during the war was not conducive to blind optimism or to Pollyannaish expectations. So much had been destroyed everywhere; how long would a recovery take?

In contrast, one did not really expect major trouble in international relations. The United Nations had been founded with hopes that it would prove more of a success than the League of Nations. Then, much to most people's surprise, economic recovery proceeded faster than expected, whereas international tensions quickly recurred. There had been indications during the last months of the war of serious differences among the Allies—over Poland, in the Balkans, concerning Turkey and Iran. But there was a tendency to overlook this kind of thing. Once Nazi Germany had been defeated, and later Japan, the commandment of the hour in the United States and in Britain was demobilization, a return to normal conditions.

So when former British Prime Minister Winston Churchill warned of an Iron Curtain descending across Europe, in a 1946 speech in Fulton, Missouri, he was bitterly attacked in the United States and Britain. So shocking was his condemnation of Soviet ambitions that some said he was parroting the Nazi propaganda minister Joseph Goebbels, who had also spoken about the dangers of Soviet aggression as an excuse for Germany's actions. Almost everyone agreed that the

Soviet Union had to be compensated and rewarded for its war effort and the losses it had suffered. Was it not entitled to create a *cordon sanitaire* for itself, a belt of submissive or even satellite states that would not attack it in the future? Why shouldn't the Soviet Union have a sphere of influence along its western borders? Furthermore, there was the widespread, but quite mistaken, assumption (also among sectors of the Soviet population) that the end of the war would bring tremendous changes inside the Soviet Union, and it would become more liberal.

There was optimism in the air, but it was not well founded. Inside the Soviet Union, this point was quickly realized. Once the war was over the regime became more, not less, repressive. Returning Soviet prisoners of war were sent to the Gulag, to give but one example. The cult of Stalin became even more intense. When he celebrated his seventieth birthday in 1949 there was an orgy of adulation that went on, in *Pravda* for instance, for many months. Adulation of the Byzantine emperor had been child's play in comparison. In the West it took longer to understand what this meant and what was actually happening in the Soviet Union.

Of course, the Soviet people, like their Western counterparts, also wanted to demobilize and rebuild their country. They desperately needed a respite. But basing one's expectations on this factor is a mistake often made in democratic states. In a dictatorship, what matters is what the dictator wants. Stalin realized that the vacuum that had been created in Europe as a result of the war provided a unique opportunity to expand, and he determined to make the most of it.

Had Stalin been satisfied with setting up a sphere of influence—regimes friendly toward the Soviet Union but not necessarily slavishly following the Communist model in every detail—people in the West would not have cared very much about it. But he was a very suspicious man, indeed a paranoiac, and he thought that spheres of influence would not be enough. The countries of Eastern Europe and also East Germany had to become part of the Soviet empire, and hence the use of what came to be called the "salami strategy," making increasingly greater demands, with each well-intentioned concession leading to another one.

In Eastern Europe, at first a government containing all the so-called progressive forces was established. But after a few months or a year the "bourgeois elements" were squeezed out, later also the social democrats, and, finally, even those Communists who wanted a "national road" to communism, meaning a degree of independence from Moscow. This Soviet strategy was quite successful in the short-run but self-defeating in the long run. Stalin could have lived with the Cold War. Indeed, he needed a state of siege mentality to justify his rule at home. But if he thought the Cold War inevitable he had not taken into account that strictly imposing the Soviet model and denying Eastern Europeans even minimal independence would bring new tensions and splits within his own camp: first the conflict with Yugoslavia, later with Romania, Albania, and eventually with China, and then once again in Eastern Europe, leading to the collapse of the Soviet empire.

And so we entered the period of the Cold War. In later years there were heated discussions whether this was all Stalin's fault, whether the West could not have prevented it, whether it did not provoke him to some extent. This was a popular revisionist view in the 1960s and 1970s and has been revived in recent times. These issues have been discussed endlessly, and one feels more than a little reluctant to reenter these debates, which really should be over by now. Those interested in details will find them in the recent books by John Lewis Gaddis, such as *We Now Know: Rethinking Cold War History* (1997) and *The Cold War: A New History* (2005).

While we do not know everything about this subject, so much has come to light that in my view it is more interesting to ask why the revisionist school arose in the first place, why it gained so much influence, and why it lasted so long despite the fact that in its essentials it was manifestly wrong.

In the early days of the Cold War the prevailing opinion in the West was that the fight for freedom and democracy was wholly justified since the Western political systems—even if capitalist—were superior to Stalinism and post-Stalin communism. Western European social democrats in Britain, France, and Germany were in the front rank of this struggle, often more militant than the right-wing forces in the West, simply because they had a better understanding of Stalinism.

Their views were challenged by the new school of revisionism beginning in the 1960s. It argued that the outbreak of the Cold War was as much (if not more) America's fault as Stalin's, that America did not accommodate sufficiently the legitimate security interests of the Soviet Union, that there had been many opportunities to put an end to the Cold War but that the American military-industrial complex would not accept them. (The school of "missed opportunities" had a revival in American-Iranian relations after 2001.) In its extreme form, to give but one example, the revisionists argued that America had been responsible for the outbreak of the Korean War and even falsely charged that it had used bacteriological weapons there, echoing a Communist accusation of the time. According to a milder version, both sides were responsible. "No one and everyone" being at fault, as a leading American historian of the Korean War put it, writing in 1990.

But in fact America was responsible, if at all, only because Dean Acheson in a speech in January 1950 had not mentioned South Korea as part of the American perimeter and so might have persuaded Stalin to believe that there was little risk involved if an attack was launched. This view did not mean that the idea to launch an attack was Stalin's. It was Kim Il Sung, the North Korean leader, who had suggested it. Stalin made it clear that Kim could not count on Soviet help if he ran into trouble and that the Chinese would have to bail him out—as they later did. But Stalin gave him the green light by praising his revolutionary spirit. Without that Kim would not have dared, as he himself said.

What were the motives of the revisionist school, and what were the reasons for its misjudgments? I can think of several explanations. To begin with, most were not students of the Soviet Union, of Soviet foreign policy, or of Soviet ideology. Their covering of the conflict was a bit like reporting on a boxing match in which only one boxer was visible. How could one make sense of Soviet behavior without knowledge of its mainsprings? This is very nearly impossible since, for American historians and political scientists, the mainsprings of Soviet politics were remote from their own political experience. There was no George Kennan among them who had spent almost a lifetime studying and observing Soviet affairs.

Second, the revisionists were deeply distrustful of American motives. Some came from the extreme left. The emergence of the revisionist school coincided with the mushrooming of radical ideas on American campuses. Others were isolationists of the right. Those of the far left thought that the Soviet system was essentially socialist and progressive, hence the belief that it was impossible that such a regime could follow an aggressive policy in its confrontation with American (and Western) capitalism and the sense that the Soviets should be given the benefit of the doubt. The far left considered American and Western pseudo-democracies so bad that they had to be at fault.

Third, there was the inherent tendency in academic thinking, both among historians and political scientists, that in most conflicts responsibility had been divided. Why assume that this case should be different? Hitler and Nazism had not been given the benefit of the doubt except by a few neo-Nazis, but Soviet communism was believed to be something quite different, far more rational in character. Truth was never found on one side only; a true academic approach had to look for it somewhere in the middle ground. Well, not quite in the middle, they really thought, for the assignment of intellectuals was to be critical—above all of one's own side.

These circumstances tend to explain why so many students of international affairs would find it difficult to engage in "one-sided condemnations" even at a time when it was difficult to find any justification for Soviet behavior, such as the Prague trial accusing Czech Communists of being traitors or Stalin's increasing madness during his last years.

However, with *glasnost*, the opening of the Soviet Union to more internal debate, much historical material on the postwar period became available for the first time. Western and Soviet historians cooperated in their investigations; new institutions were set up to study the Cold War; journals appeared that were devoted to this subject. How can one explain that, unlike the Soviet Union, the revisionist school did not quite collapse but merely retreated from certain untenable positions?

Again, the reason seems to be found in the realm of psychology and the sociology of knowledge. It is a well-known fact that people find it exceedingly difficult to give up long-cherished ideas; doing so, after all, reflects badly on their previous judgment and current prestige. It becomes even more painful if the new information making rethinking necessary is in contradiction to one's own deep-seated political beliefs and if it implies that the wrong side won the Cold War. This phenomenon certainly ought to be studied in much greater detail.

Does a more sober view now prevail? Broadly speaking, yes, a middle-of-the-road school appeared first in the 1970s as "postrevisionism." But originally these historians such as Gaddis were fairly close to the moderate revisionists. His position today, following the revelations from the archives, is far more outspoken. He writes in *We Now Know*: "Once Stalin wound up at the top in Moscow and once it was clear his state would survive the war then it looks equally clear that there was going to be a Cold War whatever the West did. Who then was responsible? The answer, I think, is authoritarianism in general and Stalin in particular." Some people have not forgiven Gaddis and his followers such conclusions, which, they argue, play into the hands of official U.S. foreign policy, of "triumphalism," whatever that means.

My own attitude after all these years is more radical than that of Gaddis. Some of us reached his present conclusions fifty years ago. What I mean very briefly is this. There is no doubt that during the Cold War the West and above all the United States made mistakes, big and small. And I mean not only half-baked adventures like the Bay of Pigs invasion of Cuba in 1961 by U.S.-backed exiles to overthrow Fidel Castro. Vietnam, too, was a mistake; I never understood why America should be in Vietnam. This was a kind of gut feeling. In all these years as a commentator on international politics I never once wrote about Vietnam but steered clear of the subject—not a very heroic attitude perhaps, but I was no Asian expert and did not want to comment on a subject about which I did not know enough.

There were some foolish people, including, for example, the great British philosopher Bertrand Russell, who were given to loose talk about launching a nuclear war, especially in the early days. But this was never American policy. The American strategy was, first, containment, an idea initiated by the American diplomat George Kennan's "long telegram" of 1946 and later carried through in the détente in the 1960s and 1970s, until Soviet policy became too aggressive and had to be resisted in places like Afghanistan. It is also true that after World War II American policy had often interpreted the Soviet danger mainly (sometimes exclusively) in military terms and given absolute priority to strategic answers. There was a tendency toward defining the struggle as one involving either peace or war, with very little in between.

But on essentials, however, the West was right. Soviet aggression had to be resisted. Of course, the Soviet leaders were, on the whole, not prone to act recklessly. When there were great risks involved they would not take the offensive. Someone compared them to a hotel thief trying all the doors on a certain floor. When he found a door locked he would not persist but instead would pass on to the next door.

Did the West miss a major opportunity to end the Cold War earlier? There has been talk to this effect beginning with the period after Stalin's death in the early 1950s, but I have not seen any convincing evidence. As long as the Soviet leaders believed that their system was superior and destined to prevail all over the world, there was no chance for anything more than a truce. And of local truces, certainly, there were plenty.

I shall have to return to these issues later in my narrative. But there is one point in Gaddis's argumentation that strikes me as factually wrong, an unnecessary concession to the academic revisionists. This is his reference to "authoritarianism" rather than "totalitarianism," and the use of these terms has been the subject of a long debate among political scientists that is not over yet.

"Totalitarian" became a dirty word, not for those to whom it was applied but for those who used it. This concept was supposedly Cold War propaganda because it allegedly overstressed the features common to both communism and fascism. It is perfectly true that the concept of totalitarianism is not an ideal term and has weaknesses. Neither Germany nor the Soviet Union, and least of all Italy (though Benito Mussolini was the first to popularize the term), were totally totalitarian, meaning that everything was controlled by the state, the party, and the leader. But with all its weaknesses, "totalitarian" is far more correct than "authoritarian," which is a downright misleading term when used with regard to the Soviet Union in the postwar period.

"Authoritarian" can be applied to all political regimes that are not democratic, which is to say most member states of the United Nations. Francisco Franco's regime in Spain was authoritarian, and so were Kemal Atatürk's in Turkey, Juan Perón's in Argentina, and Augusto Pinochet's in Chile. French President Charles de Gaulle was called by his many enemies an authoritarian leader. And certainly the regimes of the kings of Morocco, Jordan, and Saudi Arabia—virtually all Arab political regimes—have been authoritarian. Calling the Soviet Union, "authoritarian" merely obliterates the enormous differences between this regime and other dictatorships or semidictatorships, past and present. Again, this is an issue that I raised earlier and to which I shall return.

Sovietology after Stalin

The last years of Stalin's rule were a nightmare, especially if one happened to live inside the Soviet bloc. Earlier it had become difficult to apply rational analysis to Kremlin domestic policy (the Moscow purge trials of the 1930s, for instance, when many Soviet leaders were declared to be traitors and shot), but after 1949 it became virtually impossible. The cult reached unprecedented heights: Stalin the wisest leader in all history, the greatest linguist, the greatest philosopher and economist. Cultural censorship became absolute. I think in 1951 there were no Soviet movies produced at all, or if they were produced the censor did not release them. And this policy was not just Stalin's. His cultural commissar Andrei Zhdanov had been imposing ever stricter controls on literature, history, philosophy, music, and more. Doctors were accused and arrested for allegedly poisoning Soviet leaders. Then Stalin wanted to deport all Jews to the Arctic Circle. Toward the end of his life, Stalin was probably clinically mad. To this day, however, there are men and women, including academics, who firmly believe in his greatness, and in Russia history textbooks are again making this claim. Such monsters seem to have a fatal attraction for some. This, too, is a subject deserving further study.

When Stalin died in 1953, millions of his subjects were reported to be weeping: What will we do, they cried, without this wise leader? They were like a flock of sheep that had lost its shepherd. But we now know that not everyone was weeping: changes were quickly made, prisoners were released, and the whole period was later called "the thaw," following publication of a novel of that title by Ilya Ehrenburg.

My own understanding of things Soviet had progressed to the extent that while I welcomed these changes it was clear to me that one should not expect too much. This view brought me into collision with one of the leading interpreters of Soviet affairs during that period, Isaac Deutscher. Deutscher, born in Galicia in 1907, had been a Communist and subsequently a Trotskyite in his native Poland. He had gone to England and there had acquired the status of an oracle. He wrote well, having started his career as a poet preoccupied with mystical themes. His Stalin biography, published in 1949, was hailed as a paradigm of objectivity. It is still in print today and has its admirers. He is the author of a much better three-volume biography of Trotsky, even though the element of hagiography is quite strong in that book. While he is willing to admit that Trotsky was not infallible, on major issues Trotsky apparently could do no wrong. Deutscher thought that while some—perhaps even many—of Stalin's actions had been regrettable, by and large they had been necessary to modernize the Soviet Union, to get it kicking and screaming out of the morass of centuries. This, it should be noticed, again became the official line under Vladimir Putin, except that in its new version the emphasis was on Russian nationalism rather than "proletarian internationalism," as it was with Deutscher.

This kind of attitude toward Stalin has been frequent not only among those who sympathized with his policies. In 2006, a book published by an Irish historian argued that Stalin's role as a strategist in the conduct of World War II was quite remarkable and on the whole positive. I have very little patience with this kind of reasoning. There is every reason to believe that under Zhukov or a dozen other generals and marshals the Soviets would have fared better. If the Soviet Union was taken by surprise in June 1941 and suffered such enormous losses, this is Stalin's responsibility. Now that much of the historical source material is accessible, Stalin's misjudgment appears even more breathtaking than it did earlier on. It is also known that Stalin ordered the execution of Soviet military leaders throughout the war, not because they were incompetent but because he disliked or feared them or because they knew too much about his failures. To gain a true picture of what Stalin and Stalinism were like, Western readers are now, seventy years later, better advised to read Soviet novelists such as Vasili Grossman than some Western academic historians.

There is no total certainty as to how the Soviet Union would have fared in the war with other leaders at its helm. But a strong case can be made that its losses would have been much less and that the defeat of Nazi Germany would have come earlier on. It could be one of the ironies of history that Stalin's incompetence played in the hands of the non-Communist world, for if the Soviet Union would have emerged stronger at the end of the war, the threat to the West would have been even more formidable.

As for Stalin's general role, again I see no reason to be greatly impressed. He created a state that eventually collapsed, not because it was defeated in war but because of sheer incompetence, because it was so rigid that it could not reform itself. The Soviet Union made progress under the five-year plans, but much less than the rest of the world in later years, and with the waste of enormous human and natural resources. Other such countries have made much quicker progress without a Stalinist regime.

True, Stalin seems still to be quite popular in Russia these days. A majority of people think that in the final analysis he did more good than harm. This view demonstrates that Stalin helped to create a society that no longer knows what freedom means or how a free society should be constituted. The czars were quite popular, too, among Russian peasants: perhaps not that much has changed. The belief that the authorities, whoever they are, should be loved and obeyed has endured. Perhaps Stalin "objectively" played into the hands of the enemies of socialism, for the collapse of the house he built discredited not only communism but socialism in general.

But the dispute of 1953 was not mainly about Stalin; it was about the future of the Soviet regime. Deutscher in a book quickly written, *Russia: What Next?* (1953) argued that the negative features of the Stalinist regime would now be discarded and there would be a return to the days of pristine Leninist socialism. I maintained in a review and in an ensuing exchange that I saw no reason for such optimism: of course there would be change even under Stalin's most trusted disciples, bureaucrats like Georgy Malenkov, but not a return to freedom and democracy. I compared this view with the misplaced optimism among part of the Russian intelligentsia at the time of Czar Alexander II's ascension to power in 1855. He freed the serfs and was hailed as czar-liberator. But as it subsequently emerged, the liberation was strictly limited. The same thing happened after 1953. Moreover, a great many people had been killed under Lenin, too. Russia lost most of its intelligentsia, and the regime installed by Lenin paved the way for Stalinism. Subsequent history has more than amply shown how misplaced Deutscher's optimism was.

The history of Sovietology, that is to say the craft (it was hardly a science) of how to interpret Soviet policy at home and abroad at a time when there was no access to the people or accurate sources in the Soviet Union, remains to be written in detail. In the beginning, this guild consisted mainly of old Mensheviks, former Communists, or former Trotskyites, people steeped in Marxism-Leninism who had closely followed, over many years, developments in Soviet and world communism. They did not necessarily agree with each other; they were often heavily biased, and they were by no means always right. But they had acquired an intuitive understanding that helped them to grasp essentials inside the Soviet Union, and even their prejudices, far from being an impediment, often sharpened their perceptions, just as the British political philosopher Edmund Burke's bias toward the French Revolution had helped him in 1790 to predict its future more accurately than many detached contemporary students of France.

The theoretical model on which this generation of Sovietologists based themselves was often totalitarianism, with its emphasis on the inexorable spread and consolidation of state power. But certain changes were obviously taking place after Stalin's death, and new theoretical approaches were apparently needed. A search for new models began that lasted for years and, in retrospect, makes strange reading. First on the scene was modernization theory, which stressed an inevitable trend in modern society toward pluralism, toward economic and political decentralization, toward a demand for consumer goods, including "spiritual consumer goods." But it did not take that long to realize that this approach was of little use for understanding the Soviet Union under Nikita Khrushchev and Leonid Brezhnev. Next came the bureaucracy model, which informed us that the Soviet Union, like all other societies, was subject to the laws governing all bureaucracies. Functional divisions were all-important, institutional interests played a great role, performance and affiliation to a group played a greater role than ideology, and legal procedures became more important. The modernization and the bureaucracy models were likely to lead to the conclusion that West and East were converging. But this view was not of much help either, because while there were certain similarities between West and East, they did not concern the essential character of the Soviet regime, in which the Communist Party control and ideology played a crucial role.

Some Soviet experts developed an interest in cognitive psychology; they were preoccupied with perception and misperception in foreign policy. This approach was based on the belief that since we construct the reality in which we operate, most of the world's major conflicts were caused by wrong inferences drawn from ambiguous evidence, hence the need for a special effort to understand the antagonist's mentality and perceptions. There is nothing wrong with such an effort, except that in this particular case it led to the belief that Soviet and Western common interests outweighed their divisions, that but for the fact that hardliners on both sides had constituted an "objective alliance" validating each other's expectations—invariably of the worst-case type—most conflicts could be resolved with a minimum of goodwill.

This mixture of the obvious and the nonsensical had a harmful effect on American thinking. Nowhere but in the United States has there been so little understanding of how a dictatorship works or so little appreciation of ideology (both religious and nationalist) in politics. In no other country has there been so much goodwill, so much willingness to ignore or at least belittle the existence of genuine conflicts among nations, ideologies, and political systems. If only the viewpoint of the other side were better understood, it is said, most conflicts would be resolved or avoided. Americans have always been reluctant to admit that certain conflicts are fundamental and irreconcilable; this reluctance was now given scientific standing.

The first generation of Sovietologists were usually people of much broader cultural and historical interests and experience than the more narrow-gauged experts who followed them. This is true for men like Hugh Seton-Watson and Leonard Schapiro, of Bertram Wolfe as much as for Franz Borkenau and E. H. Carr. If the Sovietologists of the 1970s often stressed the importance of a comparative approach, such admonitions were hardly necessary with regard to the first generation of Sovietologists, who thought an approach of this kind to be self-evident.

Behind the rise of these new approaches there was also a revolt against "the outdated Cold War mentality," against an American policy that, motivated by blind anticommunism, had led the country into Vietnam. But it is also true that many members of this (third) generation of Sovietologists were genuinely intrigued by the new "scientific" approaches that promised to put the study of Soviet affairs on a secure, objective, truly academic basis, far in advance of the subjective, instinctive, prejudiced ("folkloristic") approach of an earlier generation of Sovietologists. It was in more than one way a generational revolt.

If the Soviet system was a "developmental dictatorship of social justice" aimed to make the Soviet people freer and more prosperous, the same people saw the Western systems as both reactionary and in decline. Books began to appear claiming that Stalinism had many positive aspects because it had carried out, for instance, a cultural revolution. Others claimed that the Gulag and the purges had been greatly exaggerated; only relatively few Soviet citizens had lived in fear. Altogether the Soviet system was said to be more democratic and less aggressive than a former generation of Sovietologists had assumed. It was a different kind of democracy, and while still somewhat behind the West in living standards and economic performance, it was also quite popular and gradually catching up. The West supposedly had a great deal to learn from it

Looking back, the revisionists reached the conclusion that the Bolshevik *coup* of November 1917 had not been a *coup* but an inevitable, ultimately beneficial social development. The same was true with regard to the collectivization of agriculture in the 1930s. The Soviet system, in short, was not and had never been totalitarian, but at most an enlightened dictatorship.

There were some fascinating parallels between this kind of revisionism and similar trends in the study of Nazism in Germany that took place at the same time. In Germany, too, books appeared arguing that Nazism was a "developmental dictatorship" and that it had never been a totalitarian regime. The so-called functionalist school in the study of Nazism described Hitler as a weak dictator (Hans Mommsen), just as Stalin was said to be largely the prisoner of the bureaucracy. They were almost Hamlet-like figures, much of the time hesitating about whether to act and what to do. Most of the time they did not even know what went on around them. In Soviet studies, as in Nazi studies, there was a tendency to downplay the extent and the importance of terror.

The revisionist school in the Soviet field claimed that the number of victims of the purges and then the Gulag had been grossly exaggerated. They were counted not in many millions, but at most in hundreds of thousands. Some experts argued that the Gulag had been established not for political reasons but for economic reasons: no one wanted to move to Siberia and the north and so some pressure had to be exerted. In the case of Germany it was more difficult to doubt the number of victims because they had been accounted for in great detail. But it was maintained that there had not been a master plan to kill (for instance) the Jews; after all, no document to this effect had ever been found. So it was reasonable to assume that it was done largely as the result of local initiatives; Jews were deported (and killed) from one part of Germany or Europe, and these actions were followed by similar actions elsewhere, and in the end this became general practice.

There was, of course, no unanimity among Western Sovietologists. If it was fashionable in the 1970s and early 1980s to take a view of the Soviet leadership and system that was much too favorable, there were many dissenters. Gradually some of the revisionists came to doubt their own wisdom. Thus it was realized in the West even before Mikhail Gorbachev opened up the Soviet system that at some time in the 1970s there had been a basic change of mood from optimism to pessimism in wide sectors of Soviet society. This change, in turn, led to searching questions as to what had produced it—the realization that the economic situation was getting worse, or the feeling that the old generation of Soviet leaders had run out of ideas, or the sense that the country was adrift. When the great crisis came in 1989–90, it did not come as a total surprise to all Western experts. But it certainly came as a shock to the revisionists. They felt betrayed when Russians suddenly talked about totalitarianism in their country, something Western Sovietologists had argued for many years had never existed.

The Cold War did not rage with equal intensity from beginning to end. It can be divided roughly speaking into three periods, from the beginning to about 1962; the era of détente, which lasted until about 1979; and a new time of high tension from that year to the Soviet Union's end in 1991. My interest in Soviet affairs began to wane as the Soviet Union entered the age of stagnation (*zastoi* in Russian political language). I visited the country first when I was in my thirties and for a number of years went there virtually every year. I was not shocked or disappointed; what I saw corresponded more or less with what I expected to see.

The first visit was to Moscow and Sochi, the luxury resort on the Black Sea coast, hardly typical places for the Soviet Union. We had not chosen them; they were, I believe, among the only places then open to foreigners. It was a time when very few foreigners went to the Soviet Union and those visiting it did so in groups. I believe that in certain parts of the Caucasus where my wife's parents lived we were an object of curiosity since we must have been the first foreigners seen for a very long time. Because the family took care of us and guided our steps, we had probably greater access than most visitors. On the other hand, we had to move with additional caution. When, on a later occasion, an unknown man accosted me in the main street of one of the Caucasian resorts with the request that I take a letter to his brother in England, I jumped back as if bitten by a tarantula, to be upbraided by my teenage daughters who complained about the boorish behavior of their father.

It was, I believe, during that visit in the mid-1960s, driving along the Grusinian Military Highway, that it occurred to me that the time had come to move away from my preoccupation with current Soviet affairs. I had reached the conclusion that nothing much of interest was likely to happen for a long time under Khrushchev's successors. There were other intellectually more challenging topics, and there were also offers and invitations leading me away from the editorship of *Survey*, a journal specializing in Soviet affairs that had been my main concern for the previous eight years. (I shall deal with *Survey*, the Congress for Cultural Freedom that published it, and my modest part in the Cold War in the next chapter.) This conclusion did not mean that I would lose all interest in Soviet and Russian affairs; the field had a certain fascination even at the least promising periods, and once bitten by the Russian bug one is unlikely to give it up altogether.

Two areas fascinated me in particular in the 1970s: intellectual history and world affairs. Marxism and the Soviet Union were no longer of interest; the action, for better or worse, was now elsewhere. The Soviet Union was still a major player in world affairs, and there were major Communist Parties in some countries; even seemingly new trends were emerging, such as Eurocommunism. As a commentator on world affairs, I was bound to follow events in Moscow, but it would not be true to say that I did this with great passion. Only with the rise of Gorbachev to power, fifteen years later, did my interest reawaken, and I shall write about the end of the Cold War, too, and the many questions concerning the demise of the Soviet Union: To what extent was the collapse predictable? What did we know at the time? And what can be said about it in retrospect?

CHAPTER 4

The Downfall and Partial Resurgence of the Soviet Empire

or, The Strange Fortunes of the Congress for Cultural Freedom, "Finlandization," and Putinism

According to a famous French saying of the nineteenth century, "How beautiful was the republic during the days of the Empire." In the twentieth century, in the midst of the Cold War's tension and conflict, how wonderful did peace and normal life appear to be. So when the Cold War ended and the Berlin Wall came down, there was a tremendous feeling of relief in Europe and America. At long last peace had returned to the world, or so we thought. Now, just twenty years later, it is difficult to remember the heady optimism prevailing in those days, let alone the fears that preceded them.

The Congress for Cultural Freedom

The strange fortunes of the Congress for Cultural Freedom provide a springboard for some further reflections about the cycles of history as well as some encouragement to those who believe that there is, after all, some justice in the world. Founded in Berlin in 1950, the Congress brought together leading intellectuals and artists to discuss and promote Western democratic culture at a time, and in a place, where they were under challenge by communism's appeal. The Soviets had just completed the takeover of Eastern Europe and begun a major campaign to establish popular fronts among the world peace movements of Western intellectuals, including the Wrocław Cultural Conference for Peace. And the mood of the West was receptive. Europe's collapse in the face of the Nazi onslaught had had a traumatic effect that would last for a long time. There was an element of bad conscience. The record of the French and Italian intelligentsias in resisting fascism had been less than brilliant during the war; collaboration with the Nazi and fascist regimes had been widespread. Most leading French intellectuals, including Jean-Paul Sartre, had not joined the resistance, and his plays continued to be performed all through the occupation. Even in Britain the record of the Colonel Blimps resisting fascism had been better than that of many intellectuals, as George Orwell observed, but his writings were turned down by left-wing journals. The *New Statesman* in particular had been reluctant to denounce the Moscow trials and Stalinism in general. It had opposed rearmament in the 1930s and in 1938 had found it difficult to decide whether Hitler should be appeased or not. Now, after fascism had ceased to exist, Europe's intellectuals wanted to atone by joining the front rank of antifascism.

If Europe had proved incapable of resisting the temptations of fascism without American help, after the war it struggled to define its place, and there was an eagerness to be on the right side. The *Zeitgeist* in the 1950s and early 1960s was largely "progressive" in foreign policy—that is to say, neutralist, and even defeatist. Sartre's Marxist politics, those of *Le Monde* and *Esprit,* prevailed in France. France and also Italy had massive Communist Parties. In Britain, the leading journal of the intelligentsia was the *New Statesman,* with some 85,000 subscribers. The situation in Scandinavia was similar. Equidistance—maintaining equal distance from the policies of other nations—was political correctness. It was not that the majority of Western European intellectuals favored the installation at home of a regime like the Soviet regime but that they argued there really was no such danger, that the Soviet threat was an American invention, or at least a gross exaggeration. Many were not well informed about the situation in the Soviet empire, nor did they want to know too much.

This was the mood when the Congress appeared on the scene in the early 1950s. Its organizers were outspoken anti-Communists. The moving spirit during this early stage was Melvin J. Lasky, Brooklyn born, an officer in the U.S. Army who later became editor of the Congress's journal *Der Monat* and later yet of its *Encounter.* Others who took a leading part were Arthur Koestler, the journalist and novelist who had broken with communism; Carlo Schmid, a leading German Social Democrat; Ignazio Silone, also a journalist and novelist with one-time Communist leanings; and Sidney Hook, an American philosophy professor and former Marxist who was ardent in his opposition to communism.

Many members of the Congress, in fact, were former Communists or fellow travelers. James Burnham, for instance, had once been a Trotskyite. But the organization was actually a coalition that also included classical liberals such as Raymond Aron, nonpolitical philosophers such as Karl Jaspers, and erratic figures such as Bertrand Russell, who vacillated between wanting to nuke the Soviet Union and submitting to Joseph Stalin. Thus it came as no surprise that it was next to impossible to draft platforms and resolutions except in a very vague way. The Congress had no party line. A vitriolic article criticizing American mass culture was rejected by *Encounter,* the British organ of the Congress, but published by *Tempo Presente,* the Italian organ of the Congress. There were also divergences concerning the major political issues of the day: some supported the Vietnam

War, others opposed it from the very beginning. Some were fierce opponents of the student revolts of 1968; others wrote about them with sympathy. The coalition was held together only by a common commitment to the defense of cultural freedom, which many felt was threatened.

The Congress's strength was not in political resolutions but in the ideas it discussed in its workshops and publications—issues of economic development and planning, the concept of the postindustrial society, the idea of totalitarianism and the end of ideology, modernism in the arts, the social responsibility of scientists. Such issues played a crucial role in the intellectual life of postwar Europe and the United States. The Congress published influential journals in the 1950s and early 1960s, and its conferences were stimulating and well attended. But when in the mid-1960s it was revealed that the organization had accepted money from the Central Intelligence Agency, a great wave of indignation seemed to destroy all its earlier achievements. The impression was created that the crime committed by the Congress by accepting such money for its publications was at least equal to the crimes of Adolf Hitler and Joseph Stalin put together.

It has been only in recent years, following revelations from the old Soviet archives and the confrontation with Muslim fundamentalism, that the historical rehabilitation of the Congress (now long out of business) began. "Soft power" was discovered by leading Harvard professors, and writers from various political quarters have been stressing the importance of winning hearts and minds rather than concentrating on military action. Where is the Congress now, when it is so desperately needed?

I first visited the Paris headquarters of the Congress for Cultural Freedom in May 1953. It was a modest office of three or four rooms in the elegant avenue Montaigne not far from the Champs Elysees, a street better known for haute couture (Chanel, Givenchy, Ungaro, Valentino, and Dior were there, as well as Louis Vuitton and Cartier) than for haute culture. Well, that's not quite true, for Igor Stravinsky's *Sacre de Printemps* was first performed in the Theatre des Champs Elysees, located in number 15 of that distinguished street. Yes, and Henry James lived in 24 avenue Montaigne, but this had been a long time ago.

The secretary-general of the organization was Michael Josselson. None of the great intellectual leaders was an organizer by vocation or training, nor had any ambitions in this direction. Thus leadership passed to Josselson and his makeshift office in Paris. Whether Paris was a good choice is not at all clear in retrospect. From recently published CIA documents it appears that there was a strong body of opinion that preferred Berlin since Paris seemed too "ethereal, evanescent, and neutralist in the struggle between liberty and tyranny." Josselson, in his forties at the time, born in Estonia, educated in Berlin, had lived in Paris before the war as chief buyer of a leading New York department store prior to enlisting in the U.S. Army. He was a polyglot and at the same time a man of intellectual substance, a manager of the best kind, for he had good judgment and a great deal of commonsense. He could be very charming, even when on the verge of an emotional explosion. His colleague and nominal boss, Nicholas Nabokov, rushed in and out of rooms, a great name dropper, preoccupied with celebrities.

I had been recommended to the Congress by George Lichtheim, the historian of socialist thought, a resident of London, and a close friend. Lichtheim did not belong to the Congress since he disapproved of Josselson's strategy of approaching above all the literary intelligentsia, figures such as Stephen Spender, which he regarded a waste of time and effort. Lichtheim had told Josselson that I was a latter-day Rastignac, a young man from the provinces, unpolished, self-made but of a certain promise with some interesting ideas such as publishing a journal on Soviet culture. Josselson liked to act from time to time as a talent scout, and he introduced me to some of his friends, colleagues, and gurus. At tea with Raymond Aron there was a famous American sociologist, but since my knowledge of American sociology was even less then than now, I confused him with a comic actor very popular in the early days of American television. This amused Aron (whom I came to admire in later years) but not the American sociologist.

It was my first visit ever to Paris, and there was a lot to be seen in that hot summer. The city was a far shabbier but intellectually much more exciting place than ten years later. Most people still drove around in old Citroëns familiar from old movies; in every other building there was a tiny BOF selling butter, eggs, and cheese; and in our little hotel at the corner of rue Jacob and rue Bonaparte there was neither lift nor private shower nor private toilet. The locals apart, I met some interesting transients whom I had read before but had not known in person—the Swiss Herbert Luethy and his friend François Bondy, editor of *Preuves*, another polyglot; the writer Manès Sperber; Richard Löwenthal and Franz Borkenau; as well as Irving Kristol, who was about to publish the first issue of *Encounter*.

I remained in contact with the Congress, but it was two years before my suggestion to establish a little journal covering Soviet culture was accepted. In the meantime I was consulted on certain issues. I recommended that the Congress not be active in the Middle East, which I thought unpropitious ground for cultural freedom. The Congress disregarded my views and sponsored certain activities, including a cultural magazine in Lebanon, which were quite unsuccessful. I was equally skeptical about the Congress's activities in India, where Americans were thought to be (following George Kennan) power lusting and money grabbing and war mongering. Indian intellectuals had their own agenda. Many sympathized with communism, albeit not very deeply; others were Hindu nationalists combating Muslims and keeping Untouchables in their place. Internal quarrels among Western Marxists, non-Marxists, and anti-Marxists were of little interest to them. The Congress was essentially a Western enterprise, and attempts to expand its activities to Asia could not be very successful.

Eventually, Josselson gave me permission (and a tiny budget) to put out a monthly newsletter of sixteen pages in a few hundred copies. Lichtheim helped me in the early days; so did Jane Degras, the Russian expert of Chatham House (the Royal Institute of International Affairs). She was a warmhearted, impulsive, and tough lady, respected by everyone in the field. Of Cockney working-class origin, she had worked in the Marx-Engels-Lenin Institute in Moscow in the 1920s. She followed me when ten years later I left and founded the *Journal of Contemporary History* together with George Mosse. I learned much from her and from George Lichtheim in those days.

There was no editorial office, no secretary. The periodical was put together in our small Hampstead apartment and retyped by Jane's sister, who lived in one of the English garden cities. In the beginning it was not accepted as a permanent fixture by the Congress, but after a while it started growing from sixteen to sixty pages and eventually to 150 and more. It became a quarterly and changed its name from *Soviet Culture* to *Soviet Survey* and eventually to *Survey*, a journal of history, politics, and sociology as well as of cultural trends. Its annual budget when I left it was a little in excess of $40,000. Two years after its foundation I hired Leopold Labedz as an assistant, who became editor after I left in the mid-1960s. The journal continued to appear for almost a quarter of a century thereafter.

My involvement with the Congress lasted for about ten years. I was never a full-time employee, and while I participated in some of its conferences, I never belonged to the inner circle and my knowledge of decision making was secondhand. But I was in sympathy with its aims and experienced the excitement of those early years and of being involved in an enterprise in which I wholly believed and which, given the imperfections of human endeavor, seems to me eminently worthwhile in retrospect.

Of the journals sponsored by the Congress, *Der Monat* in Germany and *Encounter* in Britain were for years the most successful. *Der Monat* faced the least difficulties, as Germany had been largely cut off from the West for more than ten years and there was a great wish to retrieve what had been missed (*Nachholbedarf*). Furthermore Germany was in the front line of the Cold War; the Soviet threat was no abstraction there, as it was for many in Britain or Italy. Under Lasky's capable editorship, *Der Monat* was in the 1950s the most interesting and widely discussed international magazine in Germany, perhaps in the whole of Europe. There was an openness to new ideas and a freshness in the early postwar period that disappeared in later years, after the economic miracle had taken place and been replaced by radical chic and some of the old German provincialism and self-righteousness, and *Besser Wisserei* prevailed again. Since the demise of *Der Monat* there has not been a journal quite so interesting in Germany; the few serious periodicals have had a circulation of a few thousand, at best. The political mood, too, changed. If the United States could do no wrong in 1950, after 1970 many German intellectuals became anti-American, and this attitude, too, caused the decline and eventually the demise of *Der Monat*.

Both *Tempo Presente* in Italy and *Preuves* in France faced uphill struggles. The mood of the intelligentsia in these countries was *progressiste*, and fellow travelers dominated key positions in cultural life. Silone, the editor of *Tempo Presente*, had been a political emigré under fascism; so had Nicola Chiaromonte, his associate, and to a certain extent they were bound to be out of touch with the intelligentsia. In France, the Gaullists and the French right disliked *Preuves* because of its Anglo-American connections, its lack of enthusiasm for the Algerian War, and other reasons. The French left disliked it for different reasons. Sartre and his friends persuaded themselves that communism, purged perhaps of its specific Russian excesses, was the wave of the future; that Stalin, all things considered, was an enlightened if somewhat harsh ruler; that the Gulag did not exist; and that the Soviet economic system was making enormous progress. These delusions faded only in the late 1960s when Aron, who had been ostracized for decades, was at long last recognized as the most prescient French thinker of his generation. In the United States his name is invoked today with respect and admiration by historians and political scientists having little in common with his ideas; I wonder whether he would have been more amused or horrified by some of these latter-day supporters.

To what extent did *Preuves* contribute to this change in the French mood? It had a certain influence but probably not a very large one, for the period was not propitious. The French were simply not ready for a liberal journal of internationalist persuasion. For many, especially on the left, domestic affairs mattered far more than foreign policy, which seemed distant and somewhat abstract. Foreign affairs were not part of their daily life and routine and could safely be ignored. Thus the impact of Aleksandr Solzhenitsyn's books, when they became available, came as a surprise. All these facts about Soviet oppression had been known for a long time, but there had been no willingness to accept them. Ironically, *Preuves*'s major influence was in Eastern Europe, and its volumes were reprinted years after it had ceased to exist. It had appeared too early on the Paris intellectual scene.

Encounter in London faced difficulties of a different kind. It succeeded to a much larger degree than *Preuves* and for many years had the largest circulation of all British serious periodicals. It became the flagship of the Congress. Kristol was in many respects an ideal editor, yet with all his Anglophilia he did not quite succeed in overcoming the antagonism of the British literary establishment, which resented American (and Jewish and foreign) influences. True, the reputation and the circulation of the *New Statesman* waned, but there was resentment from other quarters as well, including T. S. Eliot and Evelyn Waugh, not exactly heroes of left-wing thought. The prevailing mood, often one of superciliousness and negativism, of snobbery and arrogance, was not promising for a journal such as *Encounter.* It tried to accommodate itself to the *Zeitgeist;* the most famous of the articles it published in the early years was Nancy Mitford on the British aristocracy and U (upper-class) and non-U speech. Whatever the place of these figures in the history of literature, for a movement devoted to the cause of cultural freedom they were useless. In brief, Kristol mixed, perhaps had to mix, with the wrong crowd, but there was no other crowd, at least not among the literati.

This was not of course the whole story, and if the Labour Party has distanced itself to a considerable degree from wholesale public ownership in the course of time, much of the spadework had been done by *Encounter* and various Congress seminars in the 1950s and 1960s. There were some immensely gifted writers among the academics, but there was no real support for a cosmopolitan journal; intellectual fashions preferred the *Private Eye* and occasionally the *Spectator.* For serious magazines such as had existed in Britain in earlier periods there was only limited demand, and for intellectual trends abroad only limited interest. *Encounter* provided more entertainment than messages for which there was not much interest. It published widely read, often amusing articles, but its intellectual influence and reputation, as in the case of *Preuves,* was more outside the country in which it was published. As with *Der Monat,* it did not really find a successor. Since its demise there has not been a political-literary magazine of similar stature.

The Congress sponsored other magazines, such as *Forum* in Austria. Edited by Friedrich Torberg, a very gifted satirist but a loose cannon, *Forum* published both brilliant and cranky articles in a time-honored Austrian tradition. Torberg was also a quarrelsome man; one of his few friendships that lasted was with Marlene Dietrich, who called him from Paris whenever she felt lonely and unhappy, which was quite often. He was also the author of one of the great sport novels in the history of literature—*Die Mannschaft,* about a water polo team—and as a very young man he had written an astonishingly mature novel about the suicide of a high school student. With all his talents he was an embarrassment for the Congress. He wanted, for instance, to ban Bertolt Brecht's plays in Austria. I owe him an enormous debt of gratitude, however, for introducing me to Vienna's leading coffeehouse, Café Dehmel; without this introduction I would probably have been treated much less politely.

I was most familiar with the affairs of *Survey,* at least in the early years, and also the *China Quarterly,* founded in 1960. There was a constant battle with Paris to receive a greater allocation to publish a more substantial magazine. There was so much interesting material and so few pages at our disposal. I do not think there were authors' fees in the early days; if so they must have been a pittance. But it was in the early years that some of the most interesting issues were published—on Marxist revisionism, on the state of Soviet studies, on personal recollections of the early "heroic" period of Soviet history. Many of these special issues later became books.

Leo Labedz, the editor who succeeded me, was a polymath and formidable polemicist. He obtained the texts of Russian and other Eastern European dissidents and first published them in English; his merits in this respect were great and have not been fully recognized. Whenever I was in London after 1965 he would come for dinner. He did not mellow with age but became more rigid, and this attitude affected his judgment. Political discussions became difficult, but we still had many interests in common, such as literature and French movies of the 1930s and 1940s. On Israeli affairs Leo became a hawk after 1967 without ever having been interested in things Jewish. He died in 1992 after a long and painful illness that he bore with great fortitude. The last issues of *Survey* were guest-edited by friends of Leo. At the very time that the Soviet empire collapsed and many people in Moscow made it known that what *Survey* had been saying for decades had been correct, the publication ceased to exist.

There had been rumors for some time that the Congress was CIA financed or, to be precise, received a considerable part of its budget from grants channeled by the CIA through various American foundations. It is my impression that no more than three or four people knew about it. Like the others, I did not know, nor did I try very hard to find out. It did not seem a crucial question at the height of the Cold War, as financial aid was needed. Similar allocations were made by governments in every major and most minor countries, but these countries were less open than the United States and such matters were handled more discreetly. It later appeared that most non-Communist groups and parties—including the socialist left and Willy Brandt—had received similar help from the CIA when Soviet pressure was high and no other funds were available.

In 1967 the far left journal *Ramparts* published an article about the CIA's financing of the Congress, and this revelation caused much commotion especially in Britain and the United States among people who felt their trust had been betrayed. A strong argument could have been made that what was necessary and probably inevitable in the 1950s at the height of the Soviet offensive was no longer advisable ten or fifteen years later when the offensive began to ebb. Greater efforts should have been made to obtain support from other sources, and in fact in the late 1950s, the Congress had tried to enlist the help of the big foundations, but without success. The U.S. Senate and House of Representatives would not have allocated funds to foreign operations over which it had no control: some on the left would have blocked it because of the anti-Communist orientation of the Congress, while those on the right and the isolationists would have opposed it for it would have meant supporting liberals and social democrats in Europe for whom they had no sympathies whatsoever. Above all there was the general and profound American aversion to spending on cultural diplomacy (soft power), which has continued to the present day. Public diplomacy was always a stepchild of American foreign policy, deemed at best a luxury. From time to time lip service would be paid to the need to struggle for the hearts and minds of people abroad, but the amount of money spent on such purposes was always much less than 1 percent of defense spending.

Nor is it at all certain that the Congress would have enjoyed greater freedom under the tutelage of one of the great foundations, or even of the Senate and the House of Representatives. The CIA, on the other hand, virtually did not interfere, even in the Milan conference of 1955, which addressed "The Future of Freedom." Professor Peter Wiles of New College, Oxford, later of the London School of Economics, was commissioned to present a paper in which he showed that Soviet industrial production outpaced the West. Another paper, by Professor Michael Polanyi of Manchester, argued that state controls did not automatically weaken freedom. This argument induced an angry Friedrich Hayek of *Road to Serfdom* (1944) fame to reply that the real agenda of the Milan conference was not to plan the future of freedom but to write its obituary.

The Congress had been under attack for a long time, but with the revelations of CIA funding the campaign reached a crescendo. "Literary Bay of Pigs" wrote Alexander Werth in the *Nation,* deriding the journals that had done their best to keep the Cold War boiling. Conor Cruise O'Brien in *Book Week,* Jason Epstein in the *New York Review of Books,* Christopher Lasch in a long article in the *Nation,* and countless lesser lights denounced the deep moral corruption of the liberal anti-Communist intellectuals, especially the former Communists among them. The issue was no longer what the subsidies had been used for, let alone who had been right in the ideological debate: by secretly accepting government money the Congress had automatically disqualified itself. It was no longer necessary to discuss seriously the political issues involved because any cause supported by the U.S. government was *a priori* reprehensible. The anti-anti-Communists had gained the high moral ground. As for the lack of cultural and other freedoms in the Soviet Union, all kind of mitigating circumstances were advanced by Lasch: the Soviet Union was still underdeveloped, the penny-pinching Soviet bureaucratic culture was judged in utilitarian terms, and these were luxuries they thought they could ill afford. Theodore Draper was bitterly denounced for his diatribes: he had dared to suggest that Fidel Castro was not a democrat but belonged to the Soviet camp.

I missed many of these articles at the time, as my preoccupations then were in a different field. I read them not long ago; at a distance of forty years they made curious reading, for history did not end in 1966. There was, of course, much more to the Congress than communism and anticommunism, but this was the issue that most annoyed the critics. They could not have known at the time that one day the Cold War would come to an end, that Soviet archives would be opened, and that the documents revealed there would undermine so many of their cherished beliefs about the Cold War and the character and the aims of Soviet policy. Soviet revelations would not just confirm most of what the Congress's publications had been saying but go well beyond it. How much triumphalism had there been in the 1960s among anti-anti-Communists, and what embarrassing reading this makes four decades later. Seldom in modern history has an organization been vindicated by subsequent events as fully as the Congress for Cultural Freedom. However, having been right prematurely does not necessarily make for greater popularity.

True, some of the critics, including Lasch, who died in 1994, had changed their views even earlier; so did O'Brien, who in later years worked as a writer for Rupert Murdoch's London *Times* and editor of the London *Observer.* He became one of the strongest voices in the struggle against terrorism and author of a history of Zionism and Israel not at all consonant with the *Zeitgeist.* Peter Collier, an editor of *Ramparts,* then went on, thirty years later, to establish a right-wing publishing house—named Encounter.

One of the saddest stories was that of Alexander Werth. Russian born but of Jewish origin (a fact of which he seldom made use), he was not the most prescient of journalists: from Berlin in early 1933 he predicted that Hitler was not really much of a peril and should not be taken too seriously. Being a native Russian speaker he came into his own with the rapprochement with the Soviet Union during World War II when he was stationed there. During the later years of his life there were persistent allegations that he was a Soviet agent of influence, but if so he was certainly not the only one. When challenged of having knowingly downplayed the role of the Gulag and the number of victims, he admitted that he had indeed done so, but only because in the 1950s there had been so many people in the West eager to make war against the Soviet Union that one could not provide grist to their mills. Werth committed suicide in 1969.

Even after the fall of the Soviet Union and the revelations of the 1990s there were some unwilling to forgive the Congress that it had been right prematurely. Books and articles were written to this effect. But this should not have come as a great surprise. To accept that the Cold War had been won by the wrong side was not easy for people deeply committed to a Sartrean *Weltanschauung.* There was a great upswing of anti-Americanism in the 1990s and thereafter, mixed with fear of the sole remaining superpower. It is only human to persist in error rather than to admit mistakes, and the importance of shortsightedness should never be underrated. The real agony of the American left (a title by Lasch) occurred long after the 1960s, when the full extent of its misjudgments became common knowledge. As the saying went in Paris, it was better to be wrong with Sartre than right with Aron; but a price had eventually to be paid for such foolishness.

The Congress might well have outlived its purpose and usefulness by the 1970s. Everything had been said by that time about Communist ideology. It had become an exceedingly boring topic. Those still believing in the progressive character of the Soviet system were quasi-religious believers, impervious to rational argument and persuasion. There are always such people, sometimes many of them; they could also be found, as we shall show, among Western Soviet experts.

Later conferences such as the Princeton jamboree in 1968, after the Congress had changed its name (and character) were less important—gatherings of distinguished people and celebrities, including some curious attendants such as Lillian Hellman—and they lacked clear focus. The theme was America's place and image in the world, an interesting theme but very distant from the original purpose of the Congress. The Princeton meeting could have been sponsored by dozens of other well-meaning foundations. Josselson, who had resigned following the revelations about the CIA, was meanwhile sitting at home in Geneva working on a biography of Barclay de Tolly, the Russian general of 1812 fame.

One could conclude the story here, but there still are a number of loose ends. Mistakes were made by the Congress, but they were not those most frequently adduced in later years by its enemies. The Congress was set up hastily, and the choice of some of its officials was unfortunate. There was a heavy concentration on well-known names and great reputations, some of them spurious. Some of the gatherings were mainly for show, and the attendants sometimes reminded one of the smart set commuting between St. Tropez in the summer and St. Moritz or Gstaad in winter. There was an element of snobbery; outward appearance of refinement and sophistication counted sometimes for more than substance. Such lack of seriousness was in contrast with the traditional European image of intellectuals and the intelligentsia.

Of course, there were mitigating circumstances. An organization aiming at having a political impact could not entirely rely on young and unknown geniuses; it needed also some big names. But the Congress was prone to overdo this. In the overall balance the Congress was a remarkable concentration of gifted, stimulating, and interesting people. How influential was it? Did it affect the politics of the intelligentsia in Europe and elsewhere? The impact of ideas on politics is always a complicated affair. If French and Italian intellectuals turned away from communism in the 1970s, the Germans rediscovered Marxism just at that time, only to turn to anti-Americanism and a new nationalism thereafter. Solzhenitsyn's books had a tremendous impact in France but very little in Germany. The influence of the Congress was probably greater in Eastern Europe and the Soviet

Union. A journal such as the Polish *Kultura* made a substantial contribution to the downfall of communism in Poland, and since the Polish example influenced the rest of Eastern Europe, this was a matter of great consequence. A considerable amount of material published by the Congress was translated into Russian (and labeled secret, for official use only) in a few hundred copies kept in certain well-guarded places for selected members of the political elite, but it was, in fact, widely read. This literature had a great attraction, and by the late 1970s all but the most simple-minded enthusiasts had ceased to believe in Marxism-Leninism. In fact, there were probably more believers in Marxism-Leninism at the time in Western universities than in the Soviet bloc. All this was not unconnected to the spadework done by the Congress in the earlier decades. Soft power did not overthrow the Soviet regime, but it certainly contributed to it.

Those who opposed the aims and activities of the Congress and their ideological descendants have largely shifted their ground. They will grudgingly admit that the Congress was right when the Jean-Paul Sartres and Alberto Moravias were wrong. But they now claim that its work was unnecessary because a real threat never existed or was grossly exaggerated. Those who argued during the Cold War that the Soviet system was working well, and that Soviet power was so strong that nothing should be done to provoke the Kremlin because of the danger of war, have now taken the opposite position, claiming that Russia has always been so weak, economically, politically, and even militarily that it had been foolish to take it seriously.

Similar arguments have been adduced with regard to Hitler and Nazism, as mentioned earlier. In this view, Nazi power had been greatly exaggerated, and Hitler had lost World War II the moment he unleashed it. This view is not just misplaced hindsight; the arguments are as wrong now as they were then. According to the same logic, there was no need to spend so much on defense because the Soviet system was so weak. But this logic confuses cause and effect. The Soviet system was not always weak, there was offensive military planning, and Soviet propaganda even among Western intellectuals was not always ineffective. If the regime collapsed it was not owing to the efforts of those who wanted to appease it and who believed that intellectuals should have kept out of the conflict between the two superpowers. Nor was it owing to the efforts of those who tried to bring it to a quick end since it was unnecessary and needlessly prolonged by the blind anticommunism of certain Western circles (such as the military-industrial complex) and their intellectual helpers. They have had some success inasmuch as the Cold War has been for many, all things considered, something disgraceful, very much in contrast to antifascism.

All this now belongs to history, and yet it has a bearing on the present. Those who recommended in recent years the importance of soft power have pointed to a real issue. But it is doubtful whether a campaign for cultural freedom would have a great response in the Muslim world, to give but one example; cultural freedom does not have much support among Arab intellectuals, whose agenda is quite different from that of Eastern European and Russian intellectuals.

There is unfortunately a strong tendency in these parts to believe in conspiracy theories—the more far-fetched, the more attractive. Western black propaganda exploiting this weakness would be infinitely more effective than appeals to abolish censorship. But democratic societies will hardly ever make use of such stratagems except in time of war.

The Congress was a coalition of disparate individuals and groups, of liberals and "reactionaries," as Lasch noted when he was hostile, and the latter gradually disappeared. But it was not the breeding ground of neo-conservatism, the bugbear of the early twenty-first century. There has been a tendency among lazy media to describe the critics of Soviet and Communist politics as neo-conservatives; but Leo Strauss did not belong to the Congress, communism and the Soviet Union were not among his fields of interest, and anyway no one at the time had heard of neo-conservatism. Neo-conservatives believed in the export of democracy, a belief that was not shared by Strauss. It was shared by John Kennedy, who in many ways was a forerunner of the neo-conservatives, at least in the field of foreign policy. On the other hand, many conservatives and some neo-conservatives were or became America Firsters, even though few were willing to accept this label. The AFL-CIO was in the forefront of the Cold War battles. A recent writer on the role of neo-conservatism rightly notes that contrary to what the label implies, more than a few "cold warriors" (including Senator Henry Jackson) were liberals on social issues.

There were, to repeat once again, no neo-conservatives in the 1950s and 1960s. The label certainly does not apply to Raymond Aron or to Daniel Bell or even to Edward Shils, the three people most central in setting the agenda of the Congress at the time. What would the label mean in world affairs? Were Leonid Brezhnev and Yuri Andropov liberals, and if so, how would one define their opponents? If the critics of the Soviet leaders were neo-conservatives, their enemies must have been radicals or at least liberals. But if anything the Soviet leaders were conservatives. Were the Chinese more progressive or more reactionary than the Soviet leaders? Was Polish Solidarity a conservative or liberal movement? Is Osama bin Laden a liberal or a conservative? To ask these questions is to demonstrate the absurdity of the labels. Yet they are used, and probably will be used in future, often out of ignorance or want of another label. Sometimes they are used deliberately to obfuscate matters.

The Congress played a part in the ideological confrontation between communism and the West. While thousands of studies have been written about political and military aspects of the Cold War, very few have focused on the contest for the hearts and minds of people on the other side of the Iron Curtain. Historians have paid little attention to the "liberal conspiracy" as one author called his book about the history of the Congress. Strictly speaking it was no conspiracy at all but a small organization operating with a tiny budget and a handful of administrators. A recent best-selling critical history of the CIA devotes a page or two out of many hundred to Congress, and what the author has to say about it does not show (to put it mildly) any familiarity.

Two histories of the Congress have been written so far, one by Peter Coleman, a former Australian member of Parliament, and another by Pierre Gremion, a French academic. In addition there has been a massive study of the Congress's activities in Germany, originally a dissertation, and a very hostile book by Francis Stonor Saunders, a British television journalist, as well as a number of essays and profiles by Edward Shils, the well-known sociologist. Both the Coleman and the Gremion book are judicious, well informed, and reliable. Neither author was present at the creation, however, and those who were might not have agreed with all their observations and comments. All history is based on documents, but documents seldom contain the whole story, even with regard to relative small organizations such as the Congress. In these histories, those who wrote many letters and memoranda now figure more prominently than those who did not but were of equal or greater importance. As so often happens, those who knew most did not write diaries or publish their recollections.

According to received wisdom the initiative for the Congress came from the Office of Policy Coordination (OPC), the covert action branch of CIA. But according to the documents the first interest had been generated by a small group of European intellectuals who contacted OPC, which was hesitant and doubtful. It was also believed that Lasky acted at the time as a CIA agent. But again according to the documents it emerged that Lasky, too brash and outspoken, not easy to control, was not *persona grata* in Washington and an ultimatum was issued: unless Lasky was removed, the CIA would not support the Congress. Thus it was decided to "terminate" *Der Monat*, which survived nevertheless owing to the support of John McCloy, U.S. high commissioner in Germany at the time, and some others who had known Lasky in Berlin during the early postwar years. It was rumored at the time that the KGB thought *Der Monat* of sufficient interest to infiltrate an agent (or managed to win over a person in that office; the details are not quite clear to this day). There was apparently no spy at the *Encounter* office. If there would have been one, it might have provided the scenario for a high-quality thriller.

The story of the Congress will be told again in greater detail and with different emphasis. It offers a variety of lessons that will almost certainly be ignored.

The funds given to the Congress should not have come from CIA, but as they could not at the time come from any other source, the funding had to be done in secret. Some isolationists among U.S. lawmakers condemned cultural diplomacy root and branch, because they regarded it as cultural imperialism; others opposed it because it reduced the opportunities for pork-barrel spending. The elimination of the United States Information Agency in the 1990s and the history of National Endowment for Democracy show the same line of thought: that cultural diplomacy is elitist and the diffusion of culture abroad is a luxury as well as reprehensible because it means interfering in the affairs of other countries. Why invest in culture abroad if CNN can be watched in every five-star hotel outside the United States? True, in theory everyone agrees about the importance of soft power in contradistinction to defense, but it still has no domestic constituency fighting for it. The NED budget was increased under President Bill Clinton and again under President George W. Bush. And it is now, twenty years after it was founded, 0.02 percent of the budget of the Pentagon. But it is argued that if one takes into consideration other sources of funding, the U.S. government can claim to spend almost a billion dollars for these purposes abroad. True enough, and the French spend a considerably higher percentage of their budget.

George Kennan once wrote in a private letter to Shepard Stone of the Ford Foundation:

> Congress is an institution of great value which should have a permanent place, it seems to me, in the Western world. The flap about the CIA money was quite unwarranted and caused far more anguish than it should have been permitted to cause. I never felt the slightest pangs of conscience about it. The country has no ministry of culture and CIA was obliged to do what it could to try to fill the gap. It should be praised for having done so and not criticized. It is unfair that it should be so bitterly condemned for its failures and then should get upbraided if it does something constructive and sensible. And the Congress would itself have been remiss if it had failed to take money which came to it from good intent without strings or conditions.

As Kennan observed, alone among all developed countries, the United States has no ministry of culture (or arts or national heritage), and contributions by the private sector have been sporadic and declining in recent years. But this is another story. As for the Congress, we shall not see the like of it again except perhaps in a state of emergency. "Public diplomacy" was never thought to be of much importance in the United States, and after the Cold War ended it almost ceased to exist. I wrote "Save Public Diplomacy" for *Foreign Affairs* in 1994 without any noticeable effect. Only about a decade later did the invocation of soft power get under way.

Finnish Interlude

In the 1970s the term "Finlandization" entered the political lexicon, and the issue of Finlandization became for a while much debated. The creation of the term was attributed by some to the present writer, by others to Franz Josef Strauss, head of the Bavarian Christian Social Union, but in fact it seems to have been coined, at least in German, by my friend and sometime guru Richard Löwenthal, one of the most astute political thinkers of the postwar period.

The term refers to the special relationship between Finland and the Soviet Union, specifically Finland's appeasement of its powerful neighbor to the extent that the country could no longer be defined as neutral and independent in the accepted sense. The Soviet Union had the right to interfere in Finnish affairs. Political parties and politicians not approved by Moscow could not join the cabinet. While Urho Kekkonen, the Finnish politician most trusted by Moscow, was president of the country for a quarter of a century, KGB representatives—first Vladimir Stepanov, later Viktor Vladimirov—confirmed most important political decisions. There was no censorship in Finland, but the Finnish media had to exercise self-censorship. Soviet control was not absolute, however. When Finland decided to join the European Economic Community, it did so despite Soviet opposition.

Having become interested in the topic, having visited Finland and read all that was available on this issue in languages other than Finnish (which was not very much), I wrote a longish essay entitled "Europe: The Specter of Finlandization" in December 1977. It was measured in tone. I acknowledged that given Finland's specific geopolitical situation certain concessions toward the Soviet Union had to be made, certainly in the military field. But I also argued that Kekkonen had carried this policy much further than necessary. He was not a socialist let alone a Communist and in his younger years had in fact engaged in militant anti-Communist activities. Later on, however, he had come to believe that Finland could maintain its special status only owing to his policy, which was based, *inter alia*, on relaxing with Soviet leaders in the sauna and telling them funny stories. I argued that this policy—even when shorn of exaggerations such as being represented as the epitome of wisdom, maturity, and responsibility, as Kekkonen and his supporters loved to do—was not a good example for the rest of Europe of how to conduct affairs with the Soviets.

This essay was widely commented upon in Finland, in Scandinavia, and eventually also in the United States. The reception in Finland was mixed. Some thought the article on the whole well informed; others thought it ignorant; and a few believed that "Laqueur" was the pseudonym of a highly placed U.S. official. Ironically, most Finnish commentators, familiar with the true state of affairs in their country, were far less strident in their defense of Finlandization than some of Kekkonen's well-wishers in the West.

Thus a *Washington Post* commentator maintained that Finland was where most of Europe wanted to be. George Kennan, in *The Cloud of Danger* (1977), praised the Finns—that is to say, the Kekkonen policy—for composure and firmness, and he objected to the common usage of the term "Finlandization" as something humiliating and spineless. U.S. Vice President Walter Mondale, speaking in Helsinki, declared that the emotionally charged term interfered with accurate communication. A political science professor called Finland a paradigm for the future, "a solution for the problems facing an isolated minor state pitted against a great military power" (as I quoted much later in "A Postscript on Finlandization").

The debate triggered by "The Specter of Finlandization" and several rejoinders of mine eventually died down. But the issues involved continued to preoccupy people in Finland, and not only there. In 1981 Kekkonen finally retired and was followed by Mauno Koivisto, who, broadly speaking, followed a similar policy but without Kekkonen's aplomb. The Soviets had originally distrusted Koivisto but later accepted him, having realized that his eagerness to pursue the Kekkonen line was genuine. After Kekkonen's death in 1986 rumors began to spread that he had been a Soviet agent. This rumor was rejected by his official biographer as base calumny.

In the early 1990s the former resident of the KGB in Helsinki began to talk, and it appeared that Kekkonen and other leading proponents of Finlandization had indeed received millions from Moscow, some for their reelection, some apparently for personal use. Subsequently the files of the foreign department of the Central Committee of the Communist Party of the Soviet Union were opened, resulting in the publication of secret documents that bore these facts out, and on the occasion of Kekkonen's one-hundredth birthday in 2000 various biographical and general studies were published, as well as several volumes of Kekkonen's diaries, shedding new light on the age of Finlandization.

It appeared that Soviet interference had gone much further than I and most other outside observers had assumed. True, all this did not necessarily make Kekkonen a traitor or a Soviet tool; after all, in 1917 V. I. Lenin had accepted German money while pursuing his own agenda. Kekkonen probably would have acted as he did even if the Soviets had not paid him a single *markka*. Of course, Kekkonen was a Finnish patriot (a fact repeatedly stressed in my original essay); perhaps he thought he was the only true patriot. He did not want his country to become a Soviet satellite like the countries of Eastern Europe, and he thought that only he had the key to good relations with the powerful neighbor in the East. Many Finns now think that Kekkonen was an egomaniac and a cynic who apparently kept a copy of Machiavelli at his bedside table. Perhaps it was an effective way to handle the Soviets in this specific case. But a highly moral policy, a shining example for the rest of Europe, it certainly was not.

Another twenty years have now passed, and Finland has been doing well in many respects. After facing an economic crisis in the 1990s, the result of having been too dependent on the Soviet market, which had ceased to exist, it rapidly adjusted to the new conditions on the world markets. Owing to Nokia and some other firms of world renown, Finland's per capita income is now as high or higher as that of Western European countries. According to a Program for International Student Assessment study, the educational level in Finland's schools is higher than in other European countries. Some commentators think that this success is owing to Finland's having kept out immigrants except a few Somalis and former residents of Yugoslavia, but others refute these reasons. According to all statistics, the quality of life is very high.

In brief, Finland has every reason to be proud. And many argue that the country's current status is the result of its wise policy during the Cold War. They tend to ignore that Finland was lucky, for it became fully independent as a result of the disintegration of the Soviet empire and neither Kekkonen nor his friends made a notable contribution to that development. Prime Minister Paavo Lipponen, on the occasion of Kekkonen's centenary, said that it is legitimate to talk about Finlandization but that in the end the mouse did better than the cat in the Cold War. True enough, but he should have also said that this was not because the mouse swallowed the cat or because of anything the mouse did other than keeping very, very quiet.

How has Finland come to terms with its record during the Kekkonen years? Some Finns are proud of it, others feel somewhat uneasy, many want to draw a veil of forgetfulness over this period. What of the defenders of the Kekkonen line in the West? They, too, have kept silent; perhaps they lost interest in Finland.

Not everybody is celebrating in Finland. When I wrote my essays in the 1970s I had the help of some courageous people inside Finland who sent me translations from the Finnish press. Although there was no official censorship in Finland, one of these communications by a former ambassador was intercepted, whereupon his pension was taken away and but for the help of a few devoted friends he might not have survived. When I inquired years later I was told that the removal of his pension had nothing to do with his translation from Finnish newspapers. Having been denied justice in Finland he tried to take the matter to the Court of Justice of the European Communities, only to be told that too many years had passed and the case was now no longer within its jurisdiction. A sad story, and not the only sad story relating to the price that was paid by some during those years.

Why take up Finlandization now, when it would appear to be a thing of the past? In fact the appeasement phenomenon has not disappeared from the face of the earth, and perhaps never will. When I wrote about Finlandization I did by no means argue that appeasement should never, under any circumstances be practiced. I also said that with all of Kekkonen's opportunism and the weak-kneed Finnish Social Democrats (who professed to see in socialism as practiced in the Soviet Union an admirable example), I really aimed to show that in some circumstances appeasement might be inescapable. But I also tried to prove that quite often appeasement (such as that, for instance, practiced by Kekkonen) went well beyond what might have been objectively necessary and that it was anything but morally superior. On the whole, Finns were probably showing more steadfastness in the circumstances than some other European countries would have shown. However, what would have been their fate but for the breakup of the Soviet empire? The years to come, with Europe's growing dependence on energy supplies from the Middle East and Russia and other threats, will show whether my suspicions were justified or not.

The Fall of the Soviet Union

The collapse of the Soviet empire was not the only world-shaking event of the twentieth century, but it was certainly the least expected. This event raises (at the very least) three questions: Why did it break up so suddenly? Why was hardly anyone aware of the immediacy of its disappearance? And what are the prospects of a second coming? Thoughts on responses to the first two questions have so far been implied in this chapter. I will now recapitulate and get to the final question.

I have mentioned earlier on my awakening interest in Communist and Soviet affairs during World War II and how in the 1960s this interest waned. The Soviet Union was a superpower and still a major force in world politics, but as an ideological challenge communism had ceased to exist; the Soviet dream had turned into a nightmare. My interest reawakened when, in the mid-1980s, it seemed clear that things could not go on as before in Moscow, but in what direction would they turn?

For a considerable time communism had been the great hope, the great temptation. In my own generation there were not a few young men and women who fought and died for communism—fine, selfless people and great idealists. While they were not religious believers, their vision strongly resembled that of paradise, the Greek Elysium, the Muslim seventh heaven, a place in which there would be neither sin nor death. In this earthly Eden freed from the shackles of oppression and exploitation each individual and society as a whole would be able to develop to its full capacity. At long last human beings would be able to become fully human. The ascent to this heaven would be arduous; it would lead humankind, as it had Dante, through inferno and purgatory. At times there would be dark night, and the sight of the stars would be lost. But then a signpost would be reached, reading *Incipit Vita Nova:* Here begins the New Life. The 1920s and to a certain extent even the 1930s were an age of enthusiasm in the Soviet Union. It was in poems and songs that this enthusiasm found its most perfect expression. Anatole d'Aktil, in his "March of the Enthusiasts," proclaimed (I quoted the poem in *The Dream That Failed*):

> We are always right in our daring
> There are no obstacles for us on land or on sea
> we fear no ice, no clouds.
> We achieve in a year the work of a century,
> happiness we take as of right,
> We carry the banner of our country
> Through the whole world and all ages.

"We are born to make a new reality out of old fairy tales," said the "March of Young Aviators" written by Pavel German (a song known at the time all over Europe that still serves as the anthem of the Israeli Air Force). Even foreign visitors hostile to communism, even some of the émigrés, were impressed by the Soviet Union. Today this revolutionary romanticism has become a matter of ridicule, and a major effort of imagination and empathy is needed even to understand it, but at the time it did not ring hollow.

Though enthusiasm waned and routine took over, the defense of the homeland against the Nazi invasion in 1941 acted as a unifying factor, as did the later need to rebuild the country. If there were shortcomings in the Soviet Union they could be explained as the result of the devastation. But a quarter century after the end of World War II this kind of argument was getting very thin. Under Nikita Khrushchev some new initiatives were made, but they did not go very far; some were harebrained, others less so. Under Leonid Brezhnev there were hardly any new initiatives at all. Was this what the people wanted?

To what extent were the people even aware of their own misery? Most were not in position to compare, since foreign travel was difficult if not impossible. Those who could travel, mostly members of the new class, were unhappy when they compared their situation with that of people in other countries. But they had a stake in the preservation of the status quo, and while there was grumbling among them, there was no revolt.

In 1970 Andrei Amalrik, a young dissident and a student of medieval history, published a short tract entitled *Will the Soviet Union Survive until 1984?* It was widely read—outside Russia. It was received in the West as brilliant, but no one really took it seriously. True, Amalrik based his thesis not on scholarly research but on observation and reflection. He was mistaken in some of his basic assumptions, notably a coming military collision with China. But, astonishingly, he got the main issue right: the regime was decrepit and could not be reformed. A few others made similar predictions, such as the French demographer Emanuel Todd and the British essayist Bernard Lewin. But they were based more on impressions, and they were hardly taken very seriously.

My own doubts concerning the future of the Soviet Union were generated by an unexpected source—the writers of the Russian right wing. (I had not visited the Soviet Union between 1965 and 1989 but continued to read Russian literature.) The basic views of these writers could not be more distant from mine. Some were in the tradition of the prerevolutionary Black Hundred; they were chauvinists, believed in permanent conspiracies by Jews and Freemasons against Holy Russia, and hated the West, liberalism, and democracy. These groups had found protectors in the Soviet leadership and were given the opportunity to express their views in various literary journals.

But not all of them were fanatic fools and knaves. They felt deeply the misery of their country. There were some gifted writers among them, and what they reported from town and countryside (most were so-called village writers) was very disturbing indeed: crime, alcoholism, ecological disaster, and corruption well beyond what had been customary throughout Russian history. Work in certain parts of the Soviet Union apparently came to a standstill on payday or whenever spirits were locally delivered. Above all, there was moral decay and a seemingly total breakdown in solidarity. Today these writers, such as Vasily Shukshin, Fyodor Abramov, Valentin Rasputin, and Viktor Astafyev, are largely forgotten (except perhaps Rasputin, who is still alive and one of the favorite writers of the Putin era), but at the time they played an important role and they certainly influenced my thinking. If these people painted such a dismal picture and were given the freedom to publish their novels, the situation must indeed have been exceedingly bad and the only question was whether the regime (and society) could be reformed.

Non-Russian nationalism was another emerging problem that remained not unknown to us outside the Soviet Union. According to the Soviet anthem, which replaced the "Internationale" during World War II, Great Russia had established an unbreakable union of peoples, and there could be no doubt about its leading role. This contention was widely shared by outside observers by no means sympathetic toward the Soviet Union—from Hans Kohn, who wrote one of the first books about the subject, and Hannah Arendt to Walter Kolarz and the Sovietologists of the 1970s and 1980s. The prevailing feeling was that the Soviets might have failed in other respects but at least they had solved the nationalities question, which had ceased to be an acute problem. One of them upbraided fellow Sovietologists for being too eager to see its multiethnic society as a threat to the

Soviet state. The Soviet leaders were less satisfied with the state of affairs, however. On a visit to Central Asia, Brezhnev complained that the Central Asian republics did not carry their own weight and that the subsidies Moscow had to pay to these regions, as well as to the Caucasus, were becoming too heavy a burden. Generally speaking, at the same time that Russian nationalism was growing, so was national consciousness in the other republics, though it still seemed a far cry from such feelings to separatism.

Khrushchev had announced twenty years earlier that by 1980 the Soviet Union would not only catch up with the United States but overtake it. According to official announcements Soviet capital investment equaled American investment by 1970, and the Soviet economy had overtaken America by the early 1970s in coal and steel output, the number of tractors produced, and other essential raw materials and machinery. Given these impressive achievements, why was the general situation so bad? By the late 1970s there were broad hints by the supreme leadership that the economy was not working well, that food supplies were unsatisfactory, and that the talk about a scientific technological revolution in the Soviet Union was largely false. There was no doubt any longer that, as some Western experts put it, the Soviet Union could not cope with a mature economy and that the high growth rates of the early postwar period could not be maintained. Soviet economists, it was subsequently known, had been aware that relative decline had set in in their country around 1960.

Western experts dealing with the performance of the Soviet economy constantly overrated its output. These included not only academic experts— some of them specialists of world renown—but also the CIA, which, to give but one example, made it public that per capita income in East Germany was as high as in Britain and considerably higher than in Italy. On the other hand, these experts underrated Soviet military investment, which was not 10–15 percent of the GNP as they believed, but closer to 25–30 percent.

These mistakes were of political importance because a more realistic appraisal should have shown that the Soviet Union would be unable to compete with the United States in an arms race—and it could not. The arms race initiated by President Ronald Reagan contributed substantially to the downfall of the empire. Among the few experts whose estimates were closer to Soviet realities was a recent émigré from Moscow whose views were not taken seriously.

And yet, as a Western economist put it some years later, there was no economic inevitability about the downfall of the Soviet empire. It was falling behind the West—and eventually also behind Japan and China—but most Soviets were probably not aware of this. The Soviet command economy was fundamentally inefficient, but under Andropov there was a small rise in national income. If the Soviet leaders could have hung on for another ten or fifteen years, they would have benefited from the enormous global demand for oil and gas. It would have brought in trillions of dollars and might have secured the survival of the system for yet another twenty years. The price of a barrel of oil in 1972 was $3; it was below $10 in the later 1980s, $11 in 1998, but in 2007 it was nearing $150 (in 2008, following the world financial crisis, it fell precipitously). In 2006, Russian earnings from oil were $1.5 trillion, 60 percent of the nation's total income. Had it held on, the Soviet Union would not have become an industrial (or postindustrial) superpower but it would have been a giant among the suppliers of raw materials. Perhaps a Leninist explanation would have been found for this curious state of affairs.

The downfall of the Soviet empire (like the decline and fall of other empires in history) cannot be explained with reference to one single factor. There was not one big crisis such as military defeat, but several crises that fed on each other and aggravated the general situation. One factor not mentioned so far was the war in Afghanistan, which was not going well at all. How was it possible that a small and backward country could resist the military might of the Soviet Union? The war was unpopular; some fifteen thousand soldiers were killed in Afghanistan over nine years. But these losses should be seen in perspective. The Soviet Union had suffered infinitely greater losses in World War II without collapsing. The United States suffered much greater losses in Vietnam, and now Russia has lost almost as many soldiers in Chechnya. In other words, the war in Afghanistan could not possibly have been a decisive factor, but it was a contributing factor.

Soviet foreign policy was not doing well elsewhere in Asia or in Africa either. Erstwhile allies such as Gamal Abdel Nasser, Kwame Nkrumah, and Sukarno had disappeared, and the massive military and economic help, always unpopular in the Soviet Union (and estimated by the Soviets to be no more than 2 percent of Soviet GNP), in retrospect seemed to be a waste of money. Yet empires do have their rewards, such as military bases. For the Soviet Union, the Soviet empire seemed to confirm that the country was not weak or backward, but a superpower. Having an empire was like membership to a club for which a fee had to be paid.

Still, the cost of empire was considerable, and over the course of the Cold War it appeared that the Soviet Union was overextended. Valentin Falin, a former Soviet ambassador to Bonn and later head of the Communist Party's foreign relations, was asked by a German weekly whether Reagan had been right—from the West's point of view—when he forced the Soviet Union to arm itself to death. Falin replied (as I reported in *The Dream That Failed*) that it was not really Reagan who had started this policy; it had been general U.S. policy since 1945. The interviewer then asked whether this meant that it had been the correct policy to follow and that "all of us who had favored détente had been mistaken." Falin replied, "Détente would never have resulted in the tearing down of the Iron Curtain." Other leading Soviet officials shared his opinion. There is no doubt that the Soviet leadership found it increasingly difficult to compete in an arms race.

And yet, with all this, the Soviet regime seemed in 1986 infinitely stronger than Russia in 1916 or the Ottoman empire in 1918. The levers of power were firmly in the hands of the rulers—the KGB, the army, and the various elements of the party. These organs of political control obeyed orders from above. And yet there was a crisis of confidence that could not be quantified. The Soviet Union in the 1980s could be compared to an athlete—muscular and well trained but not strong in spirit. Had this to do, perhaps, with the absence of a strong leadership? Brezhnev stayed on in power well beyond his prime (to put it cautiously), and his two successors, Andropov and Konstantin Chernenko, were old and decrepit when appointed to the top position. Their appearances in public were embarrassing and anything but confidence inspiring. Andropov was perhaps the most intelligent of the postwar Soviet leaders, and he seems to have been aware that far-reaching reform was urgently necessary, but he rightly doubted whether it could be achieved without endangering the very existence of the regime.

But this crisis of confidence, the change from a relatively optimistic to a pessimistic mood in Moscow, dates back even further. It can be detected as early as the 1970s and had to do with the growing distance between promise and performance. Pessimism affected above all the Soviet middle class and middle leadership, and this mood subsequently permeated all classes. But pessimistic moods, however prolonged and intense, do not necessarily lead to profound change; they have occurred in many countries at different times and very frequently have led to apathy rather than revolution. And it is true that the events of 1991 in the Soviet Union did not amount to a revolution; the empire simply disintegrated. The prevailing attitude in the Soviet Union at the time was not anticommunism (except among a small number of dissidents who were kept well under control) but indifference to official ideology.

Thus in the final analysis the breakup of 1991 was also the result of certain historical accidents—namely the attempt to reform a regime that could not be reformed. Mikhail Gorbachev opened this Pandora's box, not out of misplaced curiosity but because of an unwarranted optimism. Most observers in West and East failed to consider the possibility of a debacle, and they can claim mitigating circumstances inasmuch as there is no accounting for historical accidents. But they should have known that the whole system was much weaker than they thought and that the continued survival of this enormous enterprise depended not on historical inevitability, not on "objective trends," but precisely on accident. The cardinal error of the Sovietologists was not their failure to predict Gorbachev's arrival in the Kremlin, which was of course impossible, but the failure to realize that decay had proceeded much further than generally assumed. What had caused this misjudgment? The question is not of purely academic interest, for it provides lessons for the future.

Some of the misjudgments were rooted in political bias. Those overrating Soviet strength were either broadly speaking in sympathy with the system even if they abhorred certain aspects of it or, more frequently, because they thought the West, above all the United States, was decadent, incapable of gaining the upper hand in a historical competition with "mature Sovietism" (as it was called at the time in these circles), moving forward toward "institutional pluralism." However, the proportion of those who misjudged the situation in the Soviet Union because of ideological blinkers was relatively small; there were not that many fellow travelers and admirers of the Soviet system left in the 1980s. In some cases the reason was simply ignorance or, to put it perhaps more fairly, lack of knowledge, especially with regard to the state of the Soviet economy. In the absence of any reliable Soviet figures (and in the presence of many forged ones), how could outside observers possibly gain a realistic picture of the situation? In these circumstances all appraisal had to be based by necessity on more or less intelligent speculation.

Having overrated for many years the size of the Soviet GNP, which was believed to be about half that of the U.S. GNP, the Sovietological fraternity came gradually to believe that the Soviet economy was stagnating after 1978, yet the earlier, inflated figures were still widely used. The *World Fact Book* published by CIA estimated as late as 1981–82 that the Soviet Union had a GNP of $2.6 trillion, or $9,130 per capita. Merely one year later Western reference works provided figures that were 10 percent of the previous year. Never had there been such a statistical shrinkage almost overnight!

The political implications of exaggerating Soviet economic performance were clear. As one leading Sovietologist put it as late as 1988, Soviet citizens enjoyed massive social and personal security. There was an egalitarian wage system with subsidized prices for most necessities. Seen in this perspective, there was no reason to expect major political discontent, for a population enjoying such unprecedented benefits would be very foolish to revolt. Or as another expert put it, the predictions about coming radical changes in the Soviet Union, while possible, were the most unlikely scenario. For what had been built through generations with much blood, sacrifice, ruthlessness, cunning, and conviction would not simply disappear: a systemic crisis was most unlikely. Such miscalculations were no American monopoly; expectations in Western Europe, with the partial exception of France, were more or less the same.

Both Bonn and the West German academic fraternity were convinced that Erich Honecker was firmly entrenched in East Germany. There was, however, greater skepticism among the economic experts than among the others. These miscalculations are in many ways even more difficult to understand. The Soviet Union was still something of a mystery at the time, and access was difficult. But there was much more frequent coming and going between the two Germanies, and there were few secrets. And yet the stability of the regime was grossly exaggerated.

Again, some of the reasons for these misjudgments were political, rooted in the rise of the anti–Cold War school of thought. As one of their adherents (Stephen F. Cohen, *Rethinking the Soviet Experience,* 1985) described this new school of experts: "They were freer of cold war constraints. And they benefited not only from new Soviet materials but from the more self-critical and less culture-bound perspectives in American intellectual life in the 1960s." But in retrospect neither the "new Soviet materials" nor the "less culture-bound perspectives," nor their allegedly greater self-criticism was conducive to a realistic appraisal.

There was one other circumstance that seems to have led to frequent error. Brief mention has already been made of it: the mistaken belief that social science had new insights to offer that would make the study of communism and the Soviet empire more scientific. Some Sovietologists discovered Clifford Geertz's famous essay on cockfights in Bali; others pondered the use of Albert Hirschman's thoughts on Exit and Voice with regard to East Germany; yet others were impressed by what Ferdinand de Saussure had said about linguistics. Whatever the value of these and other insights for other disciplines, they certainly did not make the study of Brezhnev and his successors more scientific or their practitioners more prescient.

Mistaken assessments could be found not only among Sovietologists critical of American policy and the proponents of social science paradigms but also, admittedly on a higher level of sophistication, among more conservative students of Soviet Russia and communism. Martin Malia with his total rejection of socialism—"There is no such thing as socialism and the Soviet Union built it" (*The Soviet Tragedy,* 1994)—was one such case. I commented at the time (in *The Dream That Failed)* that celebrations concerning the triumph of the market and capitalism in Russia seemed premature, and there is little to add some fifteen years later. While Richard Pipes was perfectly correct in his critique of the aberrations of the revisionist Sovietologists, his negative approach toward much Russian history has remained controversial.

Looking back on the commentary on Soviet affairs at a distance of thirty years is a strange experience, both amusing and troubling. The situation has improved since, but has there been radical change? It will be difficult now to find historians in the West—or indeed in Russia—claiming that the Cold War was wholly or mainly the fault of the West; this kind of revisionism has vanished except perhaps from the schoolbooks introduced in Russia during the Putin era. But the advocates of equidistance have by no means given up the struggle. (Melvyn Leffler's study of the Cold War, *For the Soul of Mankind,* published in 2007, is perhaps the most authoritative statement of this school. It was widely and respectfully reviewed.) Stalin, they say, would have greatly preferred peaceful coexistence and even cooperation with the West, provided, of course, he got what he wanted. The West should have accepted this situation, but Western leaders were unwilling or unable to seize the outstretched hand—of Stalin, Georgy Malenkov, Khrushchev, and even Brezhnev. Both sides are equally to blame for many missed opportunities. The Cold War ended in the late 1980s because two leaders with vision, Gorbachev and Reagan, had appeared. The obvious notion that the Cold War ended because the Soviet Union collapsed is either overlooked or rejected. In the perspective of these writers ideological belief is ignored; so is the specific character of the Soviet regime.

The new Putin version of Soviet history goes further. There are some dark pages in Soviet history, but there are dark pages in the history of other countries and there is no reason to be ashamed or embarrassed. The Cold War was imposed on the Soviet Union by the West and the Stalin regime was the only possible answer in these conditions. The Soviet Union was not a Western-style democracy, the Putin version reads, but it was an example for millions of people around the world of the best and fairest society. Seen in this perspective, the breakup of the Soviet 1991 was the greatest disaster of the twentieth century.

The state of mind on which such viewpoints are based could be explained as the obvious reaction of Soviet patriots. It is more difficult to understand the deeper motivation of Western revisionists. To some extent it could be rooted in ignorance; as mentioned earlier, more often than not the proponents of equidistance are Americanists, familiar with U.S. diplomacy but without any real knowledge and understanding of Soviet affairs. But in other cases it seems to be the deep-seated belief that in international conflicts blame should almost always be apportioned to both sides, and it is the moral duty of an academic to be particularly harsh on his or her own side. True objectivity can be attained only in this fashion.

It is tempting to use harsh words in criticism of such mental aberrations as recognizing the patriots of every country but one's own. But it is a futile exercise that should be resisted, for the underlying beliefs are as resistant to rational argument as to irony.

The Rise of Putinism

There is much to admire in Russian history. As the poet Fyodor Tyutchev put it, "so much dirt and so much talent." The Russians themselves were the sharpest critics of their own country, and it is not surprising that much of the time they were wavering between optimism and pessimism as far as the future of their country was concerned. Aleksandr Herzen predicted that if despotism continued for another hundred years, all the good qualities of the Russian people would be gone. How could one ignore the fact that centuries of serfdom were buried deep in the hearts and souls of this people?

And so it was no accident that great hopes arose with *glasnost* and *perestroika* in the days of Gorbachev; the spirit of liberty, it appeared, was not dead in Russia. But how realistic were these hopes? One's heart wished well to Russia, but all historical experience provided a brake. Human nature does not change in a few decades, and there had always been a tremendous gap between Russia's ambitions and its realities. At the beginning of Russian history there had been the legendary request of the princes of Kiev to foreigners from the north: "Our land is great and abundant but there is no order. Come and rule over us."

A thousand years later foreigners were no longer wanted for this purpose, but the belief in the need for strong rulers persisted. Was it realistic to assume a fast and complete transition to a wholly different political, social, and economic system? Or did the Soviet Union face another long period of authoritarian-bureaucratic rule based on some kind of nationalist-socialist ideology with a minority of intellectuals valiantly (and ineffectually) raising the banner of freedom?

With Gorbachev's rise to power, it had become clear even to those who did not professionally follow events in the Soviet Union that important changes were being tried by the new leadership in Moscow. During the preceding twenty years I had not been among those who had followed Soviet domestic affairs very closely, but I still felt, as others did, the excitement that was in the air; after so many years of *zastoi* (stagnation) and Cold War, things in the Soviet empire at long last began to move. Almost every week brought some unexpected and usually welcome news; almost any issue of Soviet newspapers and magazines contained announcements and revelations that would have been unthinkable even a year earlier. But the crucial questions were: How far would the reforms go? And who would prevail in the struggle for power?

For a number of years the Soviet Union again became the main focus of my interest and work. I visited the nation twice after an interval of twenty-five years, and I had the chance to talk to, among others, the then foreign minister Eduard Shevardnadze. I read about everything in print I could obtain, and I talked to many of the Soviet visitors who now appeared in the West. In three books I tried to provide a running commentary on events in the Soviet Union during these fateful years.

One dealt with the right-wing groups that emerged once the reins were loosened; another addressed the revelations about the Stalin era; and the last, entitled *The Long Road to Freedom*, examined the political changes that were taking place in the Soviet Union under Gorbachev and in the early years of Boris Yeltsin. I shared the excitement felt by so many observers of the Soviet scene, but as the title indicated I had few illusions about the limits of the political reforms. The future of democracy and political freedom in Russia seemed by no means certain. At best the road to freedom would be very long, with many setbacks, and the eagerness to choose this road was not great. I wrote that something akin to a cultural revolution would be needed to effect real change, but such revolutions have occurred only rarely in human history and there were no signs that anything of this kind would take place in the near future.

I assumed that Stalin could not be resurrected, that some progress would indeed be made in the years to come, and that some degree of *glasnost* would no doubt remain. Come what may, the atmosphere in the country would be less stifling than in the past. There would be, as in some pilgrimages, four steps forward and three back. But I thought it mistaken that, as some Sovietologists believed at the time, "objective trends" such as urbanization and the spread of literacy would make the progress of freedom more or less inevitable. I thought it far more likely that an authoritarian style would be maintained, the kind that prevailed virtually through all of Russian history, not a system based on free and broad, voluntary popular participation.

To these questions, history since has provided a clear answer. In Russia freedom, democracy, and human rights quickly became dirty words. On the other hand there was a surprisingly quick comeback of Russia as a great power. It had taken Germany just fifteen years after the defeat in World War I to recover and to reemerge as the strongest power on the continent. It was to take Russia no longer. Russia felt humiliated after the breakup of the empire. It had lost not only Central Asia and Transcaucasia but even the Ukraine, the cradle of Russian statehood and civilization. A thousand years of Russian history had been undone.

In the years immediately following the implosion there was goodwill vis-à-vis the West in Russia, but its extent was greatly overestimated. The West welcomed events in Russia, and some help was extended to the Russians to overcome their economic difficulties, but this was not remotely as much as hoped for in Russia. And even if much more help would have been extended, it would not have prevented the chaotic conditions that developed in the early 1990s in which a few unscrupulous, clever, and well-placed individuals grew enormously rich and former KGB employees gradually gained power over the state apparatus. Then the benefits of the energy exports began to trickle down and an authoritarian regime was established. In the West some tried to launch a debate: Who lost Russia? It was a wholly misplaced debate because Russia had never been in the pocket of the West and could not therefore be lost.

The developments under Vladimir Putin (the road to "sovereign democracy") were in most ways only natural, in consonance with Russian traditions and needs. There was no overwhelming pressure inside Russia for a freer, more democratic system, but there was a great longing for order to be restored. The West could offer some financial help and economic advice; it could not assist a patriotic government aiming at restoring as much as possible of Russia's lost empire. All public opinion polls were showing that a majority or near majority of Russians believed that the Brezhnev regime had been preferable to the situation under Gorbachev and Yeltsin. In 2007–8, even Stalin got an approval rating of nearly 50 percent. All these developments should have come as no great surprise to the student of Russian history, certainly not to the student of the Russian right, and the whole spectrum of Russian politics around the year 2000 was very much moving to the right.

There was tremendous resentment against the enemies of Russia who had allegedly caused its downfall. Their numbers were large and included ungrateful ethnic groups who had seceded from the Soviet Union, Georgians, Balts, and others as well as the former Eastern European satellites. The Russian right tried to promote an old-new doctrine of Eurasianism that had not made much sense when it was first presented in émigré circles in the 1920s and was even more unreal when it was rehashed seventy years later. Where was the Asia that should serve as Russia's ally? Certainly not China, Japan, or India. As for the Muslim world and Turkey, these were not Russia's allies, though there are some common anti-Western interests. But Russia has a serious internal Muslim problem, aggravated by demographic trends. There are at present some 15–20 million Muslims inside Russia and their birth rate is high whereas the Russian birth rate is among the lowest in the world. According to some projections, one out of three recruits to the Russian army will be of Muslim background in the not-too-distant future.

In the circumstances, Russia's freedom of foreign political maneuver is limited. A realistic Russian policy is hamstrung by the deep-seated belief in the fanatical, irremovable enmity of America but also of the Europeans ("Russophobia") who throughout history had always wanted to harm Russia. Belief in conspiracies has long been strong in Russia—under the czars, under Stalin—and this did not change after the breakup of the Soviet empire. The fact that the implosion of the Soviet empire might have had something to do with events inside the Soviet Union (and that they might even have been the decisive factor) seemed to be largely unacceptable.

When the Soviet empire collapsed, Russia was not ready for democracy. There should have been no illusions in this respect; an authoritarian regime was almost a foregone conclusion. This regime did not amount to a return to Stalinism or to aggressive military expansion. But it did mean that common interests between Russia and the West were limited.

It also meant that Russia's neighbors, once part of the empire, would come under increasing pressure. There would be no physical occupation but something similar to Finlandization during the Cold War. Putin and his successors did not have unlimited time at their disposal. Unlike the old Soviet Union in its earlier days, ideology, Communist or otherwise, was no longer a weapon, nor were Pan-Slavism or Eurasianism. Demographic trends were working against the achievement of their wider ambitions, and the oil and gas weapon would not last forever.

Two decades have passed, and the optimism of these early days has all but vanished. The new Russia has become much stronger than during the years following the downfall of the Soviet empire, and there seems to be no real danger of internal chaos and civil war. And in 2008 Putin predicted that in another twelve years Russia would be not only the most accomplished but also the most exciting country in the world. Moscow is prospering like never before, but much of the country is in a miserable state, and the Far East and the North, Siberia, and the Russian countryside are losing population. A smallish section of the population is doing very well, but not that much is trickling down, and the distance between rich and poor is greater than in any other country outside the Third World. In a report for the U.S. government in 1990 in which I engaged in prediction (*Soviet Union 2000*) I wrote, "It is indeed true that there are no billionaires in the Soviet Union." Nineteen years later Moscow housed more billionaires than any other city in the world (74 to be precise, as compared with 71 in New York, 36 in London, 34 in Istanbul, and 31 in Hong Kong). One-quarter of the Russian economy was owned by thirty-six people. The new prosperity rests almost entirely on the export of raw materials, especially oil and gas.

True, there are no mass purges, and only occasional assassinations, and Russian citizens can travel abroad if they can afford it. Dissent is possible, so long as it does not endanger the regime. But the Duma is powerless; so are the political parties, and neither the judiciary nor the media are free. There was, by and large, more freedom in czarist Russia between the Revolution of 1905 and the outbreak of World War I in 1914. Attempts to reassert its international standing and to establish a new sphere of influence (now called "zone of privileged interests") have led Russia into conflicts with almost all its neighbors, and the attitude toward the West has become more and more hostile. Public opinion polls show that the majority of Russians are skeptical about democracy, and at least half of them believe that, on balance, Stalin did more good than harm, an opinion that also seems to be the consensus among the new establishment.

How should we interpret and classify the new regime that has emerged in Russia? I was reminded of a suggestion made in the early 1960s by Adam Ulam, an old friend, Harvard professor of politics and lifelong student of Soviet politics. In an essay in *The State of Soviet Studies,* a book that I edited, he asked this rhetorical question: Who would be better placed to understand Soviet politics under Stalin? Would it be a fictitious character named X, reading the works of reputable, objective non-Communist scholars and journalists with no ax to grind? Or would it be his friend Y, whose taste ran to the nonscholarly and melodramatic, who trusted the accounts of the avowed enemies of the regime? He would infuriate X by insisting that there were aspects of Soviet politics that are more easily understood by studying the struggle between Al Capone and Johnny Torrio than the one between Lenin and Yuli Martov, leader of the Mensheviks, or the theoretical dispute about "socialism in one country." And Ulam added that the average Anglo-American writing on the Soviets during this period approached categories like "police state," "terror," and "totalitarianism" with the same trepidation and distaste as the Victorian novelist felt when he alluded to the sexual act.

Fifty years after Ulam's essay (of which most probably he had never heard) Garry Kasparov wrote an article that was published in the *Wall Street Journal* (July 29, 2007) in which he tried to explain to Western readers the nature of Putin's Russia, which, he claimed they found so difficult to understand. Kasparov, former world chess champion and one of the leaders of the opposition, felt secure enough to deal openly with the topic, unlike most other public figures in the country. He argued that reading Adam Smith or Montesquieu was of no use, that comparisons with Benito Mussolini's corporate state or with pseudo-democratic Latin American states were perhaps of limited use, but that the key to a deeper understanding could be found in the works of Mario Puzo, author of *The Godfather* (1969), describing the strict hierarchy of the Mafia, intimidation, *omertà* the code of behavior, and above all the mandate to keep the revenue flowing.

Such unorthodox explanations are valuable, but they have to be put into right (and historical) perspective. What was true with regard to Stalinism was correct only in part for the Khrushchev and Brezhnev regimes. And it is also true that the origins of the Mafia go back to the Yeltsin era when a weak central power permitted (if not promoted) the emergence of a new class of superrich oligarchs.

The essence of the regime established by Putin, which is likely to last even after his incumbency, remains to be studied. It seems to be a syncretic class of the very rich, the former KGB and their hangers-on in various fields, with political rather than economic power the decisive factor. It is quite different from the new class described by Milovan Đjilas in the late 1950s, inasmuch as the new rulers have put a great distance between themselves and Marxist-Leninist traditions, to the extent that not even lip service is paid anymore to the socialist internationalist traditions. What, then, is the motive of the new class? The Mafia was out almost entirely for material gain, and it operated in the shadows. The new class is motivated as much by the pursuit of power as by material gain, and it has to function in the open. A political system of this kind needs an official ideology that is bound to be nationalism, preferably with an admixture of populism and the Orthodox church. The new class must learn that if ostentatious spending becomes too blatant there is danger for it and the system. Naked cynicism will not work. There is little doubt that the leading figures in the system genuinely believe themselves true patriots. Like some American businessmen they may think that what is good for General Motors is good for the country. Such a system may well be popular—as long as the revenue keeps flowing and there is a trickle down from above.

In brief, Western optimism of the early years of *glasnost* and *perestroika* has given way to pessimism and in some cases to the belief that the new Russia is on the road to something akin to fascism. This view is probably exaggerated, but if there is no room for alarm there certainly is for great sadness. For a long time historians are likely to debate whether this outcome was the fault of Gorbachev and Yeltsin and their advisers or whether, given Russian and Soviet history and the absence of democratic traditions, this outcome was more or less inevitable, since Russians seem to prefer order to freedom.

Pessimism about Russia's future is, to be sure, not a new phenomenon. Piotr Yakovlevich Chaadayev's famous "Philosophical Letter" of 1829 comes to mind. He was one of the most talented Russian thinkers of this time. His friend Aleksandr Pushkin wrote about him: "Brutus would he have been in Rome, Pericles in Athens, but here he is merely an officer of the Hussars." In this often-quoted letter (Herzen called it a manifesto and a trumpet call) Chaadayev wrote that Russian history was a story of barbarism and superstition, the terrible Tatar yoke and Muscovite tyranny. Russia had no heritage of antiquity, Middle Ages, Renaissance, or Reformation. The Russians had no historical sense or useful ideas or moral concepts. Russia had never been civilized; all culture had been imported; ideas of duty, justice, law, and order had never developed. Russia had made no cultural contributions whatsoever. It did not belong to European civilization, and it had failed to play any significant role in world history. Serfdom was the main evil; it made all Russians act like slaves. Russia was useless; it had no future.

This philosophical letter was published in Russia with considerable delay. The czar thought Chaadayev a lunatic and had him put under house arrest, to be seen by a doctor once a week. Having read Chaadayev's letter, Herzen said it was written by one whose soul overflowed with bitterness, who could no longer be silent. "Who among us did not have such black moments of anger when we cursed our land—a prison for all where every police commissar was a commander and a crowned police is the ruler, where there are only serfs and soldiers of different ranks."

Comments on Russia's past by both foreigners and Russians have been very harsh, ranging from the poverty of the sanitary conditions, to the slackness and slovenliness of much of the population, to the absence of human rights, and to the dead hand of the bureaucracy. Victor Hehn in the nineteenth century wrote that all Russians are congenital liars, and Anton Chekhov said that he did not know one honest man in his native Taganrog (I hesitate to add that the Russian branch of my family lived in that city). Nothing but Russophobia? But the same critics often added that the country had for them an indescribable fascination; in spite of everything they loved it and admired and respected its people. Would Chaadayev still have claimed at the end of the nineteenth century, following the golden age of Russian literature and at the beginning of the silver age, that Russia had contributed nothing to world culture? Russians are tough. What other people would have survived the Tatars, czarism, Stalinism, and countless other afflictions? As Herzen wrote reviewing the Marquis de Custine, the French author of a classic work on early nineteenth-century Russia: "Our lungs are stronger."

And yet, it is not easy to be optimistic after seventy years of Bolshevism and Stalinist rule. It resulted in an economic shambles from which only the oil boom saved it—temporarily in any case. The Russian intelligentsia has disappeared, and the result is a cultural desert and a people whose moral backbone has been broken. If so many of them feel a longing for the Stalinist period of their history, perhaps this was indeed what they wanted and needed. In 2008 a majority of Russians still (or again), thought Stalin one of the three greatest Russians ever, the other two being Peter the Great and Pushkin.

Marxism-Leninism is dead. The new "Russian idea" that has emerged consists largely of anti-Westernism and a variety of conspiracy theories. This idea, too, goes far back into Russian history, but the Slavophiles who propagated the "Russian idea" were highly educated people, very familiar with European culture. They believed that Russia had its own specific character and would follow its own historical way and mission. Their Russian idea was by no means purely negative; they were convinced, for instance, that serfdom was their country's great misfortune. Latter-day Slavophiles produced some strange ideas such Eurasianism, Pan-Mongolism, and other geopolitical fantasies. Today's new Russian patriotism promoted by the state is mainly rabid anti-Americanism and anti-Westernism in general, since the West, it is believed, is implacably hostile to the very existence of Russia. As Gleb Pavlovsky, one of Putin's main spin doctors, wrote in 2007, it was Russia's historical mission to contain the United States and the whole world would be grateful for its doing this. It is a poor doctrine, and it is based on a paranoia that ignores the real forces, domestic and foreign, that endanger the survival of Russia.

All this is bound to be the source of much sadness. I had perhaps fewer illusions than others about Russia's future when the Soviet system collapsed. But

Russia after all its misfortunes had deserved better. Perhaps Herzen's fears were justified that irreparable damage might be done to the Russian people if the dictatorships would last too long. The majority of Russians seem to like the new order that has emerged; perhaps it corresponds most closely with their ideas and expectations after all. The oil and gas boom may have been a good thing, for what would Russia have been without it? It would have gotten poorer and poorer, perhaps falling apart and into a state of civil war, with an arsenal, not supervised, of nuclear bombs. Will Russia be, as Putin predicted, the most exciting country in the world in 2020? Or will it be closer to the Russia of Ivan the Terrible with his bodyguard, as Vladimir Sorokin, a leading novelist recently envisaged in *Oprichnik's Day* (2006)? Or will it be an aging society with a rapidly shrinking population and much lesser ambitions?

Ivan the Terrible and his bloodthirsty secret police, the *oprichniki:* surely these are the nightmare of a novelist with an overheated imagination. Not quite. Ivan, his policies, and the way he carried them out have become the idol and the guiding model of the contemporary neo-Eurasians inspired by their guru, Aleksandr Dugin. There is the temptation to dismiss these fantasies as the Russian equivalent of a postmodern carnival. But doing so would be a mistake, as their influence extends well to the center of the Russian political class and, more important, to the Duma, the Kremlin, and its youth organizations.

If the breakup of the Soviet Union was the greatest disaster of the twentieth century, as Putin has said, the time has now come, as Russia has gained strength, to undo at least some of the damage that was caused. Russia should again be a great power. World revolution is no longer on the agenda, nor is the export of Communist institutions and ideology. But Russia has "privileged interests" (claims Dmitry Medvedev) in most regions adjacent to it. The smaller countries formerly part of the Soviet Union should know that they cannot ignore these interests. This does not necessarily imply physical occupation (though it cannot be excluded in certain cases), but it certainly involves a Russian sphere of influence extending to the former people's democracies and also to Western Europe.

How far will Russia's ambitions reach? The more extreme planners dream about a new Eurasian empire including Turkey, Iran, and perhaps some other countries. But the enthusiasm for such ventures among the prospective partners is strictly limited, and given the demographic trends, would Russia not be the junior rather than the senior partner in a generation or two? According to projections of the Russian Academy of Sciences, the population of Russia will have fallen to 83 million by 2050 (or even earlier), less than Turkey, Iran, or Egypt, and most of them will be elderly people. Even at the present time the number of Russians receiving a pension is 2.5 times larger than the number of children under fourteen. It is not certain that Russia will be able to hold onto the Far East and Siberia in view of the rapidly shrinking population. Perhaps it will regain the Ukraine and expand toward the Arctic, with its many hitherto inaccessible mineral resources. Russia is again seen as a colossus, but its base is quite weak. No one can say with any certainty where the borders of Russia will be later in this century, let alone what kind of Russia it will be.

CHAPTER 5

A Middle East Education

or, Reflections on Arabia, Israel, Zionism, and Antisemitism

Having left Europe in late 1938, I received my political education during the next fifteen years in the Middle East. Middle Eastern politics seemed relatively uncomplicated at the time. Of the Arab countries, only Iraq and Saudi Arabia were quasi-independent; Palestine was a British Mandate under the League of Nations; France was running North Africa and Syria as well as Lebanon; Italy was in Libya; and Egypt was a monarchy but the British had the final say. Yemen was far away, and no one knew much about it except that it was a kingdom and that the British still maintained a base in Aden.

However, even before the outbreak of World War II, during the seemingly stable period, there was a multitude of ethnic groups and religions to be studied. Older and wiser men warned me against getting too deeply involved in the problems of the area for it was a maze, and a lifetime of study might not be sufficient to gain a solid knowledge. In addition to Hebrew and Arabic I would have to acquire a working knowledge of at least one other language, Turkish or Persian. I had bought an Arab grammar while still in Germany, but it did not take me very long to realize that the literary language was not of great help in conversations on even the least complicated topics.

There were a few learned books about Islam and Turkey, and more about explorers in Arabia, but little on Arab politics. The major European and American newspapers had correspondents or stringers in the region, but, except for the Italian *Oriente Moderno,* there were no journals covering the contemporary Middle East. I learned that Maronites and Druze had been fighting in the nineteenth century, but there was nothing on the families, clans, and tribes that were of great importance. As for Palestine, the media reported that there were two parties—one headed by the Husseinis and the other by the Nashashibis—but this again proved to be a great simplification. There were a very few novels with versions of Islamic fundamentalism as a background. A.E.W Mason's wildly popular *Four Feathers,* which was also adapted for the cinema, dealt with the Mahdi revolt in the Sudan and the battle of Omdurman in 1898, but these events seemed very distant indeed. Howling dervishes were apparently part of the Oriental scene, but it was not a scene one knew.

During the years that followed I lived in the Arab quarters of Jerusalem, among Bedouins and Arab villagers. As a journalist I went to Cairo and Beirut, and I acquired some knowledge of the Arab way of life. I mixed with simple people; intellectuals I did not know, and members of the leading families I met, if at all, only at press conferences. It was therefore only natural that my perspective was somewhat different from that of upper-class Arabs, such as Edward Said, whose books I read in later years, who had grown up in very different circumstances and later gone to elite schools and universities.

During World War II there began to be some movement in Middle Eastern politics. The demand for national independence gathered strength and started to produce independent countries. Arab nationalism became much stronger; radical Islam appeared as a political factor, and here and there even communism. Some of the earlier problems vanished—who now remembers the dispute about the Sandjak of Alexandretta?—but many new ones emerged.

Ideas of the Arab World

What was the image my generation had of the Muslim world and of the Arabs? It was shaped in my case (which, I imagine, was quite typical) by reading *The Arabian Nights* and later progressing to Karl May and Lawrence of Arabia. *The Arabian Nights* was a very attractive book—in an expurgated version, of course, for the young, with the sections about the Baghdad underworld carefully deleted. The young European reader was not told that *The Arabian Nights* had been banned for many years in many parts of the Muslim East, and for good reasons. While Allah is frequently invoked, while women are veiled and there is a great deal of praying, there is also much drinking and gambling and whoring and other activities ill befitting a pious Muslim. Reading it in later years I found a certain similarity to *The Beggar's Opera,* with its rogues, crooks, and charlatans. There is also a lot of cruelty, but the same can be said about many fairy tales from many countries (and the children who read them seem to be more robust than the child psychologists who worry about them tend to believe).

The world of the Arabian nights ("one thousand and one nights" in German as in Arabic) introduced the young reader to people of great wisdom, courage, and above all a thirst for adventure: What could be more attractive for young people? It is a world of magic, of demons, of birds as big as mountains and of serpents equally large, a world of fantasy in which horses fly and ghosts abound. It is a colorful world of wise and just rulers such as Harun al-Rashid, commander of the faithful; of fearless adventurers such as Sinbad the sailor; of simple but clever people like Ali Baba and Aladdin who always defeat the evildoers. In this world virtue is rewarded and honesty always prevails over mendacity and crime. I, for one, found it infinitely more interesting and attractive than the sinister world of the Nordic sagas or the Nibelungen with their dire prophecies, unending violence, falsehood, betrayal, and cosmic disasters in which everyone gets killed and everything burned down.

In school, when the history of the Jews in the age of al-Andalus— Muslim rule in Spain—was taught, it was *tor ha'zahav,* a golden age of tolerance and good neighborly relations. In contrast, the Reconquista began an age of intolerance, for the victory of the Christian forces was followed by the Inquisition, the burning of heretics and of those suspected of heresy, and the expulsion of all Jews from the Iberian peninsula.

What else did one learn growing up in Europe about Muslims, or Saracens or Moors, as they were sometimes called? There was the story of Saladin, the noble and valiant Muslim prince, the conqueror of Jerusalem and most of the Holy Land, fully the equal of the Frankish crusaders. True, he had hundreds of them beheaded rather than taken prisoner, but the crusaders had, after all, engaged in even more bloodshed, for the European *treuga dei* did not extend to the East and the Red Cross did not exist. On the other hand, what *noblesse oblige* Saladin showed in his relations with Richard Coeur de Lion: when Richard fell ill, Saladin offered to send him his own physician; when Richard lost two of his horses, Saladin gave him two of his own. Dante placed Saladin among the greatest and most honorable in his epic works, despite the fact that he had been the conqueror of Jerusalem. If stories of knighthood and chivalry abounded in the West, they had their earlier parallel in the work of Firdusi, the greatest of Persian poets.

In the *Song of Roland,* treason and war crimes are reported that would not have been approved by the Geneva Conventions. But the Saracens had their code of honor, too. This was the age of chivalry in the East as much as in the West. The Saracens were noble knights and perhaps lived up to an even higher standard than Western chevaliers. Irrespective of religion, knights held each other in high regard. When Roland engaged in that famous duel with the Muslim hero that lasted several days, it was self-evident that, like a tennis match at Wimbledon, the fighting would stop at sunset and the two heroes would sit down, rest, and sleep side-by-side. When the medieval German emperor Frederick II with a few companions intended to visit a place on the River Jordan associated with John the Baptist, the Templars informed Sultan al-Kamil, the Muslim ruler, that this was a good opportunity to seize and perhaps kill the emperor. Full of indignation, Sultan al-Kamil immediately passed the news to Frederick II; such meanness was utterly alien to him.

Among the best sellers of this period in intellectual circles was a biography of this Frederick II, called by his contemporaries *stupor mundi*, one of the wonders of the world, a man combining great learning, humanism, and all possible good qualities of character. Residing in Sicily, he did not fight the Saracens but incorporated them in his army, studied Arabic, maintained friendly relation with Arab rulers, and gained their confidence so thoroughly that they accepted him for a while as king of Jerusalem. This book was controversial, according to many experts as much a work of fiction as of scholarship, but it was greatly admired and the author, Ernst Kantorowicz, certainly contributed much to the popularity of medieval Islam in Europe. Kantorowicz was Jewish by origin but fought in the right-wing free corps after World War I and belonged to the exclusive inner circle of the poet Stefan George. He lost his professorship when Adolf Hitler came to power, emigrated to the United States, and ended his career at the Princeton Institute of Advanced Studies.

On a lower level of sophistication was *El Hakim*, a runaway best seller for many years by the Swiss author John Knittel. This is the story of a young boy from a poor family in contemporary Egypt who from an early age wants to be a physician in order to help the many suffering people in his homeland. Knittel, born in India, wrote in English and German. He lived many years in the Middle East, and in a series of books, some of which like *El Hakim* became movies, he presented an attractive picture of life in the Arab world and North Africa. This kind of literature—travelogues and fiction—was quite typical at the time.

But by far the greatest influence shaping the image of Islam and the Middle East was a popular writer named Karl May (1842–1912). His adventure books circulated in many millions of copies, influenced generations of Germans, and, adapted for the cinema, had an impact well into the period after World War II. There are to this day annual Karl May festivals in Germany, and the May cult is by no means restricted to young people. A writer of seemingly inexhaustible imaginative power, May began inauspiciously—as a petty criminal with several prison sentences to his record. Once he began publishing his adventure stories, however, he went from rags to riches. His most famous books deal with America's Indians—the good Apache and the bad Comanche—but there was also a long series, first published in the 1890s, about the Middle East, ranging from North Africa, via Baghdad, Kurdistan, and Istanbul, to the land of the Shkipetars (Albania). May was immensely popular in Central Europe but is now also widely read in many countries, including Indonesia. Attempts to popularize him in the United States were made in the 1970s. In 1978 I reviewed three of his Wild West books for the *New York Times*, but the project misfired. There was too much competition from James Fenimore Cooper and Zane Grey—the former was wildly popular in Europe, the latter wholly unknown.

In May's Middle Eastern books the two main heroes are the writer himself traveling under the name Kara ben Nemsi and his faithful companion Hadji Halef Omar ben Haji Abul Abbas ibn Haji Dawud al Gossarah. Adolf Hitler was among their enthusiastic readers, as were Albert Schweitzer, Hermann Hesse, and Albert Einstein, who said that he found travel books boring but Karl May was a wonderful exception. May had never been to the American West or to the Middle East, but he made good use of travel guides and encyclopedias. There is an enormous amount in these books about the way of life of Turks and Arabs, their customs, manners, and religious beliefs. May greatly admired Arabs and Kurds (he preferred them to Turks). They were the Middle Eastern version of the American cowboys, silent *High Noon* kinds of heroes, men of enormous courage and honor with, of course, some inevitable villains interspersed. Hadji Halef ("my friend rather than my servant") small of stature, with a headgear far too large, was fully devoted to Kara ben Nemsi, always ready to fight with him when in danger, at the same time a man with a great sense of humor. He is also described as a fanatical Muslim, but his conviction manifests itself mainly in frequent theological discussions with his companion, whom he tries to convert so that he should eventually enter paradise and not the less desirable place reserved for infidels.

Not surprisingly, attempts were made in recent years to deconstruct the Middle Eastern novels of Karl May by German followers of the anti-Orientalist school inspired by Edward Said. May, they argued, like virtually all Western travelers, was an imperialist intending to denigrate everything non-Western. They stressed the appearance of a variety of Oriental villains in these stories, and it is of course true that there were bandits and slave traders as well as other unsavory characters. But they represented elements in the real Middle East, and how else could the reader's interest be engaged if not through frequent clashes between the forces of good and evil, ambush, the chase after villains, captivity, and miraculous escape. The overall picture created by Karl May was one of positive, attractive heroes, the kind of Hadji Halefs one wanted to have as friends, and not just in an emergency. So I was, I suppose, a young Orientalist *avant la lettre,* admiring the proud, honest, and brave Oriental, a hero greatly superior to the Westerner, just as Karl May's noble savages, the Indians, were better men than their oppressors.

Unfortunately, what I had learned about the Middle East, Arabs, and Islam did not prepare me for my encounter with reality. Reality was the camels (I found them nasty animals) and their drivers, and women assembling at the village well and carrying water home in big clay vessels, called *djara,* on the head. Some of these scenes probably had not changed since biblical days, except that the biblical women were called Sarah, Rebecca, and Rachel. Reality was also large groups of children shouting *bakshish, bakshish* and following me despite the fact that I tried hard to explain to them that my financial situation was such that I needed *bakshish* as much as they did. I found this situation as demeaning as the omnipresent corruption, the haggling on the markets, and other such practices for which my European upbringing had not prepared me. At first I tended to put the blame on imperialism and colonialism. They had caused the miserable economic state of much of the population and the moral degradation and so many other negative features. I found the following explanation in a current work of reference: "While some visitors may find requests for *bakshish* grating or distasteful, they should recognize that the economic system which *bakshish* represents is an important part of their cultural experience." I thought this a strange observation. I have not heard about anyone finding requests for *bakshish* attractive and worthy of emulation. But it is perfectly true that they are or were part of a tradition going back many centuries. This part of the world had not been colonized or subjected to Western imperialism for most of its history. It had been either independent, such as Turkey or Iran, or part of the Ottoman empire.

I gradually lost patience with the frequent harping on corrupt governments in the Middle East. Given the fact that without corruption (admittedly within reasonable limits) little or nothing worked in the Middle East, I found such accusations disingenuous or worse. (And what Western societies have been free of corruption? Israeli public life in recent decades has been no shining example.) The alternative was not exactly attractive. I doubt whether Hitler was personally corrupt, which is more than can be said about many politicians of the French Third Republic, yet he was a mass murderer; Osama bin Laden, Mahmoud Ahmadinejad, the Muslim Brotherhood, or Hamas were less corrupt than Fatah or the Arab governments often called moderate in the West, but the fanaticism of the former inevitably led to violence, cruelty, and very often mass murder.

In the 1950s I was on the way to becoming a Middle Eastern expert, and if I decided against this, there was more than one reason. One was that I found it quite depressing, seeing no solutions to the many conflicts besetting this part of the world. I continued to be interested in developments in the region, to follow the discussions about its present state and future prospects. I knew many of the experts, some of whom became my friends. I even read about the region's history, about Muhammad and the Koran, about the battles of Khaybar, Badr, and Uhud, about the Truce of Hudaibiya, but more out of a feeling of duty because the experts told me that Arabs ideologically lived very much in the past and that the fairy tales, myths, and legends were exceedingly important for understanding their mindset. Had I been a student of religion or of medieval poetry I would have found this field of absorbing interest, but my interest was in modern times and in this field there was little to attract me compared with Russian studies.

Intellectually, I found it little more interesting than an excursion in the desert. True, from time to time one would come across magnificent ruins such as

Petra. The region was of great interest to archaeologists, but what had this part of the world contributed to world culture in recent memory? Others had made progress, but the Middle East had fallen behind, and this seemed to be largely the reason underlying its present malaise. Why should this have been the case? Was it all the fault of Western imperialism, which had deliberately prevented its progress? This explanation was nonsense, but what were the real reasons? Listening to all the arguments and reading much of the literature did not make me any wiser.

For a while in the 1950s and 1960s it seemed that Arab nationalism with an admixture of communism would cause important changes, but this prospect proved largely illusionary. In a book on nationalism and communism in the Middle East written in the early 1950s I certainly overrated the importance and impact of Marxism in the area. I did say that its roots were not very deep, but I did not realize how shallow they were. That many of these Marxists went over to the camp of Arab national socialism (Nasserism) was perhaps not surprising, but that not a few ended up among the Muslim fundamentalists I had not anticipated. There were such cases in Europe, too—Roger Garaudy, once a faithful Stalinist and member of the Politburo of the French Communist Party, or Carlos Ramirez (the terrorist "Jackal"), for whom the Soviet Union was not radical enough and who ended up a Muslim in a French prison. But these were exceptional cases, whereas in the Middle East Muslim fundamentalism was more or less the fate of a whole generation of intellectuals. Religio-political fanaticism could be found in many parts of the world, but nowhere was it as widespread and as militant as in the Middle East.

What were the reasons for falling behind the rest of the world, the violence, the blind hatred not only against the West but also against each other (not to mention the minorities living among them)? What was the powerful attraction of a religion that was largely ritualistic? What brought about the lack of tolerance, the fear of freedom, the lack of creativity, the resistance against democratic institutions? I have not found convincing answers; others more deeply steeped in the mentality of that part of the world no doubt will do so in time. Unfortunately, self-criticism is a rare commodity in the Arab world, and Western experts, for fear of causing offense, are all too often reluctant to speak out on these issues. But perhaps there is no full accounting for such developments.

The State of Israel

Most violent conflicts in the contemporary world are between and within Muslim countries, and it was in this troubled part of the globe that the state of Israel came into being. For decades the country and its inhabitants were told by well-wishers abroad that in order to become integrated and accepted it should give up fully or in part its ties with the West, cultural and political, and become more like its neighbors. Such advice also came from the Middle Eastern experts of the 1940s and 1950s. Most of them, British and French, were anti-Israeli because they thought the Arabs natural allies of the British and French colonial empires; today's experts are also anti-Israeli but for the opposite reason, because they think of the Arabs as basically progressive and anti-imperialist in character.

The idea of the Levantization of Israel did not strike me as very desirable, but to a certain extent it has happened in any case since most of the immigration into Israel has been from non-Western countries. The Jewish community in Palestine had been an elite, not saints or geniuses but in their majority deeply motivated. The number of Jews living in Israel when it became a state was about half a million, and it has since increased tenfold. Israel is now more populous than European countries such as Norway or Finland. During the first years of statehood it absorbed more immigrants, many times over, than the number of those living at the county before statehood—a demographic change probably unique in the annals of humankind. Many hundreds of new towns, settlements, and suburbs came into being. When I accompanied a United Nations commission on a visit to a hot and dusty Beersheba in 1947, it had no more than a few hundred inhabitants and on market days more camels and sheep than human beings. Today Beersheba is a modern city with more than 150,000 inhabitants, many shops, and a reputable university that has a fine mathematics department and is a bulwark of the post-Zionist historians. Amman, not much larger in the late 1950s, now has more than 2 million residents as well as a university.

For years Israel depended on outside economic help, but gradually it became economically viable. Its standard of living is comparable to European countries, except the very richest. It has a vibrant cultural life with many universities, theaters, and orchestras, and its scientific institutions are second to none. On various global statistics measuring progress, Israel figures among the first ten or twenty countries. Yet there is another side: the quality of political life is far from ideal, with a great deal of corruption and scandal that fifty years ago would have been unthinkable. The quality of political leadership has also deteriorated; there are no doubt people capable of leading the country, but they have opted for careers other than politics. All societies change over time, but Israel for demographic and other reasons has changed more than most.

The achievements were the work of a relatively small sector of the population. Once this was an idealistic society and one of the most egalitarian; a family with three rooms and a car was considered "bourgeois," well to do. In the 1930s it had not been customary to shut the front door of apartments. When a car appeared in the street in which I lived the children shouted "taxi, taxi," for there were very few private cars. Today, among developed nations, Israel has one of the most pronounced disparities in income and property, next to the United States. Even in Jerusalem, not a wealthy city at all, there are indescribable traffic jams. This trend has obvious negative political repercussions. Political polarization has progressed well beyond what is normal elsewhere. Little has remained of the motivation of the prestate days. The history of contemporary Israel leads from Theodor Herzl, Chaim Weizmann, and David Ben-Gurion to Benjamin Netanyahu, Avigdor Liberman, and Arkady Gaidamak. When Herzl wrote about the future Jewish state he said that the generals would be confined to their bases and the rabbis to their synagogues, but this is not what happened.

The Six-Day War and the Occupied Territories

Aleksandr Pushkin once said that he deeply disliked, even hated, a great deal about the Russia of his day, but he liked it even less when he heard such criticism from a foreigner. I have found myself quite often in a similar frame of mind listening to attacks against Israel from Westerners such as President Jimmy Carter and others: the list is very long indeed.

What increasingly disturbed me was the aftermath of the Six-Day War, which has profoundly shaped Israeli domestic politics to this day and of course its foreign policy. The war of 1967 was in retrospect a decisive turning point, and its consequences were fatal. Unlike some of the new historians, I do not think that the war could have been prevented once Gamal Abdel Nasser decided to close the Straits of Tiran and to order the UN peacekeepers to withdraw from Sinai. The official line of the Arab League and most Arab countries at the time was that Israel should be destroyed and the Jews thrown into the sea. There is no reason why Nasser should have retreated and declared his imposition of a naval blockade a mistake, for he had nothing to fear from the great powers. The Soviets were fully supporting him, and the United States had failed to assemble an international force to break the blockade. In any case, the Americans were preoccupied with Vietnam and in other parts of the world. Having succeeded initially, there is much reason to believe that Nasser's aggressive steps would have been followed by others.

The basic problem was not the war that had become inevitable but its aftermath. A few months after its end and following a long stay in Israel I published *The Road to War, 1967* (*The Road to Jerusalem* in the U.S. edition). As an envoi to the last chapter I chose a statement from Friedrich Nietzsche: "A great victory is a great danger. For human nature it is more difficult to bear than a defeat." Unfortunately, Nietzsche proved all too correct.

The great victory of June 1967 caused a wave of messianic hopes in Israel. There were petitions not to give up a single inch of the territories that had been conquered. Even a left-wing politician such as Yisrael Galili proclaimed that the survival of the state of Israel could not be ensured unless the Gaza Strip was annexed. In the August 1967 issue of *Commentary* I wrote:

> The magnitude and excitement of the victory made most people in Israel forget for a while the enormity of the problems facing the Jewish state. It was clear from the very beginning that Israel would be under tremendous pressure to surrender the occupied territories. . . . Israel faced the danger [of isolation in the United Nations] with equanimity, believing that the country could hold on indefinitely to its conquests in the absence of a real peace treaty.
>
> But were the conquered territories worth holding? The administration and policing of large areas populated by Arabs were bound to create nightmarish problems. It could be predicted with near certainty that there would be an increasing number of acts of sabotage, and that the Israeli authorities would have to respond sharply. And it was easy to imagine world reaction to such incidents. . . . Israel now faces hard times. There is a massive propaganda onslaught from the East about the new Hitlerites and their barbarous atrocities; already we have heard about Israeli Gauleiters . . . and Israeli extermination camps.
>
> Some brilliant minds suggested calling in advertising agents and public relations experts. As if public relations, a doubtful institution in the best of times, could replace a clear policy. And a clear policy about borders and refugees Israel did not have.
>
> Israel had obviously planned far more efficiently for war than for peace, a peace planning committee was not established until a week after the ceasefire. Already some opportunities had been missed. Immediately following the ceasefire Israel should have made it absolutely clear that the war had not been fought for territorial gain, that Israel's only concern was to live in peace with the Arab world. . . .
>
> But the nation was hardly in a mood for such actions and gestures. . . . Perhaps it was too much to expect magnanimity toward an enemy who had vowed to destroy the state and its inhabitants.

I concluded as follows:

> Pressure for revenge on Israel will be overwhelming. The military lessons of the defeat seem to be lost on Egypt and Syria. It is generally believed in the Arab capitals that the combined might of the Arab armies is more than match for Israel; they would have won the war if they had got in a first strike before the Israelis did. All this makes a new military adventure extremely probable not in ten or twenty years but well before.

(It was just six years to the outbreak of the Yom Kippur War. It is also true that, in retrospect, there might not have been peace with Egypt but for this war.)

After the 1967 war, there was euphoria; the message that "the Temple Mount is in our hands" generated something akin to mass hysteria. There had been a national religious party in Israel for many years, but it had been among the most moderate forces. It had accepted the 1947 and 1948 UN resolutions that placed Jerusalem outside the Jewish state. The representative of this party in the government in 1967 was the first to suggest that Israel should have as little as possible to do with the supervision of the non-Jewish holy places, that accepting this responsibility would cause no end of trouble. But these warnings were not heeded. There was a wave of unprecedented enthusiasm: never, it was said, would Jerusalem the eternal capital be divided. And thus a local and limited political conflict turned into a full-scale confrontation with Islam, with fateful consequences.

At the same time settlers streamed into the occupied territories, and they, too, became an intolerable burden for the Jewish state—politically, militarily, and economically—greatly aggravating the conflict. Ironically, most of the settlements, and especially those most exposed and most likely to create the most problems in future, were established during the term of President Carter, who in later years complained bitterly about them but at the time showed little interest.

The Israeli leadership had assumed that soon after the end of the war negotiations with the Arab countries would begin and that some or much of the occupied territories would be given up in the framework of a peace settlement. But the Arab countries refused to negotiate as a matter of principle, and in these circumstances the Israeli leadership saw no reason to give up any territory. The leaders failed to understand the consequences of their policy; they failed to anticipate that, given the high Palestinian birth rate, they would eventually face problems of a magnitude which with they could no longer a cope—or cope only at a price that was unacceptable.

When I first passed Gaza and Khan Yunis at the end of World War II, the former had about 37,000 inhabitants and the latter perhaps 12,000, and my impression at the time was that, like Beersheba, there were more camels and sheep than human beings in these places. Today the Gaza Strip has 1.4 million people. Within a generation the population may double, and there seems to be no chance that this territory will ever be a viable entity.

Had Israel given up most of the occupied territories in 1967–68, it would have acted from a position of strength. Forty or fifty years later such action would be seen—not without reason—as acting out of weakness. Israeli leaders at the time failed to understand that by surrendering the territories they would be doing a favor not for the Arabs but for themselves.

Writing in *Commentary* I concluded:

> The basic purpose of the Zionist movement had been to restore dignity and security to the Jewish people in its own land. The land had been restored and the dignity, but there still was no security. In the country that had been built to make the Jews secure,

they were less safe than in any other part of the world, and they had to reconcile themselves to an unlimited period of siege.

I had known Yitzhak Rabin, albeit not very well, since 1947–48 when we were both in our twenties. When he became ambassador to Washington after 1968, we met from time to time for longish discussions (largely monologues on his part), and less often in Israel when he was prime minister. When I mentioned a Palestinian Arab state he drew down the map (which I knew almost as well as he did) and said it was an impossibility. After a few years he changed his mind, and if the Oslo Accords failed, it was not mainly his fault. From time to time I expressed my view that Jerusalem could be the capital of two states, a view that was not very popular, to say the least. I had to wait till late 2007 to hear similar views expressed by an Israeli prime minister and his deputy. But their own party, as well as their own coalition, violently opposed them. The learning process as to what is vital for the survival of Israel has proceeded agonizingly slowly. The settlers and their supporters were in a position to block concessions; it was not difficult to see what the consequences of such a policy would be.

How It Might Have Been

In 2008, for the sixtieth anniversary of the foundation of the state of Israel, I wrote a brief counterfactual history. Entitled *Disraelia: A Counterfactual History, 1848–2008*, it appeared as the first in a series of Middle Eastern strategy papers at Harvard University. It was fairly widely read and translated into several languages. I shall try to summarize it very briefly (and imperfectly).

From the late eighteenth century on, Turkey was considered the Sick Man of Europe. It fought a number of wars, all of which it lost. In the chanceries of Europe the coming downfall of the Ottoman empire was widely discussed and what would happen thereafter, for the Russian ambition to inherit large parts of this empire was widely feared. There were other threats: Muhammad Ali had established himself as an independent ruler of Egypt and occupied Palestine and parts of Lebanon and Syria. So the European powers made some attempts to prop up the Ottoman empire, and they by and large succeeded up to World War I, when Turkey joined the losing side and following that war in the Treaty of Sèvres lost most of its empire.

What if Europe's attempts to prop up the Ottomans had failed? What if after the Russo-Turkish War of 1768–74 (which ended with the Peace of Kuçuk Kainarji) or after the Russo-Turkish War of 1828–29 (which ended with the Treaty of Adrianople), or at the latest after the Crimean War (which ended with the Paris Peace Treaty of 1856), the Ottoman empire had disintegrated? What if after it disintegrated a few million European Jews would have moved to the Middle East? The idea would not have seemed outlandish to everyone; it had occurred, for instance, to Benjamin Disraeli. Or what if Muhammad Ali would have been persuaded for a suitable consideration to hand over the territories that he had conquered outside Egypt to a company developing these regions? There would have been difficulties to overcome, but would they have been insurmountable? The idea would not have been to establish a Jewish state; this would have happened later, after national movements and states emerged in the region.

Let's say that this Charter Development Agency (CDA) would have been under the tutelage of Constantinople and the European powers and also of Egypt. The territory allocated would have comprised Palestine, Jordan, and parts of Mesopotamia. The local population was sparse and mixed. In 1840, according to the best statistics available, Palestine had some 400,000 inhabitants, but at least one-quarter, probably more, were not Arabs but Jews, Bedouins, Greeks, Armenians, and other foreigners. The population of Mesopotamia was very small, perhaps not more than 1.2 million, one-third among them Kurds, Assyrians, Turkomans, and other minorities. Only in the second half of the nineteenth century did their numbers begin to rise, after the Ottoman rulers introduced a new water supply and other hygienic reforms. In other words, very few people lived between the Mediterranean and the Euphrates. Many could have stayed and become members of the new enterprise. National feelings were not running high at the time, and the religious conflicts that did exist could have been contained. After all, about half the population of contemporary Iran is not Persian, and very few Middle Eastern countries are ethnically homogeneous. Those who wished to change their place of residence would have been compensated.

But would 2 million Jews have been willing to leave Europe, where their total number at the time was about 5 million? This prospect is much less likely but not wholly impossible. It is less likely because Europe was the center of civilization, and with all their traditional religious ties to Palestine and their longings, most European Jews saw their future in the European diaspora. The walls of the ghettos had come down wholly or in part in most countries, and if the Jews did not yet have full rights, it seemed to many that they would have them within a few decades. There were anti-Jewish feelings in many European countries, but modern racialist antisemitism had not yet appeared; the first major pogroms in Eastern Europe occurred in the 1880s.

Let us assume that a prophet would have arisen at the time, such as Herzl did at the end of the nineteenth century, and explained to his co-religionists that there was no future for them in Europe and that the opportunities that existed in the Middle East were such that it would be a tragic mistake not to make use of them.

Let us assume that Disraeli, having lost the crucial Maidstone by-election in 1837 (he had been defeated at Taunton, Somerset, two years earlier), having been mocked and derided by his fellow Tories as a ridiculous Jew, would have decided to leave British politics. He had been to Jerusalem in 1830, and the city had made an overwhelming impression: "The view of Jerusalem is the history of the world," he wrote; "it is more, it is the history of earth and of heaven." This fateful encounter with the past of his people might take years to gestate but eventually it would be a passion. "Man is only truly great," he also wrote in his fiction, "when he acts from passion."

Let us assume that in 1850 Disraeli was instrumental in convening a small meeting in Paris that in retrospect proved to be a historical turning point. Moses Montefiore had introduced him to the Rothschilds, who after some initial hesitation decided to support his vision. Participants at the Paris meeting were Lionel and James Mayer de Rothschild as well as Achille Fould, Moses Hess, the early socialist, and Rabbi Zvi Hirsch Kalischer. Also present was Friedrich Stahl, a young German who was to convert and become the chief ideologist of German conservatism. But what if his spiritual crisis would have had a different outcome and he would have identified with the Jewish cause and become one of the chief protagonists of the second exodus of the Jewish people?

A manifesto to European Jewry was prepared and later read out in all the synagogues of the Continent. It was received with incredible enthusiasm, and almost half of European Jewry registered for transfer to the Middle East. There was opposition. Karl Marx wrote a sarcastic article for the *New York Tribune* entitled "A Jew Crusade?" in which he argued that the Jews would never go along with this crazy scheme since no money was to be made in this godforsaken part of the world, a place where there was no water or mineral resources except a foul-smelling substance called petroleum, which no one needed. The fact that major pogroms had taken place in Eastern and Central Europe in the wake of the revolutions of 1848–49 also played a major role in promoting the Disraeli project. Several royal houses of Europe warmly supported the Disraeli scheme, and so did both the Catholic and the Protestant churches, having been assured that their traditional interests in Jerusalem and the other holy places would not be affected. Major loans were floated to finance the scheme. The French government gave its blessing having been assured that every child in this region would be taught the French language. Over five years, most of those who had been registered moved to the territory that had been allocated to the CDA.

This is not the place to relate in detail the eventful history of CDA during the years that followed. There were setbacks, and not all dreams materialized. Suffice it to say that the modern bi-national state that emerged counted some 50 million inhabitants by the beginning of the twenty-first century; given the high birthrate (6–8 percent), such growth was by no means miraculous. This state was the fifth largest oil producer in the world, had a developed industry, and was leading in the nuclear field and other modern technologies. It was economically healthy with an annual growth rate of 7–10 percent, competitive with Europe and Asia. It had powerful armed forces, lived in peace with its neighbors—at least to the extent that peaceful relations could be expected in the unquiet Middle East. It was by no means a model state but by the standards of time and place considered much better than the usual.

What would be the standing in the world of this country? It goes without saying that it would be an honored member of the United Nations, being considered for membership in the Security Council, chairing the Commission on Human Rights. True, some extreme Islamist sects would engage in incitement against this state, but no responsible Arab politician would dare to support such propaganda—no more than any would dare to attack India, or China, or Russia because Muslim minorities were allegedly persecuted there. (The president of CDA and its chief representative in the United Nations were Muslims.) Muslim theologians and preachers from Al Azhar to Indonesia would praise the CDA state as a model of friendly coexistence between the Muslim world and the people of the book. A minor *hadj* to Al Kuds (Jerusalem) might be launched, bringing several hundred thousands of pilgrims to pray each year at al-Haram al-Sharif.

The foreign policy of this state would be neutral (albeit not neutralist); lobbyists on behalf of the United States and NATO in Jerusalem were actively trying to establish even closer relations with the United States in the political field, whereas NATO was strongly pressing for military bases. Russian lobbyists were trying equally hard to explain to CDA policy makers the benefits of a close rapprochement with their country.

The U.S. Association for the Promotion of Middle Eastern Studies would pass almost unanimously a resolution asking for an urgent expansion of CDA studies and, generally speaking a more constructive attitude toward this country, including intensive cultural exchanges. British academics followed their examples. Zbigniew Brzezinski, the eminent American politologist, might publish a book entitled *J'accuse: The Bitter Fruits of Prejudice,* a scathing condemnation of White House neglect and lack of warmth in its relations with the CDA. In view of this disgraceful failure he could mark their performance only with an F. Political science professors from Harvard and Chicago of the neo-realist school would encourage American Jews to give stronger support to their lobby, for it would be in the best interests of both countries.

What of the attitude of European intellectuals of the left and of the right, of American ex-presidents, of bishops and moral philosophers? Most of them would be enthusiastic, holding up the achievements as a shining example for the rest of humankind. There would be a strong demand to Western and Eastern governments to strengthen ties with this state. International commissions would be regularly dispatched to the state to study its experiences in various fields, and there would be a growing demand to transfer the seat of the United Nations to Jerusalem or another major city in the CDA Federation. CDA would also be in line to host the Olympic Games early in the twenty-first century.

True, a few contrarian voices would argue that the state was colonialist in its origins, founded in the main by settlers from Europe. But these dissenters would not be taken seriously; against them it would be argued that the CDA had come into existence long before most other member states of the United Nations, that if a few hundred thousand people had been resettled a long time ago, that such incidents had been the case all the world over. What sane person would demand the right of millions of refugees from India and Pakistan to return (this is ruled out according to the preamble to the constitution of India), or of the millions of Germans expelled from Eastern Europe after World War II? Why not demand the annulment of all migrations since the early Middle Ages?

At one stage in its history the CDA had been compelled to build a wall to protect itself against incursions by bandit tribes. The experience of this Wall of Peace was now widely studied by experts in conflict resolution as a constructive step to be emulated elsewhere whenever necessary. In brief, the existence of such a state would be beyond discussion. There would be many political crises on the international agenda, but the CDA would not be among them.

However, the Ottoman empire did not collapse that early, and half of European Jewry did not emigrate in the nineteenth century. The great antisemitic wave in Europe came fifty years later. The opportunity for settlement in the Middle East arose only after 1917, and even then emigration was small until Hitler came to power in Germany. The Jewish communities saw no particular reason to do so, because the Mandatory power (Great Britain) insisted on strictly limiting immigration and the Palestinian Arabs were bitterly opposed.

What emerged in the end was a small country of more than 6 million inhabitants, nearly 80 percent of them Jewish, with no significant natural resources such as oil or other important minerals. It seems therefore futile to engage in speculation about what might have happened if political conditions would have been more auspicious and if more Jews would have been willing to migrate (or had been aware of the coming dangers to their existence). It is a futile exercise except for one reason: to put Israel's present isolation and the attacks against it in political (or historical or moral) perspective. (For the full version, search online for "Disraelia: A Counterfactual History.")

Antisemitism and the International Isolation of Israel

Israelis have been at a loss to understand their isolation, the boycott, the ideological hostility, the condemnation by all and sundry for misdeeds that were committed by many other countries on a far larger scale. Why should their country alone among all 192 member states of the United Nations be singled out for constant denunciations by the UN? Why should their very existence, alone among all nations, be declared unjustified by many? Why should they be considered the greatest danger to world peace? Was it antisemitism, as many believed? True, Jews had not been very popular for a long time, and the hostility—religious, racial, or whatever—was fed by the animosity of neighbors unwilling to accept the presence of intruders. But the concentration on antisemitism as the sole explanation could be exaggerated. The basic reason was that the state that emerged was small and relatively weak. It had no oilfields or other vital raw materials to offer. And it has been the historical misfortune of the small and weak to be ignored—if they were lucky and their interests did not clash with others, bigger and more powerful. The Middle East was probably the least likely place on earth for living in peace with one's neighbors, given the violence and aggression accumulated there for a great variety of reasons. In the circumstances the small state was bound to be considered an intruder, whereas no one in his right mind would have dared to show a similar attitude toward a state ten times as populous and powerful.

For most Muslims the parallel with the crusader state seemed obvious: provided sufficient military and political pressure was exerted, Israel would collapse in due time. For many others in the West the state of Israel was a disturber of the peace: if not for Israel, there would have been no Islamism and other forms of fanaticism, no terrorism, and Arab attitudes toward the West would be positive. Sunnis would not fight Shi'ites; no one would insist on the imposition of the Sharia. Osama bin Laden would still engage in the import-export trade and land development schemes. Muslim immigrants in Europe would not be restive, and the price of oil would be a fraction of what it is now.

Ehud Barak once said that had he been born a Palestinian Arab he would be with the militants; for saying this he was bitterly attacked even though it was no more than stating the obvious. The Israelis have taken, as the Palestinians see it, what rightfully belongs to them; resentment and hate in these circumstances are natural. True, it was not exactly a genocide, as some occasionally claim; the number of Palestinian Arabs now living in what was once the British Mandate of Palestine is about four times larger than it was in 1948.

I made my home in al-Issawiya, a village on Mount Scopus, until I was asked more or less politely to leave. There were about a thousand inhabitants then; now there are 13,000, all Arabs. Later I was expelled from the Jerusalem German colony, and still later from a house opposite Givat Shahin that came under fire. It was not easy with a little baby around. I listen with attention and sympathy whenever talk is about expulsion. But Israel is a Jewish state, albeit with a considerable Arab minority, and a Palestinian Arab state as originally envisaged has not yet come into being. Many hundreds of thousands were expelled or fled.

Such events have happened frequently throughout history, even in the twentieth century: Greeks were expelled from Turkey after World War I, and Germans from Eastern Europe after World War II. Tens of thousands of "foreigners" were expelled from Egypt under Nasser; Muslims fled from what became India after the partition and Hindus from what is now Pakistan; more than 3 million Afghans had to escape from their native country, as did many hundreds of thousands Burmese, Burundians, Somalis, and others. The list is long, and as the years have passed these problems have been solved but not without suffering. Of the more than 10 million Germans who were expelled from Eastern Europe, few if any wish to go back (except as tourists) to the countries where their ancestors had lived for centuries.

Those forced to migrate realized long ago that their claims to receive back what once belonged to them would have little if any international support. On the contrary, they would be denounced as troublemakers and warmongers, not because their claims are immoral or illegal but because the powers they confront are strong and would react violently. But the case of Israel is different, because the country is not a great power, whereas Palestinian Arabs have the support of the other Arab nations and the whole Muslim world. In brief, whereas in the case of other groups there is no hope that the wheel of history can be turned back, there seems to be such hope in the case of Palestine/Israel.

All this ought to be stated not to argue the claims, the rights and wrongs of the two sides, as has been done countless times, but to note the obvious, that Palestinian Arab attitudes toward Israel (and to Jews in general) should come as no surprise. In addition there is the traditional negative attitude of Islam toward Jews and other nonbelievers. Israel and the Jews have been more obvious targets than others. Given Islamic solidarity, one would expect, for instance, that young Pakistanis in Britain would direct their ire against India, against which they have innumerable complaints, or against Russia, which has not treated their fellow Muslims in the Caucasus very well, or against China, which has harshly treated its Muslim minority, the Uighurs. But despite all these misdeeds, Muslims have been very careful not to give offense to these powerful countries, and it is easy to see why. A Hindu or a Chinese walking the Muslim quarters of Bradford or London, or the Paris *banlieue*, or the respective sections of Berlin is running no risks, but an orthodox Jew or someone wearing the Star of David will not be welcome with open arms and may fare considerably worse. It is obvious why the attitude toward Jews should be different, much less restrained.

But how can the international isolation of Israel be explained, the fact that it is singled out for condemnation infinitely more often than all other nations? The continuing occupation of Arab settled territories after 1967 has been a disaster;

successive Israeli governments have not followed wise policies vis-à-vis their Arab neighbors and their Arab minority. But can it be maintained with total conviction that the situation would be radically different had other policies and attitudes prevailed?

According to peace researchers at least 25 million people have been killed in internal conflicts since World War II, of them 8,000 in the Israeli-Arab conflict, which ranges forty-sixth in the sad list of victims. But Israel has been more often condemned by the United Nations and other international organizations than all other nations taken together. In recent years it has been the only country condemned by the UN Commission on Human Rights, which, if it corresponded with realities, would mean that there have been no human rights violations anywhere in the world but for that tiny country in the Middle East, an almost paradisiacal state of affairs.

In fact, there is a great deal of evil in the world, and millions have perished even within the last decade or two as the result of civil wars, repression, racial and social persecution, and tribal conflicts from Cambodia to much of Africa (Darfur, Congo, Sudan, Somalia, Rwanda, and other places). More than 2 billion people live in repressive dictatorships, but there is persecution also in countries that are free or partly free. From Indonesia, Pakistan, and Bangladesh to Central Asia and beyond, national and religious minorities have been systematically persecuted, abused, raped, burned, shot, gassed, and their property demolished. In fact, it would be difficult to think of countries outside Europe and North America that have been entirely free of such suffering, and even Europe had such human rights violations on a massive scale in the Balkans.

But there have been no protest demonstrations concerning the fate of the Dalits (Untouchables) in India, even though there are more than 100 million of them, or the Burakumin (the social outcasts of Japan), the suffering of the Uighurs in China, the Christians in Iraq, the Copts in Egypt, or the Bahai in Iran (to list but a few persecuted groups). These persecutions have not generated much indignation in the streets of Europe or America, let alone elsewhere.

Why should passions be inflamed by the suffering of some people but not of others? It obviously depends not on the quantitative dimension—the number of victims affected—or the enormity of the crimes committed, but on other factors, such as the size of the clientele (or lobby) willing to be mobilized for this specific cause. If friends of the oppressed and humiliated were active in all or most instances of injustice, their case would be irrefutable. But if anti-racialist protestations in defense of human rights are made selectively, the question arises why this should be the case. Neither anti-racialist nor anti-imperialist emotions, however sincerely held, can satisfactorily explain this inequality.

Many Jews regard the singling out of Israel for universal condemnation as a new form of antisemitism. Others argue that since it does not involve traditional stereotypes (and in view of the fact that Jews, too, are among the bitter critics of Israel and Zionism), it should not properly be associated with the old racialist antisemitism. This is true, but there was antisemitism also before racialism appeared on the scene. Has anti-Jewish feeling among the left and many media in Western and Eastern Europe been generated only by events in Israel? Or has it been updated since World War II? *The Protocols of the Elders of Zion* have been reconceived as the conspiracy of the neo-conservatives and of globalism aiming at world conquest.

Some Israelis have been slow to accept the basic facts of life in international politics: that there is not one measure of justice in the world, that a small country will be treated not like a great power, and that it cannot afford to behave like one.

But let us assume for argument's sake that Israeli policies are the single most important factor underlying the emergence of the new antisemitism. The question still remains why Israeli policies, however wicked, should generate such strong passions among the likes of Mikos Theodorakis or Carlos "the Jackal," in other words, among people without a known personal stake in the Israeli-Palestinian conflict, who have not suffered from it physically, materially, or emotionally. Is it sympathy with the underdog and the feeling that injustice must be combated? But if so, why is there a concentration on a specific underdog and villain, and an ignoring of all others? There is no clear answer to this question. It does appear, however, that there must be a specific aspect or dimension to this case of injustice that other cases do not have. And the question remains what name to give to this dimension, if not postracialist antisemitism.

Zionism and Jewish Identity

Zionism faced many enemies from the very beginning. Herzl certainly had more severe critics than followers and supporters. They came from the left and the right. Orthodox rabbis told him that his movement was blasphemous, while socialist politicians argued that only world revolution would be able to solve the Jewish question and that the idea of a nation-state was an anachronism. The great majority of liberals also opposed the idea, believing that gradually the Jews of Europe and other parts of the world would be integrated in the societies in which they lived, that antisemitism was a throwback to the Middle Ages, and that it was bound to vanish. Zionism, they believed, ignored the progress of mankind toward freedom and humanity. Among the Jews of Europe and America, Zionists were a minority, in most countries a small minority, up to the 1930s and Hitler's rise to power.

For the next four or five decades criticism of Zionism among the Jewish community became muted. European Jews had to flee for their lives; there were few if any countries willing to accept them. The world revolution had unfortunately not taken place. Nation-states had not disappeared but become more numerous and powerful, and the progress toward humanism was reversed. In the hour of danger even ultra-Orthodox rabbis, sworn enemies of Zionism, even faithful Communists, even liberal believers in the progress of mankind, found a refuge in Palestine. Not every Jew became an ardent Zionist, but many who had been indifferent or hostile became more sympathetic or were willing, at the very least, to accept the growing Jewish community in Israel as a *fait accompli* or a regrettable necessity. It wasn't exactly "my country right or wrong," but the great majority of European Jewry had disappeared and among those who had survived a substantial part (eventually several millions) now lived in Israel. If this remainder was faced with attack and extinction, it could count on sympathy and support among most Jews outside Israel.

Gradually, however, these sympathies faded in some circles, especially after the Six-Day War and the continuing conflict with the Arabs unwilling to accept the existence of the Jewish state. For some Jews the state of Israel became an embarrassment; its policies seemed reprehensible, and the constant condemnation by international bodies had a psychological effect. Why could this country unlike others not live in peace with its neighbors? Why were there permanent conflicts, crises, and wars? And if it could not live in peace, obviously the fault must have been that of the new state. Zionism had promised the Jews not only a normal life but a life in peace and security, and these, as the conflict lasted, Israel was unable to guarantee.

If so, perhaps Zionism and the idea of a Jewish state had been a mistake. And so a new wave of criticism and attack began, largely on the part of the far left (Trotskyites and the New Left) but also among other circles that had always had their misgivings about the Jewish national movement. These included sections of the ultra-Orthodox, believers in a universal humanist mission of the Jews, and some who simply did not feel any strong emotional ties with the Jewish state and did not greatly care one way or another whether such a state existed or not.

To a certain extent it was a generational question: those who had lived through the Holocaust in Europe were unlikely to distance themselves from the Jewish community in Palestine, which had been too small and powerless to save European Jewry. But it had given a shelter to hundreds of thousands of them at a time when all other countries had closed their gates. As the memory faded into history, however, Jewish intellectuals and many of the younger generation, especially in the United States and Britain who had never been exposed to a mortal danger, felt under no obligation to show solidarity with a state with whose policies they sharply disagreed. Just as antisemitism (within certain limits) became again fashionable as the closed season on Jews ended—Jews had been talking too long and too intensely about the Holocaust as if humankind had not experienced other tragedies—attacks against Israel among Jews became more frequent and more bitter.

Many Israelis and many of their sympathizers outside Israel saw this attitude not just as a manifestation of anti-Zionism but of Jewish self-hatred. And those attacked as self-hating Jews rejected such accusations with great indignation as an attempt to silence all Jewish critics of Israeli politics, as if Israel alone among nations should be immune to criticism. It is a complicated issue likely to bedevil political debates among Jews for a long time to come. Some Israeli spokesmen have been exceedingly liberal in distributing the Jewish self-hatred label whenever the politics of their state were criticized. It is also true, however, that there were many Jews among the most bitter critics of Israel, especially among intellectuals. There was among these Jews infinitely more readiness to attack fellow Jews than self-criticism (not to put it any stronger) among Arabs, or Armenians living in their diaspora, and the question arises how to explain it.

Prior to Hitler the national idea among Jews in Europe had been weak; even in Poland, with its massive concentration of Jews, the socialist Bund, which saw the future of the Jews in the countries in which they lived, had been much stronger than the Zionists. Nazism and the Holocaust had reversed this trend, but, it seems, only temporarily. After World War II antisemitism had become unfashionable in the West. Jews in Europe and in the United States had been doing well in most respects, whereas in Israel, with all its achievements in the economic and other fields, the situation had remained precarious. While many Jews left Russia for Israel after the breakup of the Soviet Union, hundreds of thousands remained and many went to countries other than Israel. By the year 2000 more went to Germany than to the Jewish state.

Such distancing of themselves from the Jewish state was to a certain extent a natural development, and it may explain, as time passed, the relative lack of attraction Israel had for many Jews. In the United States all immigrant groups—Irish and Polish and Italian and Japanese and Armenian—were gradually integrated in American society. Sentimental ties with the old country remained, and sometimes political sympathies, but they gradually weakened. But all this does not explain the specific acrimony vis-à-vis Israel on the part of some Jewish intellectuals. True, there was a great deal to criticize as far as Israeli politics was concerned, as the mood inside Israel hardened following the attacks and the state of siege, and even for people of goodwill it became often difficult to defend Israeli government policies. But one would have expected on the part of Jews who still identified to a certain extent with their community that they would have realized that the fault was not Israel's alone, that the unwillingness of most Arabs to accept the existence of the Jewish state and the attacks had driven so many Israelis into positions that were in some respects a mirror image of Arab nationalism and Muslim fundamentalism—of not giving up territory because it would not make their enemies any more inclined to make peace, even of expelling Arabs from Israel. It does not explain why some Jewish intellectuals found it easier to understand Hamas and Hezbollah than Likud, let alone those groups more extreme.

Jews had always been in the forefront of the struggle for freedom and justice. They had been staunch internationalists in their majority, and they had been among the first to protest whenever human rights were violated. Had they expected that a Jewish state would behave better than others? Was it disappointment that caused their enmity toward Israel? This may have been true in a few cases, but certainly not in the majority. It ought to be remembered that many Jews on the European left had never had much time for specific Jewish concerns. Rosa Luxemburg had put it succinctly when she said that the fate of the Indians at Putumayo was closer to her heart than the pogroms in Eastern Europe. Simone Weil had belonged to the far left in her younger years but later had an epiphany, became a Catholic, and went to mass every day. She became so ardent a believer in Christianity that she wanted to abolish most of the Old Testament except, perhaps, the book of Job. Many thought of her as a twentieth-century saint, for she identified with the fate of all the oppressed and exploited so much so that in solidarity with them during World War II she starved herself to death. But there was one group with which she did not identify, for which she had not one word of support or commiseration even though they suffered more than anyone else at that time. How can such an attitude be defined if it is not self-hatred—a Jew (or Jewess) who had been thoroughly de-Judaized, a non-Jewish Jew, someone who after the conversion had not yet found his or her equilibrium.

Marx had thought Judaism vile and tried very hard to distance himself from his ancestors—without much success, because for his enemies, from Mikhail Bakunin to Bruno Bauer, he remained a Jew. He called his rival Ferdinand Lassalle a Jewish nigger. Lassalle wrote that he hated the Jews, and countless other examples could be adduced for similar such attitudes well before Zionism appeared on the scene.

However, to be fair, such attitudes were by no means limited to the left; they were common among the wealthy and educated Jews in Europe during the nineteenth century. As they left the ghetto, many Jews found little to admire in rabbinical Judaism, and there was little else at the time except perhaps a certain feeling of piety toward their ancestors. This piety could not, however, serve forever as a basis for Jewish solidarity. On one side were the ossified traditions of religious Judaism and the dismal heritage of the ghetto; on the other was European culture with its unlimited vista, freedom for all, and acceptance by the outside world. Nationalism and the nation-state were outdated. Why did some Jews fall for such anachronisms?

Charles Maurras wrote to a friend at the time of the Dreyfus affair that there was not a single Jew devoid of solidarity for his nation and that this included the antisemitic Jews, who were the most dangerous of all. He could not have been more mistaken, for Jewish solidarity was not strong and was becoming weaker all the time.

During the nineteenth century apostasy had been common. According to many estimates, hundreds of thousands European Jews left their faith. More than half of my family converted, and there were many mixed marriages. But apostasy was perhaps too strong a term. Most of those who converted drifted away from a religion that had become meaningless, from a community to which they felt they no longer belonged. Fritz Mauthner, an Austrian Jewish essayist, wrote before World War I that he had never in his life met a Jew who had converted to Christianity out of religious conviction. There were such cases as Edith Stein and Boris Pasternak, but they were the exception. A Jewish student in my German hometown had a religious epiphany, joined a Catholic order, and became its representative at the Vatican.

German Jewry lost most of its establishment during the nineteenth century. The Jews converted silently, not feeling any particular need to provide an ideological explanation why they thought that their Judaism had become a burden rather than an asset to be preserved. In the course of time antisemitism became rampant. For some it meant an additional reason to distance themselves from their community; others felt it undignified and cowardly to desert a besieged fortress.

For many it was the outside pressure that kept the community together; they had become a community of fate. But as outside pressure lessened after the Holocaust, the basis of solidarity narrowed except for the religious believers and those who thought that Jews had a right to their own state like all other nations, at least as long as the nation-state was the norm rather than the exception. But criticism of the Jewish condition, especially in Eastern Europe, could equally be found among the early Zionists, writers such as Micha Berdyczewski and Yosef Haim Brenner, and even Theodor Herzl, who wrote in his diaries about a party in Berlin that had been overrun by "some thirty or forty ugly little Jews and Jewesses." Generally speaking, Zionism believed in the negation of the diaspora, simply because Jewish life in the ghetto had all too often generated negative features of character. There had been historical reasons for this process, but centuries of life in the ghetto had left little courage and dignity, and many Jews had been reduced to an unproductive life of misery; they had never been masters of their destiny. Zionism saw its historical assignment not just to give the Jews a homeland but to create a new Jewish man and woman. Yiddish (the jargon) was dismissed as ugly not only by assimilated Western European Jews, for Zionism, too, totally rejected it; the language of the new country was to be Hebrew.

Assimilated Jews in Western and Central Europe often had feelings of inferiority: consider Walther Rathenau's "Who of us does not want to look like they do." These sentiments were certainly strong among the ladies of Jewish origin who ran their literary salons in Berlin around 1800 and also in the generation after that, when name changes were quite frequent. I doubt whether such feelings of inferiority were widespread in my generation. Growing up in the Third Reich and being exposed to the constant propaganda about the superiority of the Aryan race, I never felt an urge to look like Adolf Hitler, Joseph Goebbels, let alone Julius Streicher of *Der Stürmer* fame.

To deny the existence of Jewish self-hatred and Jewish antisemitism is absurd. There were too many manifestations in the past even if we ignore the more extreme cases such as Otto Weininger, who committed suicide at age twenty-three in the house of Ludwig van Beethoven; the French writer Maurice Sachs, who acted as Gestapo informer; or Arthur Trebitsch, not to be confused with the adventurer Trebitsch Lincoln, another Jewish antisemite; or Bobby Fischer, the mad chess genius.

Philosophers and psychologists have taught us that self-hatred has never been a Jewish preserve (consider Blaise Pascal's *Le moi est haïssable,* seconded by Arthur Rimbaud and others). True, after World War II and the Holocaust extreme Jewish self-hatred became less frequent. Under Joseph Stalin it became advisable to hide, if possible, one's Jewish identity; there was no antisemitism, only anti-Zionism (and anti-cosmopolitanism, but everyone knew what it meant). But in the rest of Europe and in the Americas antisemitism declined; until recently Jews in the Western world were no longer under the pressure that existed in earlier ages. Extreme Jewish self-hatred still showed itself, but these were individual cases, probably not much more frequent than among other people.

But if so, how can the relative frequency of bitter and shrill anti-Israelism be explained, especially the intensity of these feelings in particular among some Jewish artists and intellectuals? Why should people who took no interest or were not actively involved in Jewish affairs display such shock and militancy in the case of Israel? One could understand disappointment, regret, even embarrassment, but not the single-minded preoccupation with Israeli sins of commission and omission, with the particular bitterness, even hysterical hatred.

Some of the reasons have been adduced earlier on. Jews had been internationalists and cosmopolitans; feelings of patriotism had been alien to many of them; they felt that nation-states were outdated and no longer needed. It was in many cases not exactly self-hatred, but how could the attitude be defined and explained? It was certainly more than mere indifference; it was a strong urge to express opinions and to take a stand concerning the behavior of a community from which they had distanced themselves. Was it a feeling of strong moral duty to speak out, or neurotic self-consciousness, or a mixture of motives?

To be Jewish, or, to be precise, of Jewish origin, no longer carried a stigma as it had in earlier ages, although some public figures would still try to hide their Jewish antecedents and the contortions of the Jew Bruno Kreisky, the longtime Austrian chancellor, were probably closer to antisemitism than anti-Zionism. But for most their Jewish origin did not constitute a major problem. On the contrary, to be at least of part Jewish background became almost an asset, certainly not a hindrance, as the careers of Nicolas Sarkozy and several British foreign secretaries have shown.

But it is important to stress that for almost all of them, being Jewish, or of part Jewish origin, was an accident of birth. It had nothing to do with their mental and emotional makeup, or with their opinions on any subject whatsoever. And to stress this point they had to dissociate themselves even more emphatically than others from Israel and all it stood for. They had to prove to themselves and to others that they were wholly free of atavistic feelings of group solidarity. This would probably have been the case even if Israel had been a model of justice and freedom for all, a shining beacon in an otherwise imperfect world—which, to be sure, it has never been.

A well-known French lawyer in a little book published in 2008 bitterly complained that his name (Levi) was persecuting him; why should the accident of birth be interpreted as belonging to the Jewish community and supporting the state of Israel, for which he had no sympathy? An interesting and probably quite typical case for this kind of dilemma is provided by a Jewish professor teaching in London. Born in Cairo, he grew up in Italy and France and now teaches modern history. He was one of the sponsors of Independent Jewish Voices, a group of Jewish intellectuals with "a strong commitment to social justice and universal rights" who dissociated themselves from Israeli politics and Jewish organizations in the UK supporting Israel. The professor said that he did not want to give up his Jewish identity, he did not want to hide his Jewish identity, at least not as long as there was a single antisemite lurking somewhere. But what was his Jewish identity? He was facing, he said, a quandary. He was not a religious Jew, nor did he believe in the existence of a Jewish people, let alone race, nor did he support the state of Israel. He did not want to concede to the other side (he said) the monopoly of defining Jewish identity. But in the end he was compelled to do so, for if the last antisemite were to disappear he would cease to be a Jew. And in the meantime his Jewish identity would express itself in proclaiming "not in our name" as far as Israel was concerned.

I do not profess to have full explanations: the issue of the non-Jewish Jew, the citizen of the world, the member of the human race who does not quite know how to define himself, remains to be explored. In principle it should not have been a major problem. There is no moral commandment obliging people to show solidarity, let alone unconditional loyalty, to the group from which they originated; there should be ideological freedom of movement. It would have been more sensible and certainly more dignified if these non-Jewish Jews would have distanced themselves from the community to which their forefathers had belonged calmly, less neurotically, without creating a great deal of sound and fury, following their calling as saxophonists, linguists, or other worthy professions. But in the real world, with nation-states still firmly entrenched, non-Jewish Jews did not find it easy to establish themselves and be recognized as citizens of the world, even if they felt themselves as such. They wanted to escape their origins, but the world made it difficult for them.

CHAPTER 6

Think Tanks and Political Intelligence

or, Why It Is So Difficult to Predict

I was associated with a Washington think tank for more than thirty years, and the experience certainly broadened my horizons. One came to know many of the leading players (a term that emerged, I believe, only in the 1980s), and one had the impression (sometimes the illusion) of having a privileged seat watching world affairs. But when I think back it is also clear to me that for many basic questions confronting the student of international politics I found no answer, nor had those with whom I worked. The most basic is the question of failure—the high rate of failure among the leading players, the secretaries of state, directors of central intelligence, and national security advisers, and the high rate of error in assessing (let alone predicting) world affairs among experts in government and academe alike.

Thoughts on Think Tanks

Think tanks—the term was coined during World War II—are not an American monopoly. The Royal Institute of International Affairs (known as Chatham House) came into being well before most American institutions and served in the early days as a model for them. Chatham House had been founded in 1920 following the Paris peace conference with the mission "to analyse and promote the understanding of major international issues and current affairs." Both the location (St. James's Square, London SW1) and the orientation could not have been more "Establishment." The location had been the residence of William Pitt the Younger, British prime minister in the early nineteenth century. The orientation, set by early leaders such as Robert Cecil, Lionel Curtis, and the young Arnold Toynbee, was independent—to a point, given the sources of financial support (government and the city).

For a young student of international affairs—I did research there in the 1950s and wrote for its publications—it was an ideal place, with a fine library, a helpful staff (among whom I made a few friends), and frequent visitors, who were given a cup of tea. Over the years Chatham House changed, like all such institutions, and lack of funds restricted its activities. It also changed its name; although the Royal Institute of International Affairs remains its legal name, in 2004 it was "rebranded" as Chatham House.

When the Council on Foreign Relations was founded in 1921 it was inspired by Chatham House. Its founders felt that American isolationism—however popular in many circles—was not the wave of the future and that America would be drawn into world politics in the years to come whether it wanted to or not. The founders believed that a place for informed debate, and if necessary research, was needed. If anything, the council was even more establishment than Chatham House, but it was bipartisan in its constitution. The council was followed by the Brookings Institution, founded in 1927 in a merger of several small research organizations and with a main interest in economic problems. It became associated with the New Deal, which needed this kind of research. The Carnegie Endowment for International Peace had been around since 1910, when it was funded with a donation of $10 million by the famous Scottish-born erstwhile robber baron. Andrew Carnegie thought that much more should be done to preserve peace between nations through international law, and he appointed a high-level board to sponsor and supervise research and education to this end. But the influence of the endowment was very limited: to give but one example, when the League of Nations was founded after World War I, it could not affect Congress's decision to stay out.

The origins and background of the RAND Corporation (abbreviation of Research and Development) were very different. Its sponsor was General Henry H. "Hap" Arnold of the U.S. Air Force, who believed that the air force needed a think tank of its own. Thus at the end of 1945, RAND was founded under contract to the Douglas Aircraft Company and was primarily engaged in scientific and technological work concerned with the defense sector. The American Enterprise Institute (AEI), a conservative think tank with emphasis on the interests of free enterprise, was founded during World War II but became a factor of some importance only in the 1960s. At about the same time, in 1964 the Center for Strategic and International Studies (CSIS) was founded, in the beginning as part of Georgetown University but later an independent body.

I first came to know CSIS five years after its foundation, and it was a far cry indeed from the elegant and impressive location of Chatham House. It had a few rooms above a grocery shop on Washington's Eighteenth Street and half a dozen employees altogether. Its founders were Admiral Arleigh Burke (also known as "Thirty-one Knot Burke"), a naval hero of World War II, and David Abshire, a Korean War officer. Owing to Abshire's initiative and general talent, it grew rapidly to about 150 researchers, despite competition, for instance from the Heritage Foundation, a conservative think tank. CSIS had the reputation of being conservative but was in fact centrist or rather independent in orientation. Financially, the Heritage Foundation and AEI did better than CSIS precisely because their ideological commitment was more pronounced. Conservative donors liked them better; CSIS's activities seemed too neutral.

The 1970s and early 1980s were the high tide in the history of Washington think tanks, whose political importance has frequently been exaggerated by outsiders not familiar with the policy-making process. Their position stands in contrast to some of the lobbying groups also located on K Street, where CSIS has now its offices, two blocks from its original location. Like other think tanks, CSIS made an appeal for a new building.

What were, what are, the *raisons d'être* of the think tanks? Above all, perhaps, was the education of wider circles also outside Washington, less familiar with world affairs and the problems confronting the United States. Think tanks also served as convenient meeting places for foreign dignitaries visiting the capital and for scholars specializing in foreign affairs. Whether the think tanks generated new and important ideas concerning the conduct of foreign policy is doubtful for a variety of reasons. In the course of time the Department of State and Central Intelligence Agency, to name two of the most important institutions, also established research branches, and if those employed there wanted to meet fellow specialists from the academic world, they did not need the think tanks for the purpose. Think tanks were supposed to train analysts to focus on contemporary issues and express options like policy makers. But very few academics could achieve this perspective, as university education did not provide such training.

Leading policy makers, and not only in the United States, were often eager to meet experts or other people of known good judgment and to discuss some of the problems they were addressing. Such meetings were useful by way of reinsurance, for if things went wrong it was then possible to claim that the problems had been discussed with the best minds in the country. Washington was and is an open city in this respect, very much in contrast to many European capitals, in which it is not customary to consult with people outside the government. In fact, there is perhaps sometimes a danger of overconsultation. Having been exposed to many opinions, the person in authority may be inclined to agree with the last consultant he has met, just as a buyer of a house, having seen many of them, out of tiredness may opt for the last he has visited.

Furthermore, the think tanks found it difficult to attract first-rate students of world affairs. They could not offer academic tenure as in the universities, salaries were not particularly attractive, and reputations were established by writing books, or in a few cases articles, rather than membership in one of the think tanks. In these circumstances the think tanks had to fall back more often than not on young people at the beginning of their careers and on scholars (or politicians) who had retired and were at the end of their careers. Work in a Washington think tank could, however, be a useful vantage point or springboard for those interested in a career in government.

In addition, the publications of the think tanks had only a limited impact. Some of them, such as RAND, AEI, and Heritage, had no journals, and of the periodicals even the most prestigious, such as *Foreign Affairs,* with some 140,000 subscribers, were apparently more widely displayed than read. Circulation figures were sometimes misleading because they included free copies that went to members of the respective organization. They did publish occasionally interesting, even challenging articles, but these could have been written, and more often than not were written, by contributors outside the think tanks. *Foreign Policy,* connected with the Carnegie Endowment, had its admirers (such as the well-known and controversial international financier, George Soros), and it got various awards, but perhaps as much for its layout as for its contents. It was originally created by liberal State Department officials who had left over the Vietnam War. It had an Arabic edition and not less than three in Spanish, but whether these glossy, pleasing-to-the-eye editions had a major impact in the Arab world or in Latin America is doubtful. Some of the most interesting articles in the 1990s were published in journals with a relatively small circulation, such as the *National Interest,* but as so often in the history of periodicals, it proved difficult to maintain this level for many years.

By and large it is not certain that many of the Washington foreign policy think tanks would have survived far into the twenty-first century except Brookings and Carnegie, which had substantial endowments, had it not been for the terrorist attacks of September 11, 2001. Interest in foreign affairs had sharply declined with the end of the Cold War. But the terrorist attacks showed all too clearly that permanent peace had not broken out even if the Cold War had ended and that, on the contrary, America faced many new problems all over the world. Following September 11 new funding became available, and not only regarding the study of terrorism, and the think tanks, to use the language of track and field, got a second wind. As far as terrorism was concerned, the think tanks could not compete with the various government agencies, for much classified knowledge was involved and the few experts on Islam were found in the academic world. But there was a general consensus that more knowledge was needed, and the think tanks benefited.

Terrorism, including Islamist radicalism and similar phenomena, had been neglected if not ignored for many years. It was amazing to watch how within a very short period a whole legion of experts on these topics emerged in the think tanks and outside. It was easy to deride these instant experts, but in some respects it was also an admirable phenomenon. Men and women who had not been aware of the difference between *jihad* and *zakat* were now discussing with great assurance finer points of Muslim theology. It was impressive how America produced experts on topics that had been neglected. This had also been the case during World War II, when Japanese speakers were urgently needed, and during the Cold War, when Russian expertise was very much in demand as well as some knowledge about communism. It was also the case in the 1990s when civil wars broke out in the Balkans and men and women who had never heard of Sarajevo, let alone Prstina or Banja Luka, very quickly got a working knowledge of Serbian and Albanian affairs.

True, a little knowledge can be a dangerous thing, and it frequently happened that the newly baked experts tended to forget that their newly acquired knowledge was quite shallow, that it did not extend to a grounding in language, history, cultural, and political traditions of the countries concerned, and that their expertise, however useful, could not possibly replace the judgment of those who had given a lifetime of study to these subjects. Yet it could always be argued that a lifetime of study was no guarantee of good judgment either, for there was always the issue of bias and overinvolvement in the beloved subject.

Foreign Policy Makers

Enoch Powell, the British Conservative politician, once said that all political careers end in failure. But this assertion is by no means correct, unless the individuals in question are incompetent or unlucky or outstay their welcome on top. It is true, however, that since World War II American secretaries of state and other leading officials in this general field have not done too well. The same could be argued with regard to presidents and other leading politicians, but less so, and this is in many ways surprising, because the differences of opinion and the passions involved in domestic affairs are usually stronger than in foreign affairs.

But foreign affairs were not always such treacherous ground. Even a brief look at events in the twentieth century (let alone the nineteenth century) tends to show that the foreign ministers of even minor countries such as Eleftherios Venizelos of Greece or Nicolae Titulescu of Romania acquired considerable international reputations. Aristide Briand and Gustav Stresemann were celebrated as protagonists of world peace. Maxim Litvinov was a name to conjure with. So was Anthony Eden, despite his many setbacks in later years.

Today the names of the foreign ministers of major countries are often unknown, or if known, rapidly forgotten. As these lines are written, on the eve of the French elections of 2007, it would be difficult to find more than one person in a thousand (and not many inside France) able to state the name of the present incumbent. Later on Nicolas Sarkozy appointed Bernard Kouchner, a well-known and popular figure in France, but his earlier experience had not been in power politics.

In the United States in the early twentieth century, Secretaries of State Charles Evans Hughes, Frank Kellogg, and Henry Stimson left their positions with their reputations intact or even enhanced. All three were lawyers by training and had some (but not much) experience in foreign policy. Hughes later became chief justice of the Supreme Court. Kellogg had been ambassador to Britain and taken part in international conferences. He was awarded the Nobel Peace Prize for his efforts to have war outlawed. Stimson had served as governor-general of the Philippines and later became one of the most successful secretaries of war; he had served in the same position before World War I.

It could be argued that the high reputation of these and other leading officials in the field were not justified. Within a few years Kellogg's peace policies appeared to be illusory. Cordell Hull, who served as secretary of state for eleven years, is now remembered mainly for the spadework he did concerning the foundation of the United Nations, but the importance of this organization, the focus of so many hopes, fell far short of what had been expected. Stimson closed the cryptanalytic section of the State Department, thus largely depriving America of a vital intelligence capacity. His justification—"gentlemen do not read each other's mail"—was based on the assumption that players in international affairs were all gentlemen. But to repeat once again, Stimson and Hull, too, left their positions with their records unblemished. They were not really expected to show major initiatives but to defend American interests, which were then quite limited. There was little criticism at the time of foreign policy makers, and the media had not yet set themselves up as a semi-official opposition with a vested interest in tearing down reputations.

Foreign policy makers in the postwar period fared much less well. There have been close to twenty secretaries of state since 1945, and about the same number of national security advisers and directors of central intelligence. Their earlier background is of interest: among the secretaries of state, lawyers—such as William Rogers, Warren Christopher, and Cyrus Vance—prevailed. Their distinguishing mark was great caution. There were also university professors, but there were only two military men—George Marshall and Colin Powell—and only two who had spent much of their earlier career in the Department of State, Dean Acheson and Dean Rusk. Some were strong personalities, including Acheson, John Foster Dulles, and Henry Kissinger; others were rather colorless and were forgotten soon after leaving office.

Among the directors of central intelligence, two other groups prevailed—military men and officials who had made some or much of their earlier career inside CIA. These include Richard Helms, William Colby, Robert Gates, George Tenet, and Porter Goss. Among them the rate of failure (or mishaps) was even higher. President John Kennedy had suggested, when he visited CIA headquarters in Langley, Virginia, that their successes did not become known, while their failures were trumpeted from the rooftops. I shall deal with some of the problems facing intelligence later on; here suffice it to say that expectations with regard to the intelligence services have always and everywhere been too high, and they greatly contribute to the often unrealistic expectations of contemporaries and posterity. Solid and extensive knowledge of the resources and intentions of a rival or enemy has been the exception, not the rule. But while nobody in his or her right mind would blame a secretary of agriculture for a bad harvest, accusations of "intelligence failure" have been very frequent indeed.

How well prepared were these key figures for their job? Here again much depended on expectations, but very few had a good grounding in world affairs. Still, international politics had become so complicated and fragmented in the postwar period that no high official could possibly be equally at home in all aspects. Before World War II American interests had been limited and so were the number of major factors in world politics. After 1945 this situation radically changed, and if the secretary of state or the head of CIA surrounded himself by competent senior advisers whom he could trust, and if he ensured the more or less smooth functioning of his department, which had grown tenfold or more, that was about the best that one could do.

In retrospect, it seems that success and failure depended much more on luck than on the knowledge or other personal characteristics of the secretary of state or the director of central intelligence. That George Shultz and to a certain extent James Baker emerged from their trials in office relatively unscathed had much to do with the fact that they were lucky, for their tenure coincided with the breakup of the Soviet empire. Kissinger, probably the most formidable intellect in the postwar period, was less lucky because his main assignment was to extricate the United States from a lost war, a situation in which a Nobel Prize but not many other laurels could be earned. The fact that an open mind was more important than the intensive study of world affairs was borne out by the case of Zbigniew Brzezinski. A professor at leading universities, a person of quick intelligence, and a student of global affairs, full of new ideas, he was not a success in office. It is true that he served under a weak president, but he might therefore have had more, rather than less, influence and greater freedom of action. He was also unlucky inasmuch as his party, the Democrats, tended to be very dovish at the time, whereas he was an activist by temperament.

Some presidents, such as Richard Nixon, took a greater interest in foreign policy than others. Franklin Roosevelt, by contrast, often ignored Cordell Hull, and John Kennedy's attitude towards Dean Rusk was not much different. European prime ministers, including Margaret Thatcher and Tony Blair, Helmut Kohl and Gerhard Schröder, François Mitterrand and Jacques Chirac, listened to their chief foreign policy experts but for better or worse took the vital decisions by themselves. The same is true for most countries. All over the world important decisions are increasingly taken by presidents and prime ministers. These leaders often dispatch special emissaries to foreign capitals, especially in crisis situations, usually to the despair of the professional diplomats, who feel themselves ignored or sidelined. Moreover modern means of communications have made the work of ambassadors less important; their assignments are now more in the field of public relations than in high policy or diplomacy. Power has been centralized more and more in the hands of the chief executive. There have been, as always, exceptions, especially if the foreign minister or the ambassador managed to hang on to his position for many years—Hans Dieter Genscher in Germany or Prince Bandar bin Sultan, the Saudi ambassador to Washington, could serve as examples—but these were not many. One could detect, by and large, a decline in the caliber of the foreign ministers and ambassadors, but it is doubtful that their decreasing lack of power is the decisive reason.

What did matter in the past and what very much matters now is the question of access to the main center of power. But this obvious fact had been known centuries ago to Niccolò Machiavelli, Baldassare Castiglione, and others writing for the benefit of advisers and courtiers.

The Intelligence Community

On two occasions in my life, early on and again in the early 1980s, I was a member of committees in which capacity I had in the course of several months access to secret information. The subjects were not of world-shaking importance, but the issue of intelligence as a tool of political decision making has intrigued me for a long time. Around 1982 an American foundation, the Twentieth Century Fund, commissioned me to write a book- length report on the subject; it was published as *World of Secrets*. In retrospect I doubt whether my findings constituted a significant contribution, but for me it was certainly an educational experience. In the course of my inquiry I interviewed all living directors of central intelligence, some of their deputies, and heads of other American, and some European, intelligence services. They were polite but not too eager to share their innermost thoughts with me. More often than not we had lunch in a Washington club, and all things considered I made some useful discoveries, such as the fact that some of them would hold their hands in front of their mouth while talking in a public place for there was always the danger of lip reading from a distance. I even had several lunches with the legendary Jim Angleton, head of the CIA's counterintelligence for many years. But though (I think) he liked me, he was unwilling to tell me who exactly had smuggled out of Moscow the text of

Nikita Khrushchev's famous 1956 speech denouncing Joseph Stalin, a milestone in the history of the Soviet Union and Eastern Europe. This was a topic of great interest to me as a historian, but even though in Mikhail Gorbachev's days, when our conversations took place, the whole issue was of purely academic interest, he was unwilling to share his knowledge. I had to find the information elsewhere, a year or two later.

After a little while it became clear to me that my endeavor was foolhardy. To be valid and innovative, a report of the kind I had undertaken could be prepared only by a group of former highly placed intelligence officials with a lifetime of experience behind them, not by an outsider. But it was highly doubtful that such senior individuals would undertake such a project. They would be hampered by professional habits acquired during a lifetime of service—the habit of keeping truly important information to themselves even after it had ceased to be of any practical importance, not to mention other inhibitions too numerous to list.

How can suitable candidates be recruited for intelligence services at a time when a young lawyer earns a salary far in excess of even the most senior (supergrade) intelligence officials? There are other motives that may induce young men and women to sign up, such as the lust for excitement and adventure, but most jobs in intelligence involve neither. On many campuses CIA is not permitted to send its recruiters, and the general climate is rather hostile, as students are told by some of their professors that America is imperialist and aggressive. To serve one's country is not a duty but a career burden to be evaded. True, such attitudes do not prevail everywhere, and intelligence services in America and Europe have so far found sufficient candidates for all openings. But whether they have found the best and the brightest is yet another issue. All things considered, the motivation and the talent of the first and second generation of the CIA were certainly higher than in later years.

Study in a university does provide some of the knowledge needed in certain fields of intelligence—for instance, in the scientific field and so far as the mastery of languages is concerned. But academic political science and international relations are seldom a good preparatory school. However, this problem could be put right without undue difficulty if the services provided good training courses of their own.

A hundred or even fifty years ago a higher proportion of Americans were immigrants from overseas who had a better understanding of their countries of origin than schooling can provide. Generally speaking, the work of an eighteenth- or nineteenth-century spy was much easier than it is now. The number of countries that mattered was much smaller; the ruling classes were cosmopolitan by background and outlook and often quite literally spoke the same language. Today America, despite all the foreign travel, suffers from the parochialism of bigness. After the terrorist attacks of 9/11 and the Iraq War, a great many books and articles appeared written by former intelligence officials and others who had been connected in one way or another with the intelligence community. They found much to blame (except usually themselves), and some of the accusations of lack of coordination and so on were no doubt correct. On the whole, however, it was embarrassing to watch the appearance of those as gurus and advisers who had failed in their assignments prior to 9/11. The deeper sources of the weakness of intelligence were seldom mentioned—the fact that there were so few people with the knowledge of the essential languages, deeply steeped in the culture, the religion, the mentality, the way of life of the societies with which they should have been dealing, and also reasonably unbiased in their political outlook.

The same is true with regard to the think tanks and the media. Among the position papers and books written in recent years about subjects such as *jihad* or other aspects of the present crisis, many were produced by authors who had neither the linguistic background nor the general knowledge needed to deal with these subjects. During the Cold War I knew a very few experts (such as Richard Löwenthal) whose judgment on things Soviet could be trusted even though they did not know Russian. They had been Communists in their younger days and had acquired familiarity with the subject in other ways. Among the China experts there were quite a few whose knowledge of Chinese was far from perfect, but this was probably inevitable in view of the difficulty of this language.

Success in managing intelligence has been very rare indeed. Of the directors of central intelligence, Allen Dulles, John McCone, William Raborn, Richard Helms, Jim Woolsey, George Tenet, and Porter Goss were forced to resign, and William Colby, Stansfield Turner, and William Casey were under bitter criticism as they ended their careers. George Bush senior was not reappointed, John Negroponte asked to be relieved, and the few in the list that remain were only for a short time in office and seem not to have been too happy either. A great deal of ambition or patriotism (or a mixture of the two) must be necessary to accept this job, frequently considered "mission impossible." The situation is not helped by the media portrayal of intelligence operations and operators (above all by television and in movies) as tawdry, evil, sloppy, and/or demonic.

One of the main preconditions for intelligence success is access to the leading policy makers. The best intelligence is useless unless it reaches the president and his top advisers, but this is seldom the case. Most presidents have had no great confidence in the intelligence community or simply were not interested. In many instances even the head of central intelligence has had only sporadic access. According to reports, President Bill Clinton did not see his chief of intelligence even once in two years. There were exceptions—John Foster Dulles was the brother of the then head of the CIA, and William Casey had for a while a fairly close relationship with President Ronald Reagan; he was the first head of

CIA given a seat in the cabinet. Later John Deutch also got a seat, but it did not really strengthen his position.

Even the best intelligence is pointless unless the political decision makers show interest in it. There is the classic case of Joseph Stalin, who had all the information about an impending German attack at his disposal, but since it did not fit his preconceived notion—he thought that the enormous German buildup in Eastern Europe was a giant feint—he threatened to have those who supplied the unwelcome information shot. One was Pavel Fitin, the head of the KGB (at that time NKVD) foreign intelligence, whose warning Stalin dismissed as disinformation. There is the frequent, though perhaps less dangerous, problem of decision makers believing that they are better interpreters of intelligence than the professionals, hence their demand to see "raw intelligence" and to be their own analysts.

Why have the operations of intelligence services in democratic societies become so difficult and the results often so meager? It has to do with a number of circumstances, beginning perhaps with an inherent contradiction. Most jobs in intelligence demand no superior intellectual talent; solid competence and common sense (admittedly not as common as commonly believed) will do. But at least some measure of daring is occasionally needed, some courage—not necessarily of the physical variety but the willingness to disregard routine, to stick one's neck out. In short, what is needed is a nonbureaucratic approach.

In our day, however, intelligence is part of the bureaucracy, and this situation creates problems for which there are no easy solutions—and perhaps no solutions at all. Furthermore, intelligence must involve secrecy to be effective, but government service in a democracy according to established wisdom should not be secret but open to public scrutiny, transparent, and there should be strict supervision.

How can such conflicting demands produce satisfactory functioning? No ideal formula has been found. Intelligence services have frequently engaged in what the KGB euphemistically called "active measures," but by and large even the Soviets were not very successful at these; they did not prevent the collapse of the Soviet Union. As for the Western intelligence service, above all American intelligence, the majority of clandestine activities ended in failure as far as can be established. Sometimes it was the law of unforeseen consequences that defeated them. An example is the massive delivery of weapons to the anti-Soviet insurgents in Afghanistan following the initiative of Brzezinski and his successors—which led to the emergence of the Taliban and al-Qaeda. Almost always these active measures were in contravention of the law in democratic societies in peacetime. They might have been salutary and prevented disasters, but they were not compatible with the laws and regulations of intelligence services. Sooner or later they became known and led to scandals and worse.

Intelligence Failure

One of the central issues widely discussed following World War II, and ever after, is intelligence failure. There were the failure of intelligence to give a warning at the outbreak of the Korean War, the Bay of Pigs intelligence failure, and the failure to secure data on the missile gap. A colleague on one of my committees, Roberta Wohlstetter, wrote a fine study of Pearl Harbor as an intelligence failure that has become a classic (*Pearl Harbor,* 1962). She showed in great and convincing detail that while there had been many signals pointing to an attack there had also been a great deal of "noise," causing confusion. She also made it clear that, however much intelligence was improved, it would never provide total certainty—the kind of certainty decision makers always want.

The causes of intelligence failure have been constantly studied, but all the analysis has not prevented subsequent failures—from the lack of preparedness of the Israelis on the eve of the Yom Kippur War, to the disintegration of the Soviet empire, to the rise of Islamic radicalism leading to the terrorist attacks of 9/11. In fact, the history of intelligence failures (and strategic deception) is as old as the hills. The Old Testament mentions espionage on at least a hundred occasions, and there is a great deal of surprise and deception. A classic example is found in the book of Judges, where Gideon beats the Midianites and Amalekites with a mere three hundred men. He provided each fighter with a trumpet and a jar and they made an infernal noise, scaring the wits out of the enemies, making them believe that the forces facing them were much larger than they had assumed.

The famous Trojan horse is yet another example. It involved a very unlikely technological breakthrough, for what kind of wooden horse would carry forty warriors, though estimates vary greatly. Moreover, chances are that the Trojans would have taken the wooden horse apart wherever they found it rather than bring it into the city walls. The Greeks who had besieged Troy for many years accompanied the operation with a detailed deception maneuver: they pretended to lift the siege and to return home, whereas they only retreated to the nearby island of Tenedos. Lastly they sent a double agent to Troy to spread this falsehood.

Not every political and military culture in history thought equally highly of intelligence. The Romans, for instance, had their spies and informers (*speculatores* and *frumentarii*), but being proud and arrogant they did not pay much attention to the intelligence gathered, believing that they would defeat their enemies anyway. For this they had to pay a price from time to time. The German prince Arminius, chief of the Cherusci, who lived in Rome as a Roman citizen and commanded a detachment under Varus, the Roman commander in Germany, secretly planned a rebellion. Eventually, in the Teutoburg forest, he inflicted one of the most painful defeats on the Romans that they ever suffered. The event allegedly caused Emperor Augustus have a nervous breakdown, shouting: "Oh Varus—give me back my legions!" In the twentieth century Adolf Hitler was among those who did not pay much attention to intelligence; thus he underrated, among other things, Soviet military preparedness and capacity. He also underrated U.S. military strength; Germany had made the same mistake in World War I, as Walther Nicolai, the head of German military intelligence, later conceded. That Nicolai was merely a colonel tends to show the low standing of intelligence in the German military hierarchy at the time.

My impression was that more often than not the importance of intelligence has been overrated, or to be precise, the expectations attached to it have been too high. This became the main theme of my book *World of Secrets*. True, Sun Tzu, the overquoted sixth-century B.C. author of *The Art of War*, wrote that he who knows his adversary can win hundreds of battles. Frederick II of Prussia wrote if one knew the enemy's intentions beforehand one could always defeat him, even with an inferior number. Napoleon once said that a well-placed spy was worth at least two divisions, but in his campaigns he did not pay much attention to intelligence, perhaps because he knew that the enemy's intentions could always change.

Sun Tzu should have added that intelligence was important—other things being equal and assuming that the right lessons were drawn from it. But intelligence by itself could not account for much. Polish intelligence and the French Deuxième Bureau were professionally second to none, certainly better than German espionage at the time, and yet the Poles and the French were defeated in record time whereas Germany, despite its intelligence weakness, was very successful during the *Blitzkrieg* period. There is also the paradoxical effect of intelligence failures: Pearl Harbor was a stunning defeat and so was 9/11, but seen in a wider perspective, would it have been possible to galvanize America into action but for these disasters?

The recent history of intelligence is also the history of countless committees and reports aiming at reform. Some of this endeavor was successful, but very often these were pointless enterprises because intelligence services need continuity and frequent changes adversely affect their performance. Furthermore, it always takes a number of years to carry out a reform, and by the time it is accomplished the overall situation has changed. Moreover, it is doubtful whether basic shortcomings, such as the weakness of American human intelligence and the too heavy dependence on technical means of collecting information, could be changed by a committee resolution. As terrorism became more frequent and more dangerous, human intelligence gained even more in importance.

Some committees were appointed to strengthen oversight—notably the Senate committee on intelligence gathering headed by Frank Church, following revelations in 1975 about misdeeds, real or alleged, committed by the CIA in Vietnam and elsewhere. But this oversight largely caused paralysis among officials, many of whom were already inclined to err on the side of caution, not to stick their neck out, not to endanger their careers. For if, for instance, a committee had decided that it was impermissible for a member of the intelligence committee to maintain contact with a person involved in terrorism, it was unlikely that American intelligence would know much about happenings among the terrorist groups—a difficult problem in any case. Thus a direct line leads from the Church committee to 9/11.

What, then, have been the main causes of bad intelligence and intelligence failure? It has been said that God created the world very unfairly because there is an unlimited number of things that may go wrong and only one way that they may get right. First, it ought to be made clear that intelligence is a craft, not a science. There are many scientific elements in intelligence (as in medicine), but in the final analysis intelligence rests on experience and good judgment—*Fingerspitzengefühl,* as one former director of central intelligence has put it. This German term means having a sure instinct, an intuitive understanding of something. Richard Helms, the DCI in question, had served as young newspaperman in prewar Berlin.

There is no scientific prediction in intelligence despite all efforts to make intelligence more scientific, to transform the study of international affairs from folklore to science. During the 1960s and 1970s intelligence theoreticians were looking very hard for a strong and coherent theoretical framework, for operational indicators that were accurate, standardized, comparable, and measurable so as to predict, for instance, *coups d'état* or revolutions. These theoretical innovators borrowed from social psychology (decision making), management (operations research), mathematics (game theory), communication theory, and even biology (general systems), anthropology, and other fields. While some put the emphasis on simulation, the psychologists focused on the importance of perception and misperception. Recruits to the field had to familiarize themselves with the Bayesian theorum. The Reverend Thomas Bayes (1702–1761) had developed an approach to probabilistic prediction, recalculating the probability of a certain event or development in light of new information. The basic idea behind these attempts to make intelligence scientific and to make prediction possible was simple. Everyone accepted the advantages of a lifetime of accumulated knowledge concerning foreign languages, cultures, and general exposure to "thinking as foreigners did." But most intelligence operatives were not specialists, did not have such a valuable background, and were unlikely to acquire one in the foreseeable future, if ever. Were no shortcuts available provided by the social sciences to help those lacking such knowledge? True, the social sciences offered only probabilities, which were not laws; they could not predict individual events.

But was not prediction in terms of odds an advance over the "prescientific generalizations" used in the past?

The problems were more basic. No one doubted that statistics and probability theory in particular provide a powerful tool for handling numerical data. But how could fears and ambitions, religion and nationalism, or as Hans Morgenthau once noted, the struggle for power, be quantified? Game theory is based on the assumption that decisions are based on rational strategies and that the rules of the game are known. However, the "rational man model" was applicable only in part to Stalin and much less to Hitler. Game theorists have argued that the outbreak of war in 1939 was an untypical exception. However, in my research in the 1980s I soon realized that in our age these untypical exceptions have become the rule rather than the exception, and this was well before the emergence of Islamic terrorism and Mahmoud Ahmadinejad.

Looking back over a century of intelligence achievements and failures, one finds that even long ago intelligence was quite often right in assessing the numerical strength of the enemy. Having underestimated the German buildup for several years, British intelligence in late 1938 (well before it could intercept German communications) estimated that the Germans would have 3,700 aircraft by the end of 1939, and in fact when war broke out in September 1939 the Germans had exactly 3,647 planes. Sometimes mistakes canceled each other out. In the late phase of the Cold War American analysts overrated the Soviet GNP, but on the other hand they underrated the extent of the allocations for military purposes. Sometimes wrong or exaggerated intelligence had, paradoxically, a long-term beneficial effect. It could be that toward the end of the Cold War America spent more than necessary on defense, overrating the Soviet military danger, but this arms race contributed decisively to the breakup of the Soviet Union and the end of the Cold War, as the Soviet leaders realized that they were too weak to compete in the long run.

What can we make of the American misjudgment concerning Iraq and weapons of mass destruction—the National Intelligence Estimate of October 2002? According to the available evidence there was no deliberate attempt by the White House to mislead the public in this respect (though critics of the administration argued otherwise), and Saddam Hussein did all he could to create the impression that not all the weapons he had once possessed had been destroyed. It was a genuine intelligence failure, just as during the Cold War the CIA had at various times both overrated and underrated Soviet military capacities. Washington would have been reasonably certain about Iraq's military capabilities if there had been massive defections of scientists whose information could have been checked by other means. There were a few defections, and some provided false or misleading information. Short of this, intelligence was likely to proceed on the time-honored principle that "we never know what we do not know" in the fog of prewar.

Nazism and Hitler, in comparison, were the subject of fewer blatant misapprehensions. Few American journalists stationed in Berlin in the 1930s had illusions about the Nazi regime. And yet small was the number of those who clearly saw in what direction Hitler's policies would lead. One of these was Sir Horace Rumbold, British ambassador to Berlin who in his final, concluding dispatch to London predicted in 1933 that Hitler's policies were bound to lead to war and that there was an element of madness in Nazism and its leaders. Rumbold was not an "antifascist," a man of the left or a liberal, but a conservative with all the values and prejudices of his class and background, but he seems to have had an instinctive understanding of politics that many contemporary observers lacked. He had served all over the world, including in Berlin in 1914, but this background did not necessarily prepare him for the situation in 1933. Why did he see the situation far more clearly than most? More thought and study should be given to such remarkable incidents of clear thinking and accurate prediction.

This sort of analysis should include, of course, also the reverse—possible reasons for misjudgments frequently on the part of intellectuals. If certain right-wing French intellectuals supported Nazism in the 1930s and 1940s, the reason more often than not was not naiveté; they did know well what they let themselves in for. But if G. B. Shaw and some others became enthusiastic about Benito Mussolini and later about Stalin, the reason must have been ignorance.

Among the reasons of intelligence failures, apart from those caused by deception, the most frequently mentioned are mirror imaging and the "has not happened here" (or in the technical field, "has not been invented here") syndrome, the compartmentalization of intelligence (meaning the left hand not knowing what the right is doing), group think, and bias. It is true that intelligence services are unwieldy, hierarchical organizations, and there is always the danger that warning signals may be lost or filtered out in the bureaucratic channels. Mirror imaging has been a problem particularly in democratic societies. Americans, especially, have found it difficult to understand how dictatorships work, let alone the importance of radical ideologies or religion. They may be aware of the problems on an intellectual level, but that alone does not take them very far. Being citizens of a free society in which the rule of law prevails, they never lived under foreign occupation. Many still find it difficult to understand certain elementary truths about life in nondemocratic societies that are self-evident to members of such societies, and the behavior of political leaders of such a regime may largely remain enigmatic.

A report on the Cyprus crisis in 1974 put this point in a nutshell (I quoted it in *World of Secrets*): "There was the perhaps subconscious conviction and hope that ultimately reason will prevail, that apparently irrational moves will not be made by essentially rational men." Even now there is always the danger that the analyst desperately in need of certainties will be tempted to underestimate the element of doubt and uncertainty, of faulty and incomplete information on the other side. He may underrate irrational and immeasurable factors and attribute too much rational calculation and planning to the opponent, thus bringing artificial order into an essentially disorderly situation.

How can such misjudgments be prevented? There are no ready-made solutions, not even the lessons of history. The writings of Karl Marx and V. I. Lenin did not contribute to an understanding of the Pol Pot massacres in Cambodia. National interest is of course of vital importance, but it will not explain Stalin's purges or Mao Zedong's Cultural Revolution. The idea that conflicts stem from misperceptions could be true in some cases, but Mussolini did not misunderstand the Ethiopians when he attacked their country in 1935; nor did the two sides in the Spanish Civil War misinterpret each other's intentions, and Hitler's desire to dominate Europe did not stem from cognitive failure. Intelligence analysts have been advised to steep themselves in the theory of cognitive dissonance and to read Thomas Kuhn's *Structure of Scientific Revolutions* (1962). These ideas will certainly broaden their cultural horizons, but they will not help them understand Islamism or the Arab-Israeli conflict. For if two nations want the same territory, this is a genuine conflict, not a cognitive problem.

There has been a tendency in the intelligence community to regard bias as the worst evil, the most important single source of error. But as a great historian, G. M. Trevelyan, once noted, bias is not necessarily good or bad, but it is inevitable. St. Augustine affirmed that nothing can be known except through sympathy, but hate can also sharpen the senses. Edmund Burke's *Reflections on the Revolution in France* (1790) is a good example. Here was a deeply prejudiced political observer who wrote at a time when France was still a monarchy and hardly anyone had ever heard of Georges Danton or Maximilien Robespierre. Men and women of goodwill all over Europe were welcoming the new freedom that had come to France; the young William Wordsworth exulted, "Bliss was it in that dawn to be alive." An observer free of bias could have argued that there would be no violent convulsions, that the period of turbulence was more or less over, and that now that the last vestiges of absolutism had been removed, France would become a constitutional monarchy more or less like England. Burke, however, instinctively knew that this was not true, that the revolution was only beginning, that it would gather impetus and ferocity, that it would lead to despotism, and that it would end in a military dictatorship. It was by inductive reasoning on a deeper level of political understanding that he realized that something in the social and political order had been broken, that the restraints mitigating despotism had been removed, and that the revolution would have to run its course.

The case of Burke—and it would be easy to bring similar examples of contemporary observers with regard to the Russian and Chinese Revolutions—tends to show that bias is unavoidable and may even play a positive role. It does not follow that one may in good conscience suppress evidence, and since the ideal of impartiality is unattainable, one person's view is as good as another's. Trevelyan, whom we have quoted in defense of bias, also stressed that it must never interfere with the collection and collation of facts.

On the whole, intelligence failures have perhaps less often occurred with regard to "hard facts" such as the production and existence of arms than with regards to intentions. This observation appears at first surprising because it should be easier to hide the production of arms than political intentions, unless of course a ruler, or a group of rulers, only recently appeared on the political scene and has no track record. But at this point cultural bias enters the picture—the inability to understand the mental makeup of leaders rooted in a wholly different tradition. After World War I there was a great desire among the victors to live in peace, to be preoccupied with domestic problems; foreign affairs were considered an unwelcome intrusion. There was the widespread belief that all enlightened societies were interested in the maintenance of the status quo. This cultural bias prevented the European democracies from recognizing the dangers emanating from the European dictatorships.

There is, to repeat once again, an endless number of factors that may lead to bad intelligence or bad interpretation. The so-called lessons of history are very useful, even vital in some instances, but they can be very misleading in other circumstances, and it is the task of the analysts to know when to invoke them and when to disregard them.

Intelligence Failures on Islamic Terrorism

Much vital intelligence has always been available from open sources, and now more than ever in the age of the computer, and yet not much use has been made of them. It was, I believe, only relatively recently (under Negroponte) that a department dealing with open sources was established at CIA—the DNI Open Source Center. This center traces its history back to the FBIS (Foreign Broadcast Information Service) founded in 1941, when it monitored and translated German and Italian radio broadcasts. In later years FBIS concentrated on Soviet radio and newspapers; Chinese materials were monitored by another organization in Hong Kong. This was an important service, but it was probably used by the scholarly community more than by intelligence. Furthermore, the important raw material was apparently not analyzed like other intelligence information, certainly not in a systematic way. This service continued after the Cold War, but the circumstances had changed to a certain extent. Al-Qaeda and similar groups had neither radio nor television stations, but they were very active blogging on the Internet. Furthermore, there was a whole illegal or semilegal literature available if one knew where to obtain it.

Robert Baer, a CIA operative who had been active for more than twenty years in the Middle East, India, and Central Asia, described in a memoir, *See No Evil* (2002), how he walked along Edgware Road, London, and found in the Arab bookshop there very illuminating information—books and pamphlets banned in most Middle Eastern countries. He realized that his colleagues at the London station were not aware of this literature, and they would not have been able to read it anyway. However, much was also available in English, for most Muslims in Britain and also in other European countries do not read Arabic.

I had made a similar discovery years earlier—in Edgware Road, in Notting Hill, as well as in little bookshops elsewhere in Europe and in front of many mosques. Specialists in the field knew even better than I where to obtain such material. I refer, for instance, to books by Giles Kepel, Johannes Jansen, a Dutch professor, and Eberhard Serauky, a less-known East German specialist who had spent years teaching at a Egyptian university. The visitor to these bookshops would find the works of Sayyid Qutb and of Abdul-A'la al Mawdoudi, the Pakistani Islamist, as well as the memoirs of Ayman al-Zawahiri, Osama bin Laden's deputy, and of Abdullah Yusuf Azzam, the grandfather of the movement who was killed in Pakistan in circumstances that have not become clear to his day. The intelligence customer would not find in these pamphlets the date and place of the next major terrorist attacks, but there was, for instance, a very interesting history of the "Afghani Arabs," meaning the foreign legion that had congregated in Pakistan and Afghanistan during the 1980s and later fought in the Balkans, Algeria, and other parts of the world. Former President Clinton recently claimed that no one in the early 1990s knew about the danger of aggressive Islamism, but it could have been known if those in intelligence had read the obscure books and pamphlets, legal and illegal, available in a variety of places. There was a great deal of information available on the aims of the Islamists and how they intended to defeat their enemies. There had even been a few Western studies of radical Islamism, but its crucial importance had somehow not registered with most Western experts. It was only after 9/11 that more attention was paid to this new version of *jihad*.

How can this strange omission be explained? Intelligence officials could rightly argue that they, after all, are not the only ones following world affairs, and if research on Islamism had low priority for them, it figured even lower in the research of the media and the academic experts.

A few enterprising correspondents visited Osama bin Laden and interviewed him well before 9/11, but those in search of editorials and analytical articles on this topic in the world's leading newspapers will have to look very hard to discover anything at all. The number of foreign correspondents has greatly shrunk all over the world, except for television crews coming for short visits at a time of crisis. But there were some correspondents in the Middle East as well as in Pakistan and Afghanistan, and unless their editors suppressed their stories, they seem to have missed one of the great unfolding political developments in the 1990s.

Correspondents in our age frequently spend only a relatively short time in the country to which they have been assigned, and their knowledge of local language and culture and of political conditions is limited. But they have local stringers, and they should to a certain extent have been aware of what was happening below the surface. But quite obviously they were not, and if there was an intelligence failure with regard to the rise of Islamism, it was not limited to intelligence professionals. There have been countless articles and many dozens of books in recent years by journalists on intelligence failures, but there have been few if any such writings about the failure of the media to alert the public to coming dangers.

But what of the academic experts, most of whom had at least a working knowledge of languages, traditions, customs, and mentalities, who were spending months and sometimes years abroad? Only a few recognized that something new and very significant was emerging in the Middle East and beyond. One was Bernard Lewis writing in *Foreign Affairs* in 1998, but that was after Osama bin Laden had declared his *jihad*. The other exceptions were the French expert Giles Kepel and Olivier Roy, who provided valuable studies on the subject but erroneously believed that the new movement had already peaked. How can the failure of academics to recognize what was happening underground be explained? It would have been easy to understand had it been a conspiracy of a handful of militants; such plotting is difficult to penetrate and could be overlooked by outsiders. But it was a very open conspiracy, with thousands, even tens of thousands, of members and sympathizers in many countries, with open statements and hardly an attempt to keep the *jihad* secret.

In defense of the mindset of the experts on Islam and the Middle East it could be said that mistakes even by leading experts have been frequent all throughout history. One could think of the first generation of Russian/Soviet experts such as Bernard Pares in Britain and Samuel Harper in the United States who, having been inveterate enemies of the Russian Revolution, became blind believers in Stalinism. If in the 1930s Sidney and Beatrice Webb came to believe in Soviet civilization as one of the wonders of human achievement, this could be explained in view of their ignorance of things Russian, their lack of knowledge of the Russian language, and their general gullibility. But Pares had been a student of Russia and the Soviet Union for many years; so had E. H. Carr and not a few others, and there were no apparent mitigating circumstances in their cases. Or consider John Fairbank, probably the most highly esteemed China expert of his generation: he knew the language, having been born to missionaries to China, and he was steeped in things Chinese. He was not a Communist or a Communist sympathizer. But all this did not prevent him from regarding the late Mao period, including the disastrous Cultural Revolution, as the best thing that had happened to China. More recently we encountered the French postmodernist philosophers; one of them, Michel Foucault, claimed that the Khomeini revolution was the best, the most progressive thing that had ever happened east of Paris. Another, Jean Baudrillard, demonstrated that the Gulf War had never taken place and that 9/11 was the "absolute event," whatever that meant. Their reputations among their admirers were not affected.

Why did the Middle Eastern experts fail to read the signs of the times? A variety of reasons have been adduced, including the fear, perhaps sometimes subconscious, that reports on negative features could adversely affect future stays and contacts in these countries. This syndrome could also be found among journalists and academics during the Cold War with regard to nondemocratic regimes in general: visas could be refused, doors that had been open could suddenly close.

The failure to recognize the arrival on the political scene of militant Islamism must have been motivated to a large extent by political bias. Only very few experts sympathized with this movement, let alone its extreme representatives such as Osama bin Laden. But many apparently thought that giving publicity to these radical forces would strengthen suspicions of Arabs and Muslims in the West and, generally speaking, weaken the Arab cause, which many of them strongly supported. Furthermore, many seem to have genuinely thought that the information about Islamic terrorism was either fabricated or in any case greatly exaggerated by Western terrorism experts who had a vested interest in the creation of bogeymen. And thus the study of militant Islamism (let alone terrorism) was discouraged. It was said to be a greatly overrated phenomenon that really did not amount to much inside the Muslim world.

Intelligence Failures and My Political Education

There has been an enormous amount of literature, especially in the United States, about intelligence failures. However, the basic reasons for these failures are not shrouded in secret. In democratic societies not in a state of war it is difficult if not impossible to attract the most suitable men and women for service in intelligence. They will be hampered in their activities by a myriad of regulations, legal restrictions, and bureaucratic obstacles. And even if they will be in the possession of valuable intelligence, it is doubtful whether they will have access to those in power, their main customers. It is doubtful whether in a country like the United States these difficulties will ever be overcome in peacetime. A secret service involves secrecy, whereas American public opinion demands openness.

Some intelligence failures may be inevitable, others are not. What makes for good political judgment? This has remained a neglected subject of research, perhaps because it has been realized that there are no shortcuts even in the age of computers. There are no alternatives to human intelligence, especially insofar as intentions are concerned. It is gratifying that albeit with much delay the importance of open sources has been realized. But the quantity of such sources is enormous, and the problem for the uninitiated still is to differentiate between reliable and misleading background information. Political intelligence has not become scientific; it cannot make predictions with scientific accuracy, and this will not change in the foreseeable future. Regrettably, it will remain a cumbersome process, and all the think tanks in the world will not alter its prospects.

In my own life I learned to understand the decisive role of accident. I survived, and so did others I knew, because of having been by mere chance at a certain place at a certain time—or sometimes of not having been there—and such accidents are frequent in history and politics. But this notion is difficult to accept for academic students of politics in search of historical laws and predictability. I learned that lessons from experience might be learned too well, for history never quite repeats itself. Having lived through the age of murderous dictatorships, there is the danger of tending toward worst-case scenarios, but these, too, could be misleading because, as an old saying goes, the worst does not always happen. But this was my personal experience. In the United States, a country never devastated or occupied, the danger is not excessive pessimism but, on the contrary, misplaced optimism, the belief that most of the world's problems are the result of misunderstandings.

CHAPTER 7

Guerrilla Warfare and Terrorism

or, What Systematic Study and Theory Can Mean

My first personal encounter with terrorism took place in Jerusalem not long after the end of World War II. I had visited my dentist, and in the same building, at street level, was a bank, which I entered since I needed cash. Being immersed in my thoughts (or suffering from toothache), I did not realize that a bank robbery was in progress. One of the robbers ordered me to sit or lie down (I forgot which), and since he had a revolver and I had none, I obeyed. The whole thing was over within a few minutes. The robbery was carried out by members of the Irgun, the right-wing anti-British Jewish terrorist movement, and it was not a great success. There was not much money in the bank at the time, and one of the attackers, albeit partly masked, was recognized as the son of a Jewish police officer and arrested the same day or the day after.

The adventure left no major psychological trauma as far as I was concerned. Perhaps it prepared me in a small way for confronting terrorism, however, which was rampant at the time and not only in Palestine, still ruled by the British, but also in neighboring countries. As a young newspaperman I had to report not only the exploits of the Irgun and the Stern gang but also on terrorism in Egypt, where several leading politicians were killed by terrorists. These included Ahmad Mahir Pasha in 1945 and Mahmoud Fahmi an-Nokrashi in 1948 and also (in retaliation) Hassan al-Banna, leader of the Muslim Brotherhood, in February 1949. In July 1946, I had been only a few hundred meters from the King David Hotel in Jerusalem when it was blown up by the Irgun, the most deadly terrorist attack up to that the time. Palestinian Arab extremists killed a fair number of their leaders, such as Fakhri Nashashibi, because of internal feuds or because they were not sufficiently anti-Zionist. Fawzi Husseini, murdered in 1946, was another; he had dared to establish contact with Jewish public figures advocating a bi-national state. As Jamal Husseini, a leader of the Arab community in Palestine observed (and I quoted him in *Dying for Jerusalem)*, "Our cousin has stumbled and received his just punishment." Sami Taha, the Haifa workers' leader, was another major public figure to be assassinated, in September 1947, probably by Palestinian Arab terrorists on orders of Haj Amin al-Husseini, the grand mufti of Jerusalem, because he was too independent. My home at the time in

Jerusalem was a few minutes' walk from where Count Folke Bernadotte, the UN mediator, was ambushed and killed by the Stern gang in September 1948, but I missed the murder of King Abdullah of Jordan while he was praying in the Old City in Jerusalem in 1951.

After that terrorism in the Middle East died down, at least for the next two decades. While it lasted, the violence provided a great deal of fascination, and the appetite of the media was insatiable. But I did not find it overexciting, and politically it seemed to me much overrated. If the British left Palestine, and Egypt and the Middle East in general, the part played by the terrorists was a modest one, even though they claimed a great deal of credit. The main reason was that Britain had been weakened as the result of World War II, and once the British decided to give up India and their other possessions in South Asia, the strategic positions in the Middle East, which had served as something like a land bridge, were no longer vitally needed.

The History and Theory of Guerrilla Warfare

Guerrilla warfare has been recurrent throughout recorded history and probably also before. It stands to reason that it antedates regular warfare because the complex organization of regular armies, with their supplies and logistics, was beyond the capacity of primitive man and remains difficult and expensive even today. Surprise attacks by small units, on the other hand, do not involve a great deal of sophistication. My research on the history of guerrilla warfare and terrorism took me to Madrid and Helsinki, to Vienna and Dublin, and to many other places in search of materials on partisan warfare. And what I found confirmed what I had suspected: that the principles of guerrilla warfare had by no means been invented by Mao Zedong or Che Guevara but had been known and practiced for centuries.

World War II and the decade thereafter were the high tide of guerrilla warfare; never before or after had this kind of armed conflict been more widespread and more successful. There had always been a tendency to exaggerate its importance, perhaps because of its romantic element and a certain heroism absent when big armies confronted each other. After the war great claims were made for the role of insurgencies. But these were a myth. The partisans in the rear of the German armies had not, in fact, been important to the outcome of the war, nor Josip Broz Tito's partisans, nor the Polish Armia Krajowa. Tito's partisans were probably the most successful of the lot, for they fought heroically and even their opponents admired them. Their achievements were significant for the power struggle in Yugoslavia after the war, but their impact on the German war effort was small. Some claimed they compelled the Germans to keep divisions in Yugoslavia that might have been deployed elsewhere. The truth is that the Germans kept three or four divisions in the country while they kept ten divisions in Norway, a country without partisans or insurgencies.

Imperial overstretch has often sparked insurgencies, but almost always with limited success. The Spanish *guerrilleros* did not defeat Napoleon, and the Russian partisans of 1812–13, including the celebrated Denis Davydov, appeared on the scene only after Napoleon's defeat on the battlefield. On the other hand, the myth about the invincibility of insurgents received fresh impetus following Mao Zedong's victory in China, the French defeats in Indochina and Algeria, and the American defeat in Indochina as well as the more recent difficulties encountered in Afghanistan and Iraq. However, if historical evidence teaches anything it is that each situation is different. Insurgents have been successful when the incumbents were preoccupied with fighting a war on other fronts; the case of Mao is the best known and most obvious. They have been successful in wars against a colonial power, when the global tide was running against the imperial powers. They have been successful in a few cases in internal wars when central power was weak or very inefficient, with Fidel Castro's Cuba as the prime example. They have been successful if they received massive help from a neighboring country. But during the last fifty years the great majority of armed conflicts have been internal wars, and in this context, fighting the internal rather than the external enemy, insurgents, guerrillas, and terrorists have failed to make major inroads.

By 1970, when I became interested in the study of political violence, guerrilla warfare had ebbed, the period of decolonization was more or less over, and Communist- or Maoist-inspired fighting was sporadic and not very successful, as in Kerala in southeastern India. This trend was not to change in the following decades. As I began my research I assumed that guerrilla actions and terrorism were more or less the same phenomenon but for the fact that the one took place in the countryside and the other in the big cities. (The term "urban guerrilla" seemed to me a contradiction in terms, and I have seen no reason to change my views.) Gradually it dawned on me that there were fundamental differences between these two—about which more below.

I also realized that while a great deal had been written about specific guerrilla movements, there had been few general studies in living memory. Attempts to develop guerrilla doctrines by Mao and others had been uncritically accepted by friends and enemies alike. But even Mao had been aware that his message did not apply to all countries, that what is possible in China cannot be done in, say, Belgium. In the West more thought had been given to counterinsurgency warfare than to guerrilla warfare and terrorism. Efforts made by some Western observers to explain the guerrilla phenomenon—why it occurred in some places at some times and not in others—seemed to be less than helpful. Why do men rebel, it was asked. But the very posing of the question involved a great many assumptions about both human nature and the perfectibility of societies. Were conformism and obedience the norm, and aggression a deviation? Were political accord and social harmony the norm, and conflict and violence the unfortunate exception?

A survey of guerrilla warfare in modern times showed an almost infinite variety in inspiration, aims, composition, and organization. Some were Communist inspired, others nationalist in character; some were headed by young men, others by old; some of the leaders had military experience, others lacked it; some bands were large, others small; in some the personality of the leader was of paramount importance, in others there was a collective leadership; some lasted for a short time, others for a very long time; some transformed themselves into regular armies, others degenerated into banditry. Some won, and some lost.

How could so many variables be accounted for? The theory that gained the widest currency was the grievance-frustration concept, accepted in various forms by liberals and Marxists alike. It says that men and women will not rebel, risking their lives and property, without good reason, though these good reasons might be a tyrannical political regime, a major economic crisis, the occupation of their country by foreigners, great poverty, or a great gap between the rich and the poor.

The concept seems plausible enough, and it can be taken for granted that if people have no grievances and feel no frustration, they will engage in the pursuit of happiness. But to assess the nature of grievances and measure the level of frustration are not at all easy. In some instances relatively minor grievances have triggered major conflicts, whereas a seemingly intolerable situation has been accepted without demur. In other words, is it perhaps the perception of grievance that counts rather than the "objective" grievance? And how can one account for this diversity in perception?

It has been argued by some interpreters that if governments fulfill popular aspirations they will not lose legitimacy. There will be no violent opposition, and even the critical intellectuals will happily sing their praises. Unfortunately, the principle of virtue rewarded applies no more to political life than to private life. Political reform aiming at greater freedom will not necessarily make terrorism redundant. This might be the case if, for instance, the legitimate demands of a national minority for greater self- rule, or even secession, could be fulfilled by a mutually acceptable compromise. But very often legitimate demands of one group collide with the legitimate demands of another. The state, however well meaning, faces claims that are irreconcilable. If resources are limited, it may have to set priorities that discriminate against some sectors of the population. Moreover, socioeconomic improvement does not immediately increase popular support; these programs more often than not give tangible results only after years or even decades. It is sometimes argued that effective and virtuous governments have nothing to fear, while corrupt and ineffective ones are doomed. But corruption and inefficiency are by no means synonyms, and in any case their relevance to insurgency and guerrilla warfare is not at all obvious. Nor is there any reason to assume that a state or a society can be more perfect than the individuals constituting it. It has also been argued that the most traditional and the most modern societies are the most immune to upheaval, whereas those in between are unstable. Yet as far as rich countries are concerned this is merely stating the obvious; the rural population in these countries is usually small, and would-be guerrillas would not be welcomed with enthusiasm in the American corn belt or by British, French, or German farmers.

Western commentators on guerrilla warfare and terrorism have found it very difficult to accept that these forms of rebellion against authority have not occurred in places where oppression is most brutal and exploitation most severe. Actuality contradicts the grievance-frustration theory. There were no insurgencies against the governments of Nazi Germany or fascist Italy, in the Soviet Union or in Maoist China. There was no insurgency even in Francisco Franco's Spain, a relatively mild dictatorship; only after the dictator had disappeared and his regime dismantled could the Basque ETA expand its operations. Recently there have been no insurgencies in Syria; nor were there any in Saddam Hussein's Iraq, or in Iran after the theocratic regime had established itself.

The reasons are not hard to discern. As Mao observed, the guerrilla is like a fish: it needs water—that is, popular support—to survive and, I might add, a freedom of movement that exists only if the government is relatively liberal or relatively inefficient. If government control and coercion are effective, a guerrilla movement cannot make progress. It is not that dictatorships are free of grievances—on the contrary—but that they permit no outlet for protest; the rebels will be arrested, sent to prison, or shot. Their arrest will not be reported by the mass media, and as it has no palpable political consequences, their sacrifice will be in vain. If intellectuals are alienated they will keep the fact strictly to themselves, for fear of losing their jobs or worse.

Some Western guerrilla and terrorism literature is curiously parochial in its stress on the importance of public opinion, for in a great number of countries public opinion has no way of expressing itself. Resistance in an effective dictatorship is a very difficult and often hopeless endeavor as long as the leader or leaders have not lost self-confidence and feel no compunction about using the means of repression at their disposal. The argument that repression is a two-edged sword, that guerrillas always benefit from government repression, that power is weakest when it resorts to violence, applies to some premodern dictatorships and of course to liberal regimes whose powers of repression are strictly limited. But by and large it is no longer true. The basic lesson (to which we shall have to return because it is not easy to accept) is that a little repression is indeed dangerous but that massive repression very often works.

If political scientists and sociologists have found it difficult to come to terms with the guerrilla phenomenon, legal experts have found it even more difficult. Since World War II many attempts have been made to establish a new basis of legality, a more humanitarian status for guerrillas (and eventually also for terrorists) under the laws of war. For many years the status of the partisan was based on the Brussels Declaration of 1874 and the Hague Conventions. Guerrilla tactics, meaning hostile activities committed by small bodies of soldiers in the enemy's rear during real war, were considered legal, whereas guerrilla warfare was not. According to this argument, organized war has ceased and the individuals engaged in guerrilla war are not bound by the laws of war. If private individuals commit hostilities against their enemies these individuals do not enjoy the privileges of members of armed forces and the enemy has the right to consider them war criminals.

But these legal concepts were not acceptable to most member states of the United Nations, especially the Third World countries that took a more lenient view of irregular warfare—provided they were not at the receiving end of it. The additional Geneva Conventions of 1949 and a variety of subsequent protocols tried to grapple with the status of partisans in internal conflicts, but the lawyers and the politicians could not agree what constituted a state of war, and then there was the question of whether the insurgents could possibly be bound by a convention they had not signed.

For a guerrilla movement, the acceptance of the rules of international law would be absurd, indeed suicidal, a negation of their whole strategy. For it would imply, for instance, that they would have to wear a uniform or at least some distinguishing mark. Imagine a terrorist appearing on the scene in a uniform or with a big sign (like a policeman or soldier) on his shirt or coat, making it known to all and sundry that he is about to engage in an attack.

Guerrillas would of course have lost the element of surprise and anonymity so essential for the success of an operation if they adhered to the rules of war—for instance with regard to prisoners. Guerrillas will mostly not be in a position to take prisoners, whereas regular armies are obliged to do so. The very essence of guerrilla warfare and terrorism rests on the principle of asymmetry—the fact that guerrillas disregard the laws and rules of war that their opponents must observe.

The study of guerrilla warfare teaches above all the importance of geography. Guerrillas have almost always preferred regions that are not easily accessible, such as mountain ranges, forests, and jungles, in which the enemy cannot employ his full strength. Such areas are particularly important in the early period of consolidation and organization, and they retain their uses later as hideouts. In these areas the guerrillas will be relatively unmolested, but there are drawbacks, for if the enemy has a hard time moving about in these inaccessible regions, so do the guerrillas. It will be difficult to obtain food and other supplies. The guerrillas will be relatively safe but also relatively ineffective because they will be able to harass only isolated enemy outposts. Sooner or later they will have to move out and launch major attacks. The ideal guerrilla country should therefore be located not too far from cities and villages. Afghanistan, with its virtually open borders, is ideal guerrilla country, and since the United States and NATO have not in the recent war been willing to station sufficient forces, it was a mistake to get involved in the first place.

With global urbanization, topographical conditions have lost some of their importance. The village can no longer encircle the city, as Mao described his strategy during China's Civil War, if the majority of the population lives in cities. On the other hand, the big Third World conurbations can to a certain extent replace the jungle of yesterday. Thus in predominantly urban societies the main scene of guerrilla warfare is gradually shifting from countryside to city. The drawback is, of course, that guerrilla bases in cities are far less immune to attack.

The etiology of guerrilla war shows that it very often occurs in countries in which such violence is endemic or at least has occurred before. This relationship has to do in part with topographical factors, but also with cultural traditions and socioeconomic development. In advanced societies neither workers nor peasants nor the middle class will feel sufficient enthusiasm to go to the mountains or the jungle. Furthermore, there have been few peasant guerrilla wars in modern times even though peasants may have had very genuine grievances. During the last two centuries guerrilla wars have been the favorite tactics of separatists and national and religious groups, such as in Afghanistan. There have been a few exceptions, notably in Latin America, but they were not successful.

During a certain period after World War II excessive importance was attributed to Marxist-Leninist verbiage on the part of Third World national liberation movements. While anti-imperialism and the rejection of the capitalist mode of modernization certainly played a role, the ideology was usually a mixture of agrarian populism and radical nationalism. The leadership of nineteenth- and early twentieth-century guerrilla movements was in the hands of men of the people, tribal chiefs or religious dignitaries. More recently the guerrilla elite in Latin America and Asia has been middle class, especially of the administrative stratum, the lower mandarins.

Among the motives that induce men and women to join guerrilla bands, patriotism has been the single most important factor, sometimes with an admixture of religious fanaticism. On top of these are a multitude of personal factors—humiliation, material deprivation, a developed social consciousness, boredom, and a thirst for adventure and the romance of guerrilla life. The motives have by no means been altruistic, for guerrilla warfare offers an excellent outlet for aggression and opportunities for settling accounts with personal enemies. It also conveys a great sense of power to those hitherto powerless. There has been tendency not just to employ violence but to glorify it, to consider it a necessary process of self-purification, as advocated by Frantz Fanon. The cause legitimizes the fulfillment of personal ambition and the infliction of cruelty that in other circumstances would be considered inhuman. As Jean-Frédéric Le Miere de Corvey, a theoretician of guerrilla warfare, put it almost two hundred years ago, there can be no guerrilla warfare without hate and fanaticism. Seen in this light, there are parallels among modern guerrilla warfare, terrorism, and fascism, which implant a pattern of dictatorial practices and brutality that perpetuates itself. Graduates of this school do not become apostles of humanism after victory.

Organization and propaganda have always been essential parts of guerrilla warfare. In this respect there are important differences between guerrilla warfare and terrorism that I had overlooked when setting out in my work on political violence and that were ignored in much of the extant literature.

The aim of guerrilla warfare was traditionally to build strength gradually, to organize first small units, to train them, and then to proceed to the mobilization of larger units, which were, if possible, to liberate parts of the country in which an alternative administration was to be set up. In these liberated regions the guerrillas would indoctrinate the population and have their schools, courts of law, and social and political institutions. In the course of time these liberated regions would grow and the guerrillas would operate in still larger units—brigades and even armies—and eventually encircle the big cities and occupy them.

Terrorism, on the other hand, would mainly occur in the cities, and the units involved would by necessity be small. There could be no open political activity or propaganda; if terrorists would try to operate in big units they would expose themselves to the superior firepower of government forces and almost certainly be defeated. On some occasions urban terrorists have managed to set up liberated (or at least no-go) zones, but these have been the exceptions.

This difference between guerrilla warfare on the Maoist or Cuban model and the terrorist campaigns of the 1970s and 1980s was absolutely crucial. The fact that German and Italian terrorists called their units "armies" or at least "brigades" was mere eyewash. Their aim was to use terror as a strategy to demoralize the government by disrupting its control, create a general climate of insecurity, demonstrate their strength, and deter collaborators.

Few guerrilla movements have been opposed in principle to the use of terrorism. It has been used with considerable effect in Vietnam, Afghanistan, and

Algeria. Elsewhere as in Latin America and Greece it has on the whole been counterproductive, antagonizing much of the urban population. More Greeks were killed by EOKA in Cyprus than by British servicemen, more Arabs than Jews by the Palestinian insurgents of 1936–39, many more Arabs by fellow Arabs than by Americans in Iraq. Today democracies face difficulties confronting insurgencies not because they are too weak but because, unlike authoritarian regimes, they are not in a position to apply their full strength.

Why did some guerrilla movements win and others fail? Success and failure depend not only on courage, wisdom, and determination but not least on the tenacity and aptitude of the enemy. Castro won because he faced a weak and inept Fulgencio Batista, while the Greek partisans after World War II and the Huks in the Philippines had the misfortune of facing determined opponents in the persons of Alexander Papagos and Ramon Magsaysay.

Given a certain historical process such as decolonization, the victory of a guerrilla movement, however ineffectual, became very likely. But the era of decolonization is over, and old rules no longer apply as guerrillas more often than not confront native incumbents. In brief, accident plays a considerable role. Guerrillas have succeeded even in adverse conditions, and they have been defeated even when everything pointed to their victory. The presence of an effective leader (or opponent) is a historical accident. But for Castro the march to power in Cuba would not have taken place. On the other hand, if the Chinese Communists had faced a more forceful and farsighted leader than Chiang Kai-chek, the Kuomintang might have won the war. Mao was aware of this possibility.

When I wrote on guerrilla warfare in the 1970s, the basic issues involved were no longer a matter of great contention. The colonial empires had disintegrated, for the colonial powers had no longer the will to fight. Combating the insurgents became so costly that the colonial powers withdrew. Since then the conditions conducive to the success of guerrillas have become much less promising. But what of guerrilla war against domestic rulers: Could the Cuban example be repeated in these conditions? In other words, could a guerrilla movement in peacetime undermine an existing government to such an extent that its collapse became a distinct possibility? My conclusion at the time was that in the foreseeable future the chances for terrorism were better than for guerrilla warfare, unless the moral fiber of a regime was in a state of advanced decay and the political will paralyzed. This assessment has been by and large borne out by subsequent events. Compared with the period following World War II, there have been very few guerrilla campaigns in recent decades.

But in the 1970s one could not foresee all future developments. One was the emergence of militant Islamism, which in certain conditions, such as in Afghanistan, could and would revert to guerrilla tactics. Second, there was the emergence of failed states, above all in Africa—for example Somalia. And finally, there was the use of guerrilla warfare as a surrogate strategy by a state against its enemies. Large-scale conventional warfare has become so expensive and politically risky that warfare by surrogate forces, usually in neighboring countries, seems a more promising, and certainly a cheaper, approach. Such warfare by proxy with attacks launched from sanctuaries within state borders might appear tempting, but it is still dangerous, for the sanctuaries cannot be kept secret for long and full-scale warfare may follow.

While guerrilla warfare has certainly been on the decline for the last forty years, I did not expect it to disappear altogether. In certain countries, such as Afghanistan, many preconditions exist for campaigns of this kind: the motivation, including fanatical religious and nationalist movements; the topographical conditions; and support from a neighboring country, in this case Pakistan. In parts of Africa the failure of new countries has been so massive and the authority of the state so weak that a power vacuum now invites more or less permanent fighting on a small scale. But such violence carried out by armed bands more interested in plunder and the massacre of tribal or ethnic enemies without the aim to take over state power is quite different from traditional guerrilla warfare. It is a state of lawlessness and chaos rather than a campaign with a specific political aim.

In brief, guerrilla warfare has endured but become the exception. The same is not true with regard to terrorism.

The History and Theory of Terrorism

The principles and the motives of guerrilla warfare are by now well documented, and they largely belong to history, whereas debates on terrorism are still, to this day, emotionally charged. I know of few other fields of study in which there has been so much emotion and so much confusion as in this one. Seldom have I encountered so much anger, so much reluctance to accept statements of fact that were perfectly obvious. And I have not found a wholly satisfactory answer for this state of affairs.

Some of the misunderstandings about the nature of terrorism are rooted in ideology. In the 1970s, terrorism was predominantly left wing in inspiration—or at least in its rhetoric. It was probably not surprising that commentators belonging to the same political persuasion would produce theoretical explanations that were, at the very least, not unsympathetic as far as the terrorists were concerned. Thus it was argued that terrorism (as in the case of guerrilla warfare) always occurred when there was intolerable oppression, social or national, and that terrorists had genuine, legitimate grievances. It followed that if these grievances were eradicated, terrorism would also disappear. Terrorism was seen as a revolutionary phenomenon, carried out by poor and desperate human beings, and therefore it had to be confronted with sympathetic understanding.

The argument stressing the left-wing character of terrorism is no longer widely heard except perhaps among some academic culturologists and members of certain sects trying to establish a popular front with Islamists in whom they see a powerful ally in the struggle against imperialism, even if they find the fundamentalist doctrine primitive and sometimes embarrassing. But the belief in a fatal link between poverty and violence has persisted. Whenever a major terrorist attack takes place, one hears appeals from high and low to provide financial help, to deal at long last with the "true causes of terrorism," the "roots" rather than their symptoms and outward manifestations. And these roots are believed to be poverty, unemployment, backwardness, and inequality.

Yet all investigations have shown that poverty does not cause terrorism and prosperity does not cure it. Most terrorists are not poor and do not come from poor societies. In the Indian subcontinent terrorism has occurred in the most prosperous region (Punjab) and the most egalitarian region (Kashmir), while the poorest regions (such as North Bihar) have been relatively free of terrorism. In Arab countries such as Egypt and Saudi Arabia, and also in North Africa, the terrorists originated not in the poorest and most neglected districts but hailed from places with concentrations of radical preachers. The backwardness, if there was any, was intellectual and cultural, not economic and social.

These findings, however, had only a limited impact on public opinion and politicians, and it is not difficult to see why there was resistance to accepting them. There is the general feeling that poverty and backwardness are bad and that there is an urgent need to do more about them, hence the inclination to couple the two issues.

Reducing poverty in the Third World may be a moral as well as a political and economic imperative, but to expect a consequent and decisive change in regard to terrorism is unrealistic. Such an expectation ignores both the causes of backwardness and poverty, the reasons for stagnation, and the motives for terrorism. Still, poverty combined with youth unemployment does create a social and psychological climate in which Islamism and various populist and religious sects flourish. These conditions, in turn, provide some of the foot folk for violent groups in internal conflicts. According to some projections, the number of young unemployed in the Arab world and North Africa could reach 50 million in less than two decades.

The British historian Richard Cobb, writing about the French revolutionary movements in the eighteenth and nineteenth century, described a new crowd that had emerged in the big cities, hanging around aimlessly in the street, a historical situation that reminds one the Arab world and North Africa today. Cobb observed (and I quoted him in *The Uses and Limits of Intelligence*): "There is no greater threat to the established order than the nameless man who lives alone in a garret, receives no mail, has no friend and no occupation, and no fixed hours, and no reason to be in one place rather than another. The events of July 1789 were exactly what such people had been waiting for for years."

This description may well fit the current situation, and it will not be conducive to political stability. Conditions in the Arab world and North Africa will increase the demographic pressure on Europe, since, according to polls, a majority of these unemployed young people want to emigrate. Politically, the populist discontent will be directed against the rulers—Islamists in Iran, moderates in Egypt, Jordan, or Morocco. But what can be done for the failed economies of the Middle East and North Africa? Some might suggest foreign aid, but keep in mind that the countries that made substantial economic progress, such as China and India, South Korea and Taiwan, Malaysia and Turkey, did so without massive help from abroad.

All these factors point to a deep malaise and even an impending danger, but not to a direct link between the economic situation and international terrorism. In fact, there is a negative correlation: terrorists do not hesitate to target areas of the economy that have been successful. One of the main targets of terrorism in Iraq was the oil industry. And terrorists have caused great harm to the tourist industries of North Africa, Egypt, and Bali. Terrorism spread to the Maldives in the Indian Ocean not because of poverty (tourism has given the Maldives the highest per capita GNP in the developing world), but because Islamic preachers of violence have been permitted to act freely.

Sometimes it is argued that solving religio-nationalist grievances will eradicate terrorism. If the issue at stake is the conflict over a certain territory or the demand for more autonomy, a compromise through negotiations seems a possibility. But it ought to be recalled that al-Qaeda was founded and the terrorist attacks of September 11, 2001, occurred not because of a territorial dispute or a feeling of national oppression but because of a religious commandment—*jihad*.

It goes without saying that there have been terrorist movements throughout history pursuing liberation from tyrannical regimes. But seen in historical perspective these groups have been much fewer in recent decades than in earlier periods. In the twentieth century terrorism appeared not under the most oppressive regimes but, on the contrary, under conditions of relative freedom—or of anarchy. It should have been clear, moreover, that terrorism was by no means the exclusive domain of the revolutionary left and that it has been exercised also by the extreme right, by fascist, semi-fascist, or chauvinist-racist movements. The predominantly left-wing terrorism of the 1970s was soon replaced by a terrorism that had nothing to do with the traditional ideas of the left, however liberally interpreted. This development put some of the liberation theorists of the time in an embarrassing situation, for they could hardly argue that the grievances and demands of the neo-fascists were legitimate and if one gave in to their demands there would be no terrorism.

In the first decade of the twenty-first century a new doctrine calls for a united front between the revolutionary left and Islamic terrorism—with frequent reference to Antonio Gramsci to justify this strange marriage of convenience. Both orthodox Islamists and orthodox Marxists have certain difficulties with this new idea. It was the basic mistake of the liberation terrorism commentators to assume that terrorism was a progressive ideology. They tended to equate socialism and populism and to take the revolutionary slogans and phraseology far too seriously, failing to understand that the words should not be taken at face value in Europe or the Americas, and even less so in the Third World. In actual fact, terrorism was simply a mode of warfare, a species of political violence that could be used by people of very different political orientation—from the extreme left and the far right, by religious fanatics and fanatic nationalists. Similar mistakes were committed in later years by politicians and political analysts who were not at all left-wing in orientation but came to believe that terrorism was somehow a political doctrine, a *Weltanschauung*. In some ways it is easy to understand why this happened. The prevailing manifestation of terrorism in the 1970s was seemingly revolutionary and left-wing, and although thirty years later it was Islamic-nationalist, the temptation to generalize on the basis of some passing phenomenon was bound to lead to mistaken assessments.

But this was not the only prevailing misconception at the time. In the 1970s it was widely believed that terrorism was a new and unprecedented phenomenon, that it was one of the most dangerous problems facing humankind. According to frequent media reports, terrorists were fanatical believers driven to despair by intolerable conditions. Their inspiration was deeply ideological. These beliefs were quite untenable in the light of realities. The situation in West Germany or in Italy in the 1970s was in no way more intolerable than in the years before or after; on the contrary, there was more freedom in Germany and Italy than at any time in their recent history. The same was true with regard to Latin America; terrorism occurred first in Uruguay, probably the freest of the Latin American countries.

How can the emergence of terrorist groups at that time—and not before or after—be explained? In truth, the number of terrorists was small, not more than a handful. And just as in the physical world there is no accounting for the movement of small particles, so there was no accounting for the behavior of a hundred or even a thousand terrorists out of a population of many millions.

Given the fact that all over the world there were real major grievances (or at least the perception of grievances), why were there so few terrorists? Surely these grievances must have been felt by many more people. Were the terrorists those who felt injustice most acutely, or were other psychological factors involved? If, as the saying at the time went, "a terrorist is a person just like you and me," why weren't there many millions of terrorists? There was the tendency to exaggerate the importance of terrorism, and that led to overreaction on the part of the authorities. In truth, terrorism at the time was politically not very important, above all a media event, fueling the fear that a few terrorist attacks could possibly bring about the downfall of whole societies, of Germany or Italy for instance. But these fears were of course wholly misplaced at a time when weapons of mass destruction were as yet a very distant possibility.

Some such fears were quite obviously rooted in ignorance. There had been no major terrorist campaign in Europe or America for a long time, and the suddenness of these attacks produced surprise and shock. Newspaper readers of the year 1900 would have been much less surprised than those of 1975. Some of the wrong thinking at the time seems to have been less a matter of ignorance than of deliberate obfuscation. Certain analysts were opposed in principle to the systematic study of terrorism, arguing that many more people had been killed, many more crimes committed, by governments in time of peace and even more during wars, than by the tiny groups of individuals.

Many more people had indeed suffered under cruel or aggressive governments than endured suffering caused by a few sectarian bomb throwers. But this attempt to obliterate the differences between various kinds of violence carried out by dictatorships (and sometimes by democracies) could only cause confusion and mischief, and this was perhaps the aim of the exercise—to downplay the specific character of terrorism. But what was to be gained by equating the Nazi extermination of the Jews (to give but one example) with the activities of the Russian terrorists in the nineteenth century or the Irish in the twentieth century? All government rests on a certain amount of coercion, and anarchists have always resented this fact. But to argue that, since there has never been absolute freedom in any society or political regime (and that terror from above has been an essential part of totalitarian government), there is no difference between this kind of violence and terrorism is, of course, wholly misleading. All this should have been perfectly obvious. Yet the idea that Maximilien Robespierre and Osama bin Laden are brothers under the skin, that one kind of violence is like another, still has believers to this day, be it out of ignorance or ideological prejudice.

There are an unending number of misconceptions with regard to the character of modern terrorism. Sometimes these theories, while naive, have been relatively harmless. In the very early days of investigation Cesare Lombroso, the founder of modern criminology, reached the conclusion that lack of vitamins was one of the main roots of violence, political and otherwise. In a later age the idea gained ground that terrorism (like guerrilla warfare) is caused by poverty. All investigations have shown that there is no such obvious correlation: in the fifty poorest countries of the world there is a great deal of violence but hardly any terrorism. True, in the very richest countries—mostly small societies—there is not much either, but since there is not much chance that the very poorest countries will reach the level of the very rich oil-producing countries or of Luxembourg, stressing this fact is not of great practical importance. We have adduced some of the reasons why some have focused on poverty as the main factor responsible for terrorism. But poverty is not the cause, and financial help will not fix it. Giving people more vitamins, however, will usually do no harm, and combating poverty is equally desirable.

The list of misjudgments extends to the very recent past. The great surprise and the even greater confusion caused by the growth of suicide terrorism during the last decade serves as an example. It was widely believed that suicide bombing was unprecedented in the annals of humankind, and all kind of strange theories were put forward to explain it. But in truth most terrorism in history until about fifty years ago has been suicide terrorism for the simple reason that the weapons used by terrorists, such as the dagger, the short-range pistol, and the very unstable bomb (likely to explode in the hands) made the mission more likely than not suicidal. Furthermore, traditional terrorism, in contrast to contemporary terrorism practiced by Islamists, was aimed at kings, ministers, or military leaders who were so well protected by bodyguards that a getaway was seldom possible.

One recent theory claimed to have found an explanation, arguing that terrorism and in particular suicide attacks appeared whenever a foreign power invaded a country—such as in Iraq. But the facts demonstrate otherwise. Foreign invasion could generate terrorism but in many cases did not, and, on the other hand, terrorism occurred without any foreign invasions—in the Philippines, Pakistan, Colombia, Sri Lanka, Indonesia, Palestine/Israel, and Algeria. And even in Iraq most of the suicide attacks were carried out and directed not against the invaders but by Sunnis against Shi'ites and Kurds and vice versa.

A professor of economics writing in 2006–7 proved quite correctly that poverty did not cause terrorism (a misconception widespread among politicians), nor did lack of education. Some of us (including the present writer) had made this argument back in the 1970s, but it was useful to have it confirmed following the application of modern social science tools such as negative binominal regression models and with reference to statistics about infant mortality as well as U.S. stock market volatility. But the author also believed that curtailing civil liberties could turn people to terrorism. Unfortunately, there is no evidence to this effect; a little repression could have such consequences, massive repression seldom if ever. A social psychologist, on the other hand, recently stressed "significance restoration, significance gain, and prevention of significance loss" as crucial motives in suicide terrorism. A psychiatrist points to leaderless (decentralized) terrorist groups as the most significant new development; the violent groups of the extreme right in the United States have operated in this way for a long time, albeit without much success.

Yet another recent theory—of networking—was simply stating the obvious. It dealt less with the motivation of contemporary terrorism than with its mode of organization, communication, and operation. Again, a little historical homework would have shown that networking was not an invention of the computer age. It had been, under different names, the operational mode of the secret societies of the nineteenth century—from the Italian Carbonari to the French, Spanish, and Italian anarchists, the Russian and Irish freedom fighters, and the Molly Maguires in the United States. These small secret societies consisted mainly of professional revolutionaries. As they often moved from one place to another, it was of vital importance to have contacts on whom they could rely—for financial help, the acquisition of arms, and places to hide. This kind of networking was somewhat primitive and much slower in that age before telephone and e-mail, but it rested on the same principles. Like some of the Islamic militants, the conspirators sometimes met in the backrooms of bookshops; as they were not church-goers or mosque-goers, they picked other spaces.

But how helpful are even the erudite and commonsensical theories such as the one seeing the key to terrorism and the fight against it in the emergence of the market state, which, it is argued, provides the model for global terrorism? What is right in these theories (or constructs) has been known for a long time, and the new elements are usually of doubtful validity. The psychologists among the theorists see the main, if not the only, key to understanding terrorism in psychological factors of the individual and/or the group. The lawyers' preoccupation is with the constitution and the laws; the economists introduce concepts and methods from the field they know best; and all of them are firmly convinced that they are (more or less) the first to gain a true understanding of terrorism.

Lastly, I must repeat, there is the anti-anti-terrorism school of thought, which has changed its arguments over the years but shown remarkable persistence. Originally, in the 1970s, it maintained that terrorism was unimportant; after all, many more people had been killed through violent actions carried out by governments. This is, of course, perfectly true, but the intention was to obfuscate the difference between various forms of violence (or power). The small terrorist groups that existed at the time were left-wing in orientation and must therefore have had good reasons for their actions (anti-capitalism, anti-Americanism, anti-imperialism, anti-exploitation, anti-oppression). These were the views voiced by Noam Chomsky and others, but it soon appeared that there was terrorism of the extreme right too, which they could not possibly consider as progressive or liberating violence.

After a period of decline the anti-anti-terrorism school reappeared at the beginning of the twenty-first century in a different guise among British and American university lecturers, using "critical students of counterinsurgency" and similar labels. They found it difficult to argue that Islamic terrorists were left wing in character and ideology, but since they were (or claimed to be) anti-capitalist, anti-American, anti-imperialist, etc., they were more worthy of support than their enemies such as Ronald Reagan, George W. Bush, and other Western leaders. However, these critical students soon faced difficulties that were almost impossible to surmount. For the great majority of the victims of these near-progressive Islamic militants were not Western imperialists but, be it in Iraq or Algeria, in Lebanon, Pakistan, or Bangladesh, fellow Muslims. The only practical way out of this dilemma was to focus not on the terrorists but on those fighting them, an ingenious maneuver but hardly likely to shed any new light on the murders of Benazir Bhutto or Rajiv Gandhi, on the assassination of countless Lebanese and Egyptian political leaders, and generally speaking, on the character of contemporary terrorism.

The Study and Definition of Terrorism

In the 1970s, when the systematic study of terrorism began, only a handful of people were involved and the existing literature was restricted largely to articles and studies of general issues that were only indirectly connected with terrorism, such as the general question of why men (or women) rebel. One of the very early studies, widely read at the time, dealt with "regimes of terror" and was based on case studies of tribal African societies. I never doubted the value of such studies by ethnographers and anthropologists for their specific disciplines, but I fail to this day to understand their relevance to the terrorism that occurred in Europe, the Middle East, or Latin America in the last third of the twentieth century, let alone the Islamic terrorism of the twenty-first century.

More recently, especially since 9/11, interest in the subject has grown tremendously. Funds became available, conferences were arranged, and new journals were established. Courses and seminars at many universities became a permanent fixture. I believe that there was not a single such course in America in the early 1970s and that mine at Georgetown University may have been the first, but interest at the time was limited. Since then tens of thousands of books and articles have been published and even the most obscure Arab writings have been translated and become part of huge data bases. These include authors such as Abu Basir al-Tartusi and Maidi Ahmad Husain, of whom even many learned Western experts had not heard before. As a result, many thousands of new experts appeared on the scene—in some respects an admirable phenomenon.

But unfortunately it was also true that much of this new expertise was spurious. To become a China expert involved a great deal of work; one had to acquire at least a working knowledge of the language, the history, and the culture. But political violence was somehow considered a soft subject. No special preparation was needed except perhaps some general familiarity with recent trends in political science and social psychology and above all the terminology of these disciplines. Anyone aware what a "meta-narrative" was and what "subaltern" meant was entitled to contribute to ongoing debates and to be taken seriously.

To the extent that history is supposed to be relevant, the texts offered to students, even in armed forces colleges, were often absurd, referring to the Spanish Inquisition, the Luddites, the French Revolution (where terrorism was said to have been originated), and Adolf Hitler's rise to power and plans for genocide. In other words, no differentiation was made between the history of despotism, dictatorships, repression, massacres, and cruelty in the history of humankind, and the quite specific history of terrorism. This kind of loose thinking and ignorance was bound to spread confusion. One extended example should suffice.

While the Cold War lasted (and even beyond) a great deal of energy was spent refuting allegations that the Soviet Union was somehow involved in aiding international terrorism. Such allegations were thought to sabotage détente and, generally speaking, an understanding between West and East. It is perfectly true that terrorism had not been invented in the Soviet Union, but it was equally true (as it emerged after the breakup of the Soviet empire) that from an early stage the Soviet leadership had extended a great deal of help to a variety of terrorist groups in the Middle East and to some extent also in Europe, in Italy and Germany. Money and false passports as well as arms had been provided, and training camps had been established in the Soviet bloc. When they felt hard pressed in the West, these terrorists could always move freely in Soviet bloc countries, and when their groups had been smashed by Western security forces, they were given permanent new homes in the DDR.

True, Soviet leaders and also the KGB had certain misgivings about these terrorists, often considered loose cannons, difficult to control. But on the whole their value as a destabilizing force was thought to be greater than any danger they could present to the Soviet bloc. Only in the 1980s did Soviet policy makers begin to reconsider their attitude toward the terrorists. These close contacts became clear when, after the fall of the Berlin Wall, the West German police were helped by their East German colleagues, including some of the Stasi, to locate the Baader-Meinhof terrorists who had found an asylum and a new identity in East Germany.

Much time was wasted in the vain search for an all-encompassing definition of terrorism. I had argued in the 1970s that trying to develop a definition of this kind was bound to be fruitless because the character of terrorism had changed enormously over time and also differed according to the political and cultural environment in which it took place. The study of terrorism could and should manage with a minimum of theory. This proposition was criticized, with arguments that unless the terrorism as a concept was clearly defined there would be chaos, everyone able to include under its rubric whatever he or she saw fit. Such criticism frequently came from political science theory builders, most of whom were more interested in theory than in terrorism. Given the difficult nature of the subject, it is easy to understand the measure of their exasperation. But I had not suggested that the study of terrorism could proceed without commonsense and a knowledge of its history and character. Even if a universal definition of terrorism was beyond our ken, it did not mean that anyone could define terrorism as he or she wanted, in a totally subjective way, unless of course the aim was to provide an ideological justification for terrorism.

Since then more than three decades have passed and there has been no significant progress in this search for a definition. Even though the practical need for a definition—for instance, for legal purposes—was undisputed, the results have been meager. There was no unanimity about whether the emphasis should be on terrorist goals, motivations, or methods. The definitions that were produced were either very general and vague and therefore of little practical help or more specific and therefore more likely to become outdated as the character of terrorism changed. In the 1970s, most of the definitions were prepared with groups like Baader-Meinhof and the Italian Red Brigades in mind. Thirty years later, in the context of Islamic terrorism, these are of no relevance. At the present time the UN definition of terrorism is also meaningless. Defining terrorism by its victims, it states a civilian is "any person not taking an active part in the conflict," leaving open, among other things, the question as to what constitutes conflict. The Department of State has its own definition: "premeditated, politically motivated violence perpetrated against noncombatant targets." The Federal Bureau of Investigation's definition puts the stress on the unlawful use of force or violence against persons or property. The Defense Department's definition is similar but not identical.

Some of the differences are ludicrous. According to the State Department definition, using a vehicle to smash an ATM machine to collect more than $10,000 should not be considered a terrorist act, whereas according to the FBI definition, it is a terrorist act if the FBI regards the group that did the smashing as associated with terrorism. Such borderline cases make precise definitions difficult if not impossible. In many of the official definitions the emphasis is on the character of the victim: if he or she is an "innocent civilian," the attack ought to be considered terrorist, but if he or she belongs to a branch of the security forces, an attack is apparently not terrorist. But it is not at all clear why an attack against a soldier or policeman carried out by a terrorist group should not be considered terrorist, since the attacker does not belong to the armed forces of another country. Furthermore, it is difficult to think of any terrorist group in history that has attacked only civilians or only policemen. In real life it may attack civilians in the morning and soldiers at night: Does that mean it changes its character within twelve hours?

The most widely used criminal justice definitions are those produced by Bruce Hoffman, Brian Jenkins, and the present writer, and they rest upon the idea of illegitimate force used to achieve political ends by targeting innocent people. But the weakness of even very general definitions like these is obvious, especially the stress on "targeting innocent people." Who decides who is innocent, and why should an attack against someone who is guilty not be considered terrorist?

Once we move from official institutional definitions to those provided in the academic world, more or less free rein is given to ideological predilections and prejudices, and there is a special temptation to eradicate the dividing lines among all kinds of violence—that committed by governments (democratic or dictatorial), by substate groups, by security forces, and by terrorists and criminals. Excepted are only those with whom the writer or speaker feels ideological kinship, in which case it would obviously be improper to affix the terrorist label.

Some of the media (and also certain governments) have gone through strange contortions in their endeavor to find synonyms for terrorism and terrorists that are not "loaded" and would cause no offense to anyone. They have been called fighters, insurgents, insurrectionists, militants (a great favorite), gunmen, rebels, and radicals. Whenever possible the term guerrilla (or urban guerrilla) has been applied because it was thought to have no negative connotations—in contrast to terrorism. But terrorism has by no means always been an insult. When Boris Savinkov, the head of the combat wing of the Socialist-Revolutionary Party in Russia before World War I published his autobiography, he unself-consciously called it *Memoirs of a Terrorist* (1917 and still in print, an interesting book), and one could think of many other such examples.

Terrorism acquired its negative connotations as it became more cruel, savage, and bloodthirsty. The enemy was not just to be annihilated; he also had to suffer as much pain as possible in the process. In contrast, nineteenth-century terrorists had a certain code of honor. When a duke or minister or general targeted by the terrorists in czarist Russia appeared on the scene accompanied by his wife and children, the terrorists would not attempt to assassinate him for fear of killing innocents. Their dilemma became the subject of a famous play by Albert Camus. Even the Uruguayan Tupamaros in the 1970s strongly admonished their followers to take every precaution not to harm innocents.

Today, however, terrorism has become inhuman. "We shall drink your blood" is a frequent threat in Middle Eastern terrorism (it is not known whether blood was actually ever consumed). Abu Musab al-Zarqawi, the late leading Jordanian terrorist active in Iraq, was upbraided by some of his colleagues for slitting the throats of his victims too quickly. Similar reports have come from Algeria, where in the 1990s victims were slowly disemboweled, with members of their families forced to watch. There were protests. But some still argue that terrorism has not become more inhumane, that this so-called trend is nothing but a calumny spread by Western Orientalists, a "hegemonistic strategy" aiming to give a bad name to the "legitimate violence" of "peripheralized people."

Counterterrorism

I have tried to steer clear of counterterrorism in my research and thinking on terrorism. Frequently intermingled, these are two related yet different disciplines, just as, say, physiology and the practice of medicine. To present advice about how to prevent and counteract terrorism, specialized knowledge is needed that is often secret and to which only those in government have access.

But the history of counterterrorism certainly does offer certain lessons. I always felt uneasy about the term "war on terrorism." Obviously the military has to play a certain role in this context, especially when dealing with countries that have failed to function and become terrorist havens. The military may also be needed to deliver blows against heavy terrorist concentrations. But these are not the typical terrorist situations. The key role should be played by intelligence and by relatively small specialized units.

During the twentieth century the importance of terrorism has frequently been exaggerated for reasons that were no secret: the wholly unexpected character of terrorist attacks created the impression (magnified by the media) that this could happen everywhere at any time and that there was no limit to the damage the terrorists could inflict. But it did not happen everywhere at all times, and the damage caused by the terrorists was on the whole quite limited. Of course, it was clear even when I first confronted the problem that this was bound to change when terrorists gained access to weapons of mass destruction. No one can say whether this is years or decades off.

The problem facing democratic societies when confronting terrorism is of a different character: they do not know how to cope with asymmetric warfare and are hampered in doing so in many ways. Terrorism does not accept laws and rules, whereas governments are bound by them. This is a dilemma that authoritarian rulers do not face. They do not accept that guerrilla warfare and terrorism are invincible, and the experience of the Middle East and North Africa bears them out. When almost three decades ago the late Syrian president Hafez al-Assad faced an insurgency (and attempted assassination) by the local Muslim Brotherhood in Homs and Hama, large sections of those cities were destroyed and tens of thousands of inhabitants were massacred by his troops. This action put an end to all plans of terrorism and guerrilla war. The Egyptian government dealt harshly with its terrorist opponents in the 1990s, and in Algeria more than a 100,000 were killed in a bloody civil war unleashed by the Islamic terrorists, which they eventually lost. No rules were observed, and no pardon was given in these counterterrorist activities. No one dreamed of invoking the Geneva Conventions.

Such behavior on the part of democratic governments, however, would have been denounced as barbaric, a relapse to the practices of long gone precivilized days. But if governments accept the principles of asymmetric warfare they will be severely, possibly fatally handicapped. An old proverb says, "Do not put your hand into a wasp's nest, but if you do, come down hard." This basic rule of antiterrorist and antiguerrilla operations, as mentioned earlier, has very often been ignored: it is not that force is ineffective but that applying a little force is indeed a dangerous thing whereas massive force usually has an effect.

As I noted in a 2004 article for *Policy Review,* in the nineteenth century and earlier, terrorists would have been regarded as pirates—*hostes humanii generis,* enemies of all humankind—and treated accordingly as outlaws. Karl Marx more than once invoked a saying prevalent at the time: *À corsaire, corsaire et demi.* From the second half of the twentieth century onward, however, terrorists in democratic societies have been protected by various human rights conventions. It is true that normal legal procedures are sufficient if a terrorist group is small and not very dangerous and the issues involved of marginal importance. But this is not the case when core interests are at stake, when the very existence of a state or society is threatened, when it is a question of survival.

It is often, and recently, argued that force alone cannot defeat terrorism, for it is a confrontation of ideas, a struggle for the hearts and minds of people. But that argument is true to only a limited degree. While the use of massive force is bound to be unpopular, it might be applied in extreme cases. The Russian government could have deported the Chechens (or a significant proportion of them) to distant parts of Siberia, thus solving the problem on the Stalinist pattern. If the Chechens had threatened Moscow or St. Petersburg or the Russian state or its fuel supply, there is little doubt that such measures would have been taken. But the threat was only peripheral, and for this reason the Kremlin refrained from the most extreme measures, though still brutal by Western standards.

As for the importance of soft power in dealing with terrorism, it is not the terrorist idea that constitutes the threat but their weapons. A cultural dialogue cannot be very effective against a fervent, fanatical belief system be it of a religious or nationalist character or that of a secular religion. When, in the days prior to the March on Rome, Benito Mussolini was asked about his program, he replied that it was to break the skulls of the socialists, and this, *mutatis mutandis,* applies to many contemporary terrorist groups. Mussolini would probably not have been deterred by soft power.

Joseph S. Nye has described soft power as based on culture and political ideas, as making use of the seductiveness of democracy, human rights, and individual opportunity. This is a powerful argument in certain circles, and it is true that Washington has seldom taken advantage of opportunities to employ this kind of soft power. But how seductive are Western democracy and human rights in the Muslim world? These days, they are not very seductive even in Russia. Who is to be influenced by the spread of Western values and ideas? Cultural propaganda (public diplomacy) had an effect in Europe and even behind the Iron Curtain during the Cold War. It is possible that, as sometimes argued, even the Beatles made a certain contribution to the downfall of the Soviet empire. But soft power will have no impact on radical Islamists, who abhor democracy, who believe that human rights and tolerance are imperialist inventions, and who do not want any ideas circulating except those that appear in the Koran—as they interpret it. They do not want compromise and peaceful coexistence. They do not believe in diplomacy. They want to annihilate the enemy.

Western radio and television do not make much of an impact on the radical Muslim world. Some 70 percent of this audience believed (and probably still believes) that the attacks of September 11 were carried out by the Mossad even though Osama bin Laden made no secret of his involvement. This audience will be influenced by disinformation however far-fetched, but not by a truthful, matter-of-fact coverage of the news. Nazi Germany was open to a certain extent to British black propaganda during World War II, to rumors, half-truths, and outright lies. But the Muslim world's interest in the West, in twelve-tone music, abstract expressionism, and even poststructuralism, is strictly limited. It is, however, very vulnerable to black propaganda simply because of its strong predilection for conspiracy theories. But this kind of soft power will never be used by democratic governments in time of peace; it would be considered a betrayal of Western values and principles, of lying and worse. It is even less likely that that these governments would broadcast material for which there is an interest and demand—drug culture and pornography and other negative aspects of Western civilization. One cannot imagine the U.S. Congress allocating funds for the Voice of America to broadcast black propaganda at a time when American libraries covering academic subjects have been closed down for lack of funding.

Antiterrorist action in the West is an obstacle course, not so much because of the ingenuity of the terrorists but because of the very nature of democratic societies. Many suspected terrorists have been arrested in the United States and in Europe, but very few have been brought to trial and even fewer have been convicted. Often the evidence was inadmissible or the authorities were reluctant to reveal the sources of their information. Moreover, if the authorities succeed in preventing terrorist attacks, then it is argued that antiterrorist measures are unnecessary, for the terrorist danger must have been grossly overrated, as no terrorist attacks have taken place. Antiterrorist laws are said to be tantamount to introducing fascism or at the very least an authoritarian regime. But if the authorities fail to prevent an attack, they are accused of negligence. In brief, the more successful the authorities are in preventing terrorist attacks, the less public support they receive.

Current antiterrorist legislation is probably insufficient to prevent attacks in which weapons of mass destruction will be used. But such attacks have not happened yet, and effective measures can be adopted only when governments have broad public support. If devastating attacks do not occur, stringent antiterrorist measures will not be necessary. If they do occur, the demand for effective countermeasures will be overwhelming even if these mean severely curtailing freedoms that have been taken for granted. The problem facing Western governments is that they must not move too far ahead of public opinion, which means that effective measures can be adopted only after some major disaster will have occurred.

The Future of Terrorism

Making predictions about terrorism is even more risky than making predictions about political trends in general, for we are not dealing with mass movements. It is certain, however, that terrorism will not disappear from the earth. At a time when full-scale war has become too dangerous and too expensive to undertake, terrorism has become the prevailing mode of conflict, and as long as conflict persists among groups of human beings, so will violence.

More than forty years have now passed since the systematic study of terrorism began, and there have been attempts to draw an interim balance about achievements and failures in this field. A small working group at the United Nations has identified no fewer than 490 topics that ought to be further explored, ranging from the role of the media in terrorism and countering terrorism to comparative airport security and "terrorism and the Internet." But it is doubtful whether the studies so far had a significant impact on the incidence of terrorism, except perhaps as Paul Wilkinson rightly noted, in the field of security technologies. How much attention has been paid by policy makers and the media to the writings of the terrorism researchers? (Perhaps that's an unfair question: How much attention has been paid by ministers of war and chiefs of staff to the writings of strategists from Karl von Clausewitz on?)

I cannot complain about lack of attention: my *Guerrilla* and *Terrorism* have been about second place in the list of works most frequently quoted. (I have been rightly criticized for writing such a history despite my skepticism with regard to developing a scientific definition of the subject I was dealing with.) But have many lessons been learned from history, and how many lessons are there to be learned? Most of them are of a negative character—don'ts rather than do's. Perhaps another item should be added to the UN list of 490 topics to be explored—the reasons for the reluctance (and resistance) to consider the lessons of the past. Much of it is no doubt of an ideological character, but stating this is not taking us very far, for how else can a consensus among the nations of the United Nations be reached on a subject like terrorism? I am not entirely pessimistic in this regard, for once terrorism equipped with weapons of mass destruction threatens our survival, attitudes will change and there will be greater readiness to cooperate. But this may be years, perhaps decades, off.

At the present time all attention is focused on Islamic terrorism, but it is useful to remember that this was not always the case and that there are a great many other conflicts, perceived oppressions, and causes calling for radical action that may also lead to terrorism in the years to come. These need not be major conflicts in an era in which even small groups may have access to weapons of mass destruction.

At present Islamic terrorism has not yet run its full course, but it is unlikely that its present fanaticism will last forever. Religio-national fervor does not constantly burn with the same intensity. There is a phenomenon called in Egypt "Salafi burnout," the mellowing of radical young people, the weakening of the original fanatical impetus. Fanaticism is not easily transferable from one generation to the next. Like all other movements in history, messianic groups are subject to routinization, to changing political circumstances, and to sudden or gradual changes in religious belief. The terrorist impetus is also likely to decline as the result of setbacks. As attacks will continue, some will be successful, perhaps spectacularly successful, but many will fail. One day it might be possible to appease militant Islamism—though hardly in a period of burning aggression when confidence and faith in global victory have not yet been broken.

When Alfred Nobel invented dynamite, many terrorists thought it was the answer to their prayers. But theirs was a false hope. The trust put today in that invincible weapon—suicide terrorism—may in the end be equally misplaced. Even the use of weapons of mass destruction may not be the panacea some terrorists believe. Perhaps their effect will be less than anticipated, perhaps they will be so destructive as to be considered counterproductive. Statistics show that in the terrorist attacks over the last decades considerably more Muslims were killed than infidels. Since terrorists do not operate in a vacuum, this fact is bound to produce dissent among their followers and even among the fanatical preachers.

There are likely to be splits among the terrorists even though the structure of their groups is not highly centralized. In brief, there is the probability that a united terrorist front, if ever established, will not last. It is unlikely that Osama bin Laden and his followers will be frontally challenged on ideological grounds, but there has been criticism for political and tactical reasons, such as the attacks against the Shi'ites. If it is assumed that America and the West in general are in a state of decline, why was al-Qaeda so impatient? Why did it launch a big attack while the infidels were still in a position to retaliate massively?

Some leading students of Islam have argued that radical Islamism passed its peak a long time ago and that its downfall and disappearance are only a question of time, perhaps even not much time. Societies that were exposed to the rule of fundamentalist fanatics (such as Iran) or to radical Islamic attacks (such as Algeria) have been immunized to a certain extent.

However, in a country of 60 million, such as Iran, some fanatics can always be found for suicide missions. It would be overoptimistic to assume that we have seen the last of the failed countries. In any case, many Muslim countries have not yet undergone such learning process at firsthand, and for some of the more backward regions, such as parts of Pakistan (Waziristan and the North-West Frontier, but perhaps not only there) the imposition of the rule of the Sharia and the restoration of the Caliphate are still brilliant dreams.

By and large, therefore, predictions about the impending demise of Islamism seem to be premature, while probably correct in the longer run. Nor do we know what will follow. An interesting study, *When Prophecy Fails*, by Leon Festinger and others, was published in 1956. A similar study is now needed on the likely consequences of the failure of religious fanaticism.

These, then, are the likely perspectives for the more distant future. But in a short-term perspective the danger remains and may in fact grow. When and where are terrorist attacks most likely to occur? They will not necessarily be directed against the greatest and most dangerous enemy perceived. Much depends on where the terrorists are strong and believe the enemy to be weak. That terrorist attacks will go on in the Middle East goes without saying. Other main danger zones are Central Asia and Pakistan.

The founders of Pakistan were secular politicians. The religious establishment and even the extremists among the Indian Muslims had opposed the emergence of the new state. But once Pakistan had been established, the extremists set out to dominate it, with considerable success. Their alternative education system, the many thousands of *madrasas*, became the breeding grounds for *jihad* fighters, not just in Afghanistan but also in their own country and eventually in Western Europe. Ayub Khan, the first military ruler, tried in vain to break the stranglehold of the *madrasas*. Subsequent rulers, military and civilian, have not even tried. The tens of thousands of *jihad* graduates they produced will find employment not only at home but also in Central Asia or even in India if conflict between Pakistan and India escalates. Pakistan's most radical *jihadists* aim to destroy India, but, given Pakistan's internal weakness, this aim is more than a little fanciful. Still, their destructive potential is considerable, and they can count on sympathies and support from some sections of the army and military intelligence. A failed Pakistan with nuclear weapons at its disposal would be a major nightmare. However, Pakistani terrorism, like Palestinian and Middle Eastern terrorism in general, remains essentially territorial in its ambitions, and unlikely to reach too far.

Europe is one of the most vulnerable battlefields. It has over the years become the main base of terrorist support groups. The growth of Muslim communities in Western Europe has exacerbated tensions with the local population, creating a reservoir of new recruits. At the same time, in Western Europe the freedom of action for the extremists is considerably greater than in the Arab and Muslim world. *Jihadists* convicted of capital crimes in their native countries were given political asylum in Europe. It is true that there were some arrests and restrictions on their activities after 9/11 and the attacks in London and Madrid, but given the legal restrictions under which European security services operate, effective countermeasures were still exceedingly difficult.

Western European governments have frequently been criticized for not having done enough to integrate their Muslim communities, but cultural and social integration was not what many immigrants wanted and exactly what their preachers constantly warn against. They have wanted to preserve their political, cultural, and religious identity and their way of life, and they have resented interference by secular authorities. But with all this, the first generation of immigrants have also wanted to live in peace and to make a living for their families. Today they have little control over their more radical offspring.

The radicalization of the second generation of immigrants is a frequent phenomenon. This generation has been superficially acculturated, fluently speaking the language of the land yet at the same time feeling the resentment and hostility of the local population more acutely. It is not necessarily the power of the fundamentalist message that inspires the younger radials; they are by no means pious believers when it comes to carrying out all the religious commandments. The British suicide bombers, for instance, were not known for their religious orthodoxy; most of them did not pray regularly. Yet young Muslims in Europe are caught in between—no longer at home in the country from which their parents came yet not accepted in Europe, no longer under the authority of the parents, attracted by the power of street gangs. All these factors lead to free-floating aggression and too often to a life of crime directed against the authorities as well as their neighbors.

As a result, non-Muslims in Europe began to feel threatened in streets they could once walk without fear. They came to regard the new immigrants as antisocial elements who wanted to impose on them their way of life. Pressure on European governments has been growing from all sides, right and left, to stop immigration and restore law and order.

This, in briefest outline, is the milieu in which Islamic terrorism and terrorist support groups in Europe have developed. True, the number of extremists is still quite small. Among British Muslims only 13 percent have expressed sympathy for terrorist attacks, but this still amounts to about 200,000 sympathizers, far more than needed to launch a terrorist campaign, far too many to be effectively observed by the security forces. Furthermore, such statistics do not take into account the continuing growth of Muslim communities as Western European countries, with their low and declining birthrates, have a continuing need for immigrants. It is also true that the tensions in Europe are not equally strong in all countries. Muslims in Germany, for instance, are predominantly of Turkish or Kurdish or Alawite origin and with some exceptions have shown less inclination to take violent action than communities of Arab, North African, and Pakistani origin. Newcomers from the Far East and India have been more successful in school and professional training than immigrants from Muslim countries. Still, according to studies of the German interior ministry in 2007–8, one out of four young Turks are *gewaltbereit*, willing or even eager to use violence, but there has not yet been political terrorism on a major scale.

If acculturation and integration have been a failure in the short run, prospects are less hopeless in a long-term perspective. Muslims cannot be kept in a hermetically sealed ghetto even if their preachers make a valiant effort in this direction. They are disgusted and repelled by the consumption of alcohol, loose moral standards, general decadence, and all the other wickednesses of the society surrounding them—as they see it, indoctrinated by their preachers. But at the same time they are attracted and fascinated by these temptations, which are bound to affect their activist fervor. Other religions, in the face of these temptations, fought a losing battle.

We need to remember that it was only a short time between Islam's primitive beginnings in the Arabian desert and the splendor and luxury (and learning and poetry and architecture) of Harun al-Rashid's Baghdad, between the austerity of the Koran and the not-so-austere *Arabian Nights*. The pulse of contemporary culture is beating faster, but is it beating fast enough? For it is a race against time. The advent of mega-terrorism and the access to weapons of mass destruction is dangerous enough, but coupled with fanaticism it generates scenarios too unpleasant even to contemplate.

How likely are these attacks? Mega-terrorism has not yet arrived; 9/11 was a stage in between old-fashioned terrorism and the shape of things to come. The idea that weapons of mass destruction could and should be used goes back at least 150 years, first enunciated by Karl Peter Heinzen, a German radical who immigrated to America. Nineteenth-century Irish radicals considered using poison gas on the British Parliament. But these were fantasies of a few eccentrics, too far-fetched even for the science fiction writers of the day.

Now these have become realistic possibilities. For the first time in human history very small groups have, or will have, the potential, to kill a great number of people, to cause immense destruction, and perhaps to paralyze normal life for considerable periods. There are, and will be, small group of terrorists who will not be interested in negotiated settlements. Some might be satisfied with less than the annihilation of the enemy, but some more radical elements will always be eager to continue the struggle. They are not necessarily rational actors, and their motivation may not be political but apocalyptic.

Perhaps this scenario is too pessimistic, perhaps the weapons of mass destruction for whatever reason will never be used. A professor in Ohio has recently reassured the American public that the fear of terrorism is greatly exaggerated; if people will not be afraid of terrorism the struggle against it will be won. Experts say that the damage caused by dirty nuclear devices should not be overrated; but this, alas, is not the ultimate weapon. If weapons of mass destruction are not used it would be the first time in human history that arms, once invented, have not been employed.

In 1932 when Albert Einstein attempted to induce Sigmund Freud to support pacifism, Freud replied that there was no likelihood of suppressing humanity's aggressive tendencies. If there was any reason for hope, it was that people would turn away on rational grounds—that war had become so destructive that there was no scope anymore in war for acts of heroism according to old codes of behavior.

Freud was partly correct. War, at least between great powers, has become far less likely for rational reasons. But his argument does not apply to terrorism, motivated not by political or economic interests but by fanaticism with an admixture of madness. Not all terrorism will be like this, but some will be in this vein. Generally speaking, terrorism will last—not perhaps with the same intensity at all times, and some parts of the globe may be spared altogether. But there can be no victory, only an uphill struggle, at times successful, at other times not.

What about the study of terrorism? Books on terrorism are still published in their hundreds and articles in their thousands. It seems only a question of time until there will be doctorates and chairs in terrorism and counterterrorism, even though more recondite terms may be used. However, intellectually it is not a subject of great complexity, and it seems increasingly difficult to say anything new about it. New theories ought to be approached in principle with an open mind, but it is becoming increasingly difficult to fight off skepticism. The subject has a brighter future among novelists and Hollywood.

CHAPTER 8

Europe, 1945–2008

or, A Short Study in Hope and Frustration

The long summer of 2007 began early in Europe. High temperatures were registered in April and May throughout the Continent. In June, July, and August, as the schools were closing down for holidays, many millions went on their annual leave from north to south and from east to west. Paris and Rome as usual were almost empty in August, but there were long queues on the routes nationals, the *Autobahnen* and the *autostradas* (all of which had become more and more expensive); hotels in seaside resorts and mountain villages were fully booked; even those rowing on the rivers of Europe and the bikers and the ramblers in the forests complained about lack of solitude. The coffeehouses and bars were full and so were the local shops in the holiday resorts. The euro went from strength to strength (and continued to do so in 2008 until the fateful month of October). We had the good fortune to spend part of the summer in a village of Haute-Savoie attending a wedding, traveling through Upper Italy in all its glory, crossing the Brenner Pass and Innsbruck, and staying for a few weeks in our favorite resort, Elmau, a castle high up in the Alps facing the Zugspitze that has been turned into a hotel, spa, and cultural center. And there in the middle of forests near the border between Austria and Germany, in a lovely landscape with a strong sun shining in a blue sky, with some glaciers and remnants of snow still visible through the large windows, it was my assignment on a fine afternoon to open a debate about a recent book of mine entitled *The Last Days of Europe.* It could not have been more incongruous, given the time, the location, and the general mood. It seemed so far-fetched, so unlikely; I felt like a spoilsport and hoped for very few attendants. But many came, and the debate lasted for a long time. Some came from Duisburg, some from Antwerp. As far as they were concerned, they said, the last days of Europe (as they had known it) were already a thing of the past. They lived, they said, in a post-European age.

A Grand Tour of Europe

I was thinking back. When I left Europe at age seventeen, I had seen very little of it. I had been to Berlin and to Copenhagen and Prague, but Paris and London were wholly unknown territory. My curiosity was great but there was no money. My father had never been to France or Britain, my mother had never been outside her native country, and I doubt whether my grandfathers had ever even been to Berlin, the capital of the country in which they were born and spent their lives. There was in those days no particular reason to travel. It was expensive, and the urge to broaden one's horizon by traveling abroad was limited to relatively few people—and those among them who could afford it.

I began to travel in Europe and to explore it, more or less systematically, only in my thirties. For a while I regretted not to have known more of prewar Europe, but on second thought I realized that I may have not missed much simply because I would not have been prepared. I did not know the languages and knew very little about the culture and history of the countries I had missed.

In later years, as a historian I became familiar with the phenomenon known as the Grand Tour. Up to the late seventeenth century few Europeans traveled except if there was stringent necessity to do so. Traveling was uncomfortable, even dangerous. It was only in the years that followed that young British noblemen, having graduated from Cambridge or Oxford, usually accompanied by a somewhat older tutor, set out on a journey that led them to Paris and subsequently, sometimes by way of Switzerland, to Venice—at the time the most popular destination in northern Italy—and on to Rome. The Grand Tour took never less than year and frequently much longer. Diplomats traveled, but this was part of their job. So did scientists and philosophers—Gottfried Leibniz in Hanover, John Locke in London, or Anton van Leeuwenhoek in the Netherlands. Baruch Spinoza lived in seclusion and did not travel, nor did Isaac Newton, but in the generations after it became the fashion.

I learned that some of the leading lights of the eighteenth century went on the Grand Tour only in their thirties or later. Johann Wolfgang von Goethe was one such case. He settled in Rome, where he felt on the top of the world though he lived very modestly. His friend Friedrich Schiller could not afford foreign travel, but would *Wilhelm Tell* have been any better or more authentic had Schiller visited the scenes in Switzerland, Rigi, and Küssnacht? Adam Smith went to the Continent as a mentor to an English nobleman. Voltaire traveled a great deal when he was at the height of his European fame. Broadly speaking, the British aristocracy and upper middle class did travel, the French much less frequently because they knew that there was no life outside Paris.

The Russians were among the greatest travelers of all, following the example of Czar Peter I. Not Aleksandr Pushkin and Mikhail Lermontov, who were poor and died young, but virtually everyone in the generation after traveled. Nikolai Gogol went not only to Rome but even to Jerusalem. Leo Tolstoy went to Italy, and Fyodor Dostoevsky to Paris, London, and Baden Baden, which had a fatal attraction for him, for well-known reasons, far more than the Louvre or the British Museum.

A great-granduncle of mine named Aleksandr Borisovitch Lakvir made his name as the leading Russian travel writer of his day. He wrote the first systematic travelogue of the United States (including Cuba on his trip), but visits to America were a rare exception. Among the travelers from America was Mark Twain, who wrote, "I *hate* travel, and I *hate* hotels, and I *hate* the opera"; he also hated the wetness of the German weather and the damned cuckoo clocks and a great many other things. But for all this hatred he was a great traveler and *The Innocents Abroad* (1869) made him very famous.

Why do I dwell on the Grand Tour of ages past? It seems to me of some topical relevance that, I hope, will be clear later on. It also showed me that the fact that I had not been able to travel as a very young man had not been a disaster. When I began to travel in Europe after World War II, I was better prepared. I had been reading up not only in European history but I regularly followed the British, French, German, and Russian press so I was reasonably familiar with current affairs. In fact I had been commenting for a number of years on European politics but by necessity secondhand, for I had no immediate experience. A whole decisive dimension was missing; I was writing about people and places I had never seen. Now I would see them.

My first port of call in Europe in the early 1950s was Paris, the second Berlin, the third London. What should have been an extended visit turned into a stay lasting fifteen years. We kept an apartment in London where our children went to school, but we spent much of the time traveling all over Europe. Travel was not that easy in those faraway days. One needed entry visas for every country, and there were currency restrictions. I remember a Swiss consul in London who wanted to refuse me a visa; I had told him that I was to participate in a conference. He was Francophone, and to him "conference" meant giving a lecture for which I was presumably paid and this was strictly forbidden as far as foreigners were concerned. Traveling in the Soviet Union and Eastern Europe was not great fun. Tourism was virtually nonexistent and was not encouraged, and large parts of these countries were out of bounds to foreigners. One did not know until literally the last moment whether a visa would be granted, nor would one be told in what hotel one would stay. More often than not one's movement would be of interest to the local secret police, which, after all, had to justify its existence and budget. After Joseph Stalin's death in 1953 the danger of arrest was less, but it still existed. If the United States or Britain had arrested a Soviet spy there was always the possibility that the KGB would seize a tourist as a hostage.

The differences between the countries were enormous. The Berlin I had known, however imperfectly, had been destroyed. The rubble had been removed much more quickly than originally assumed (some experts thought it would take a century), but many quarters had not yet been restored and the city was of course divided. Passing from the Western sector to the East was, however, relatively easy until the wall was built. No physical damage could be seen in Paris. Nothing had been destroyed, but there had been little if any new building. France looked very much like what it must have been before the war—or what I remembered from the movies of the 1930s—with little shops selling eggs, butter, and vegetables late into the evening, little Renaults and Citroens, and many little restaurants (the big ones we could not afford). The great social changes had not yet taken place; the country seemed averse to change. But in France there was plenty of food and no rationing, whereas in Britain, meat and many other foods and commodities were rationed until 1954, and the food in the chain stores was barely edible. "Austerity" was the key word.

Culturally, most of the action was in Paris. Germany was preoccupied with more urgent problems, such as rebuilding its economy, and London seemed lethargic even though some of the great writers of a past age were still alive, the BBC was highly respected, and there were many theaters. The angry young men were still in the kindergarten. This was the sunset of the British empire. India and other major jewels in the crown had been lost, but Britain still had many overseas possessions. Most people I met believed that Britain was still a world power (despite temporary financial difficulties), that the Commonwealth was a reality, and that Britain did not really belong to Europe anyway. The people in the cities and countries of Europe were remarkably homogeneous. There was not as yet much tourism. I saw a few black people in Brixton in South London, but no Asian or Africans elsewhere. The great influx from the West Indies began only in the next decade.

When the war had ended and for a few years thereafter, there was a near consensus that Europe was finished—physically destroyed, mentally exhausted. So many young people had been killed. The economic situation seemed hopeless. Europe was starving and beset by inflation. It did not produce enough food and raw material to generate an economic revival, nor could it pay for imports. There was the famous dollar gap, the imbalance between the European economies and the United States. At this critical stage the Marshall Plan was launched. Recently some historians have argued that Europe would have recovered without the Marshall Plan; perhaps so, but it would have taken longer and I doubt there was that much time because there were also major political crises, especially in France and Italy. Without the economic recovery, who knows what would have happened.

Most European governments were reluctant to cooperate more closely, to liberalize trade, and in this respect American pressure was extremely important.

The idea of a European army was mooted and quickly turned down. But an impetus for at least some closer European cooperation was generated unintentionally by the Soviet Union. The Soviets had taken over Eastern Europe and turned its countries into satellites. Western European governments and societies, however tired and reluctant to engage in new cooperative ventures, understood that they would have to show some initiative if they wanted to maintain at least some independence.

This, very broadly speaking, was the general climate at the time, but there was already a cautious optimism in the air. The story of European recovery after World War II has been told many times, and there is no need to describe it in detail. The economic miracle was uneven. In the 1950s it was most striking in Germany, despite temporary setbacks in the world economy caused mainly by the Korean War. The miracle came only later in Italy; it proceeded slowly in France and was imperfect in Britain, even though the UK received more help from the United States than any other European country. "Most of our people have never had it so good," Prime Minister Harold Macmillan said in 1957, which was true, but Britain was still lagging behind the rest of Europe. A few Marxist intellectuals such as Jean-Paul Sartre were proclaiming that Europe was dying in convulsions, but they probably did not mean it literally, and in any case no one took them seriously.

Europe regained self-confidence especially during the years of "the thaw" in the Soviet bloc, following Stalin's death. The danger from the East was not yet over, but NATO provided a shield. In Western Europe there was political reconciliation between traditional enemies France and Germany. There was also increasing economic collaboration from which all benefited. Perhaps most startling was the progress made by backward regions such as Spain and Ireland.

Summarizing Europe's progress in 1990, I wrote that the postwar history of Europe read almost like an old-fashioned Hollywood movie with all kind of tensions and conflicts but a strikingly happy end. But I also wrote that history has no end and there were, as there always are, unlimited possibilities for things to go wrong.

A Historian's Assessment

I had become the historian of postwar Europe. *Europe since Hitler* was written in 1969, published in 1970, and there were subsequent editions, the last in 1992. This was followed by *A Continent Astray*, published in 1979, and eventually by *The Last Days of Europe*, published in 2007. *Europe since Hitler* ended on an optimistic note. I drew attention to the strange discrepancy between Europe's economic strength and its political and military impotence. But this discrepancy did not greatly bother European politicians or the public at large.

In 1972 the advent of a golden age was announced in the capitals of Europe. The conflicts of the postwar age seemed to have come to an end, a turning point in world affairs had been reached, peace had descended. But how quickly did the Euro-mood change. With the oil shock of 1973 the prices of raw materials shot up, and there were political, economic, and psychological repercussions. A vague feeling spread that democracies had become ungovernable. There was talk about a tragic new period of social and political regression, of the possibility that the whole European system might crumble. Leo Tindemans, the Belgian statesman commissioned to write a report about Europe's future, compared Europe to a house half-finished and without a roof; unless completed, it would be exposed to rain and storm, and sooner or later it would collapse. Shortly after he left office in 1974 West German Chancellor Willy Brandt told some of his confidants that Western Europe had only twenty or thirty years of democracy left; after that it would sink, engineless and rudderless, into the surrounding sea of dictatorship. Valéry Giscard d'Estaing, the French president, thought that the world was unhappy because it did not know where it was going. And should it find out, it would discover that it was going toward catastrophe.

I did not share these apocalyptic forebodings. I reflected that Europe had passed though countless ordeals in its long history and never suffered ultimate defeat. With all its periods of decline, European history was also full of stories of regeneration and rebirth; periods of pessimism and despair were frequently followed by eras of hope and new confidence. Perhaps the dangers seeming to threaten Europe from the outside would be less acute and formidable than they appeared at the time. What was so strange was the fact that the problems facing Europe—economic, political, and military—were by no means insurmountable, but that it was a matter of *aboulia* as I called it at the time. The term, coined by French psychiatrists in the late nineteenth century, referred to an absence of will for which there was no obvious explanation unless one agreed with those who saw it as a by-product of prosperity.

And so it happened that some of the problems of the 1970s simply vanished. Who remembers Eurocommunism these days? The economy picked up, though not at the rate of earlier decades. There was fresh movement toward European unity. More countries including the UK and Spain joined the European Economic Community (EEC), which later became the European Union (EU). A European Parliament met for the first time in 1979, and in accordance with the Single European Act (signed in 1986, effective in 1987), many barriers were removed.

But the main reason for this Euro-optimism was the end of the Cold War, the demise of the Iron Curtain, the coming down of the wall between West and East. The military danger had disappeared. Germany was reunited. The year 1989 was an *annus mirabilis*, and it was celebrated with great enthusiasm in Western capitals. Eventually there was a European passport and a European anthem: Ludwig van Beethoven's *Ode to Joy* with a Latin text—*Est Europa nunc unita*. The euro came into being (between 1999 and 2002), and despite some grumbling was adopted by most European countries. It became a strong currency.

By the year 2000 European leaders, meeting at a conference in Lisbon, were convinced that Europe was emerging as a shining light, an example to the nations. It was a paragon of international virtues, and its community of values and system of interstate relations would make it a leading force in the world. Much of the public agreed. Euro-optimists argued in their writings that Europe, not loved during the imperial era but by and large respected, had again become a model for the rest of humankind, with its regard for human rights, the rule of law, and peaceful coexistence. The topic was debated and written of by Europhiles in America, seriously discussed in books, lectures, and TV documentaries. An article by a Euro-optimist was titled "America Is the Past, Europe—the Future." The twenty-first century, it was proclaimed, would be the century of Europe.

Just as I had failed to share the earlier apocalyptic forebodings, I now failed to share what seemed to me an excessive optimism. I wrote in the last edition of *Europe since Hitler*—renamed in the meantime *Europe in Our Time*—that the jubilation was premature. And after a short while it appeared that very little remained of the erstwhile reformist impetus that had made Mikhail Gorbachev so popular at home and abroad. The period of transition to a lasting new order was likely to be troubled and prolonged. And with regard to the countries of Eastern Europe, "Tyranny had been defeated. But political freedom was not yet secure."

The danger from the East that had seemingly disappeared was by no means the only one that threatened Europe. In *A Continent Astray* I had mentioned the coming ecological crisis, the increasing cost of the welfare state, the fact that Europe found it more and more difficult to compete on the world markets, the growing dependence on energy supplies, and the faltering enthusiasm for closer European cooperation in some decisive fields. There was constant talk about common European defense and foreign policies, but there was no significant progress. Whenever a major international crisis occurred, it appeared that Europe was incapable of acting.

There was a rising tide of Euro-skepticism and Euro-pessimism, manifest, for instance, in the rejection of a European constitution in 2005. In October 2007 European ministers meeting in Lisbon agreed on a treaty of sorts, minus the constitution, but it, too, was turned down by the Irish electorate in June 2008, and the initiative came to a halt. There was a great deal of discontent for a variety of reasons. Above all the basic attitude was, What's in it for us? Among the various member states, in some more, in others less, national interests prevailed over the common interests. Was it perhaps unrealistic and unfair to expect more? The nation-states had developed over many centuries; how could one expect the emergence of a European consciousness and of European solidarity within a few decades?

Perhaps so, but in the circumstances how could commentators and observers talk about Europe as if it were a superpower, an important factor in world affairs? How could anyone claim that Europe would dominate the twenty-first century?

The Debate over Demographic Trends

I wrote *The Last Days of Europe* in 2007. The last days of Europe? It was, of course, not meant literally. Europe is not going to disappear with hardly a trace, like Pompeii and Herculaneum. But the Europe I knew, and my generation knew, is vanishing. There is a great deal of resistance against accepting this reality, but I suggest a tour through western Germany, northern France, Belgium, and Holland, with visits to schools and kindergartens. Politicians and political analysts seem not to have much interest in primary schools, but they might, alternatively, observe changes in the streets from the windows of their cars or, better yet, read the publications of the statistical departments of the United Nations (*World Population to 2300)* or of the European Union (*Eurostat*). The former argues that if fertility in Europe continues at the current low rates, Western, Southern, and Northern Europe will, "by the year 2300 each have only 28–30 million people, and Eastern Europe only 5 million. The European Union, which has recently expanded to encompass 452–455 million people (according to 2000 or 2005 figures) will fall by 2300 to only 59 million. About half the countries of Europe will lose 95 percent or more of their population, and such countries as the Russian Federation and Italy will have only 1 percent of their population left."

These predictions are so grotesque as to seem improbable, and indeed they might seem an idle enterprise. They cannot possibly take into account either great scientific or technological breakthroughs that will almost certainly take place in this time span, or great disasters that may happen. But predictions for 2050 are infinitely more solid; they concern the lifetime of those between the ages of twenty and thirty at the present time. According to the same UN predictions, in that year Ethiopia will have 171 million inhabitants, Egypt 127, Iran 105, Uganda 103, Turkey 98, Yemen 84, and for comparison, the Russian Federation, 101 (some 20 percent of them Muslim). All European countries will have a smaller and older population, and Europe's share of the world population will be much reduced.

When I went to school in the 1930s, I learned that London and New York were the most populous cities of the world, followed by Berlin and Paris. Today New York figures twelfth on the list, and Paris and Berlin are far, far down. Yangon (formerly Rangoon) is now more populous than Berlin or Paris, and Lagos much more populous, though most Europeans and Americans would have difficulty locating these cities on the map. In the year 1900 (when my father had just come of age), about 25 percent of the population of the globe was concentrated in Europe. In 2050 (when my grandchildren will be about to retire from work), it will be 7 percent.

What is the meaning of these demographic trends? Some have pointed out that demographic predictions have frequently been proved wrong; until about forty years ago the great fear was overpopulation. Given the fact that most of Yemen is desert, isn't it highly unlikely that the country will be able to sustain a population of 84 million, even with a high rate of emigration? Furthermore, all indications are that the birthrate is declining not only in Europe but in many other parts of the world, including China and India (though not significantly in Africa and the Middle East). In other words, it is not just the population of Europe that will be aging and shrinking, but world population generally. And given the fact that the resources of the globe are limited and finite, this trend should be welcomed rather than regretted.

In the eighteenth century, Thomas Malthus predicted starvation because population growth would outstrip the capacity of agriculture to produce enough food. But the Malthusian catastrophe that should have occurred a long time ago has not taken place, and the neo-Malthusian catastrophe will probably not occur either. However, while numbers may not weigh heavily with regard to quality of life and cultural achievements, they do count in world politics. During the late Middle Ages and early modern times Europe's center of gravity was in the Mediterranean area, and this had very much to do with the fact that Italy was more populous than Germany and more than twice as populous as England. The center changed radically in later periods, owing to fast growth in the north and stagnation or slow growth in the south. Equally, the growing importance of the United States vis-à-vis Europe over the past 150 years has very much to do with the fact that Europe had a population ten times as large as that of the United States (close to 25 million) in 1850, whereas today they are about equal. By the middle of the twenty-first century the United States could overtake the EU. One hundred years ago there were three times as many Europeans as Muslims; today the number of Muslims is twice that of Europeans. While the size of the population of a country or a continent is certainly not the only decisive factor, it is one of the crucial ones affecting standing among nations.

Demographers know that a birthrate of 2.1 is the magic figure, the rate at which the population reproduces itself. But beyond this there is not much agreement. Some believe that there is no room for doomsday scenarios such as the extinction of a people even if the birthrate in all major European countries has fallen below 2.1, and in many considerably below. Men and women will always want to have children for any number of reasons (or they will have sex and children will follow), and if they realize that their nation or their continent is in danger of not being able to sustain itself, economically and in other respects, there will be a self-correcting mechanism and more children will be born. In other words, the birthrate will not continue to decline, but will increase again once a critical point is reached.

However, the assumption that the birthrate cannot possibly decline beyond a certain low limit can no longer be taken for granted. Since contraception became common, the nexus between sex and procreation has been broken. Moreover, if the birthrate falls below 1.2, a dramatic recovery becomes difficult if not impossible. Some French observers proudly announced that the birthrate has gone up almost—but not quite—to reproduction level (but they cannot say how much of this refers to children and parents of French background and how much to others). Russian spokesmen have expressed their firm conviction that given the boom in their country, a rise in their very low birthrate could not be far behind (but there is no historical evidence that wealth produces more babies and poverty less).

It is clear that Europe is shrinking and aging. It is also clear that it will need many millions of immigrants to keep its economy going and its social institutions functioning.

The Debate over Immigration to Europe

Immigration *per se* is not to be feared. It has been a constant of human history. Karl Marx and Friedrich Engels described history in terms of class struggle, but even more it is the story of migrations. Migrations have provided fresh impetus to exhausted societies. In recent centuries, immigrants built the United States, Canada, and Australia. In recent decades, they have made notable contributions to the British and German economies as well as to others in Europe. As a writer in *The Economist* rightly noted in a review of *The Last Days of Europe* (May 3, 2007), European cities such as London and Berlin have acquired a new zip thanks to immigrants from around the world.

But there is a difference between the social role of computer experts from Bangalore or carpenters from Poland and other groups, say, from mountain villages in Anatolia or Pakistan, whose contribution to the economic and cultural life of the cities and countries of Europe has been negligible. Europe's problem is not that it is dependent on immigration but that it will be more and more difficult to obtain the kind of immigrants needed—workers who are qualified and industrious and enterprising. The computer experts from Bangalore are not particularly attracted to non-English-speaking countries.

At present, only 5 percent of qualified workers from Asia, Africa, and the Middle East go to Europe, whereas 85 percent go to the United States. On the other hand, there is a great and growing population pressure from the Middle East and from North and Tropical Africa, from the unemployed and often unemployable. The only major reservoir of educated people and skilled labor at the present time are political refugees from Iraq and Iran, but they, too, have shown limited enthusiasm to migrate to Europe. As for immigration from Tropical and North Africa, from the Middle East and Pakistan, there is great resistance in Europe. Nor is it clear in what way this immigration would solve Europe's economic problems.

But the fears that Europe risks becoming a Muslim-dominated Eurabia, adopting Sharia, are a vast distortion of the views of serious students of Europe's present state and future prospects. Nor is there widespread belief that (as a UN study says) if Europe will still be a continent of any consequence, it will be a black continent two centuries hence. I never liked the term "Eurabia" and never used it. More than half of the immigrants to the UK are not Muslim, and of the Muslims, most hail from Pakistan, not Arabia; they do not speak Arabic and there is in fact a rivalry (not to put it any stronger) between Pakistanis and Arab elements in the struggle for domination over Muslim organizations in Britain. Most of the Muslims living in Germany are Turkish, Alawite, or Kurdish, not Arab. Most of the immigrants in France come from North Africa, not the Arab countries. Some of the immigrants to Belgium and Holland arrived from Morocco, others from Turkey. There are common interests among various Muslim communities but also great differences, even in their attitudes toward religion. These facts have frequently been overlooked by the authorities in the countries of Europe and also the public at large, for which all Muslims, indeed all immigrants, are birds of a feather.

The term "Islamophobia" (first defined in 1997) is at least equally problematic if not fraudulent. There has been no fear of Islam as a religion in modern history, except perhaps in certain regions of India, the Balkans, or Nigeria, where clashes between communities have taken place (but precisely there "Islamophobia" has never been used). There has been and is "Terrorophobia," but Islam as a religion has suffered from a lack of interest rather than a deep antagonism in the non-Muslim parts of the world. The term is not even particularly liked by the Islamists who would prefer something indicating racialism rather than hostility toward their religion. However, their search for a more effective propagandist term has so far not been successful because Islam is a world religion and its believers include people from many peoples, countries, and races, so that an accusation of racialism would make even less sense than hostility toward Islam.

What of the argument that the number of Muslims in Europe is really small and that therefore they cannot possibly be of any political consequence in the foreseeable future? The precise number of Muslims in Europe is not known, and the estimates vary to a considerable extent. A certain proportion of European Muslims are illegal immigrants and do not appear in the official statistics, and in some countries, such as France, statistics referring to ethnic and religious background are banned. It is also true that the birthrate of immigrants from Muslim countries, while still higher than that of the native population, has decreased over the last decade and may well decrease further. What if Muslims in Germany will be 10–15 percent of the general population, those in Russia 20 percent, in a decade or two?

The Muslim communities are considerably younger, according to many estimates now constituting about 30 percent of the younger age cohort in many French, Belgian, and western German cities as well as in regions of other countries; by 2025 this could be the average for more European countries. Even now, every third child born in the UK is of foreign parentage, and the situation in large parts of Western Europe is similar. In the future, the percentage will probably be higher. Even now, children of Muslim and other overseas parentage are 30–45 percent in cities such as inner London, Manchester, Birmingham, Leicester, Cologne, Brussels, Antwerp, Duisburg, Nuremberg, Frankfurt, and Stuttgart. It could be more in some parts, less in others. Muslim communities are not evenly distributed in Europe, and in each country there are concentrations, usually in the bigger cities such as Malmo in Sweden and parts of the Midlands in the UK.

How meaningful are these figures? They would be of limited importance if this young cohort were reasonably well integrated in European societies. There have been no such problems with Chinese or Indian immigrants—or with the Poles, the largest group of immigrants to the UK in the early twenty-first century. Unfortunately, however, neither multiculturalism nor integration has worked well for the second and third generation of immigrants from Muslim countries, despite the fact that they have a better command of the languages of their host countries than of their countries of origin. But many of them reject the values and the whole culture even more emphatically than their parents and grandparents.

It is not a uniform picture. There are economic success stories; social and cultural assimilation does take place, but very, very slowly. Cultural and social change and advancement are possible, even likely, but it may take generations rather than years and decades. As a leading Berlin imam said, the road to 'the mosque is long and on the way we may lose half of them—referring to the young generation.

Losing the young generation to what? Not, unfortunately, to the positive aspects of Europe but to its negative features. The street gangs do not turn into study groups of Jürgen Habermas, Giorgio Agamben, the *New Left Review,* or Slavoj Žižek; they find more interesting (and often profitable) entertainment in other fields. Which leads to a more general question. Once the minority in a certain town or region turns into a majority, once schools consist predominantly of children of foreign origin, with what right will the authorities impose the teaching of standard curricula to a young generation that is not part of this cultural tradition and is not particularly eager to become part of it? There could be pragmatic reasons: the teaching of English in the UK may be necessary because English is the *lingua franca* for the various sectors of the Muslim community who otherwise do not have a common language. It is less clear why Turkish children in Berlin or the Ruhr should be taught poems by Goethe and the German romantics rather than Turkish literature. This is not just a question of religion, the Koran vs. the Bible. It is about as incongruous to expect young Pakistanis and Turks to sing "Land of Hope and Glory" or "Kein schöner Land in dieser Zeit" as a Palestinian Arab to participate in singing the "Hatiqva," the Israel national anthem with its reference to the dream of Zion that lasted two thousand years. (India faced a similar problem with "Vande Mataram," the national song that referred to a Hindu goddess and was therefore unacceptable to many Muslims and Sikhs; the controversy continues to this day.) In some European countries references to Christmas or Easter are no longer made in schools so as not to hurt the sensibilities of children of another religion; but does this go far enough? These children are taught by their religious teachers to reject the norms and values of a sinful Western civilization; they feel, according to all public opinion polls, primarily Muslim, not British or French or German. Why impose alien and unwanted traditions on them?

It could be argued that natives and newcomers may find common ground in gangsta rap and hip-hop, but this point in turn raises questions about the level of the European culture in the years to come. Social and cultural assimilation is bound to take place, but it will not be a one-way street and is likely to take generations rather than years. And one can only speculate what the result will be, except that it will be quite different from the civilization of old Europe and probably not very attractive.

My argument is that Europe is greatly changing: How can anyone dispute this who has recently visited Brussels, the capital of Europe (say the Marollen and Sint-Gillis quarters) or Copenhagen (say Noerrebro) or Paris (no directions needed)? These changes may turn out a wonderful thing as some observers believe, but there still are commentators from among the second generation of Euro-optimists arguing that there are no changes of great consequence, that this is an optical illusion or worse, the hysterical fantasies of extreme right wingers. Great is the resistance against admitting the obvious.

The Debates over Europe's Economic and Political Future

Certain arguments come up time and time again in debates over Europe's future. These include: But America faces very serious problems too; or, Why panic about Eurabia if the share of Muslims in contemporary Europe is no more than a few percentage points? or, Europe has faced many serious crises in its long history and has always overcome them.

For some Eurocrats, competition with America is an obsession. Europe's dependence on the United States for its defense was bound to generate ill will and estrangement. In 1979, when NATO decided to upgrade its missiles in Western Europe, there was a tremendous protest, not only among the left but also in the churches and other sectors of European society. It was clear that European and American interests no longer converged. When détente weakened following the Soviet invasion of Afghanistan and President Ronald Reagan set a confrontational policy, there was a great deal of anxiety. Following the end of the Cold War, anti-Americanism persisted and gained ground; some regretted that there had not been two losers in that war of nerves. Anti-Americanism flourished again in the first years of the twenty-first century with what many viewed as a short-sighted (or arrogant) and aggressive American foreign policy. America is bound to limit its foreign interventions in the years to come, but it is doubtful whether this will lead to a more peaceful world.

It has become common to point out America's serious economic, social, and political problems. There is also a heated debate in the United States about immigration, above all illegal immigration. But what comfort does all this offer? Every country, including those that have shown great economic progress in recent decades, has serious problems, perhaps even major crises, but Europe certainly will not benefit from the misery of others. On the contrary, in view of the heavy dependence of the European economies on exports overseas, a crisis elsewhere, be it in America or in Asia, will doubtless have a negative effect on Europe. A weaker America might provide some joy to anti-Americans in Europe, but such *Schadenfreude*, psychological satisfaction, would be of very short duration because it would expose Europe even more than it is now to pressures and extortion, from the main oil suppliers or in other respects.

Europe's economic recovery since World War II, however spectacular, was imperfect. Politically, and as far as defense is concerned, it has not been able to stand on its own. This would not have been of crucial importance if the world had entered a stage in which power politics no longer mattered, in which all are equal and conflicts are peacefully resolved by the United Nations. Unfortunately, weapons have not been beaten into ploughshares; on the contrary, they have become more deadly and widespread. Conflicts have not declined, and the passions underlying them have not subsided.

Politically, Europe has become weaker and weaker, and the obstacles to a common European defense and foreign policy seem insurmountable. Europe has been afraid to apply sanctions, be it to express indignation in the face of massive breaches of human rights or to avert future dangers. It has been unable to intervene in crises outside Europe and incapable of coping even with fighting in its own backyard—the Balkans—without American initiative and help. Most European governments (to echo *The Economist*) do not even have the courage of their lack of conviction. They are more in favor of a "political Europe" than their electorate, but only if they can get out of it as much as possible for their own country.

How independent can Europe's foreign policy be in the future, given its dependence on oil and gas from Russia and the Middle East? About 85 percent of Europe's oil and gas is imported. In these circumstances, one would have expected considerable efforts to agree on a common energy policy, but very little has been done in this respect. Even in economic issues such as agricultural subsidies there is no progress; the different national interests cannot be overcome. In these conditions, is it realistic to talk about European independence in world affairs?

Europe has very little moral confidence left. One shudders to think about its helplessness in the face of storms in the years and decades to come, the growing pressures it will be exposed to from countries less squeamish about power politics. Having been the center of world politics, it is in danger of becoming a political football. It will still be more important in world affairs than Latin America, but not by very much. Yet it will be more exposed and under greater pressure than Latin America.

On the other hand, a clear and powerful crisis could, under capable leadership, force the nations of Europe to realize that the old order is no longer workable and compel them to cooperate. They may realize that unless they forgo some or many of their national interests, they may lose not only whatever influence they still have in world affairs but also the domestic achievements of which they are proud—the comfortable life, the welfare state, the civilized norms, the human rights, and so on. There is no doubt that a strong Europe could be a positive force on the international scene. As it stands, however, speeches by European leaders concerning human rights, for instance, bring less impact than irritation, as in China and Russia. Such admonitions, however well meant, carry little weight if emanating from a position of weakness. In these conditions, Europe is well advised to keep a low profile, as *The Last Days of Europe* put it, not preaching sermons about human rights, democracy, and the need to do something about climate change.

What I argued in *The Last Days of Europe* was not that Europe was going to disappear, nor did I want to belittle past achievements of European societies in areas of freedom, human rights, social justice, and all the other things that make life in these societies so attractive. My argument was that Europe is much too weak to play a civilizing mission, even if the century we have just entered will be, as the Euro-optimists hope, one of peace and goodwill. Our new century will more likely be one of savage conflicts, however, even fanaticism, not to mention the spread of weapons of mass destruction. At such a time, there will be no significant role for a civilian or moral superpower. Europe will in all probability continue to be an important economic force, but politically a smaller Europe will count for less and less in a bigger world.

How prominently does Europe figure today, as these lines are written? It is a typical day, I believe, and a survey of the *New York Times* is revealing. There is a report about a tunnel in Switzerland and an item under the general heading "Europe" in the "In brief" section, but it is about Uzbekistan. And this is all. As these lines are revised, again there is not one major story dealing with Europe in America's leading newspaper. But there is a short, interesting report from London: the British foreign secretary announces that British diplomacy will shift away from the traditional European capitals toward Asia. He says that while the United States will have at least one more generation as a superpower, the century may become known as the Asian century.

Will Europe turn into a museum, a cultural theme park for well-to-do visitors from China and India, a Europe of tour guides, translators, and gondoliers, showing the rest of the world the attractive remnants of a highly developed civilization that once led the world? I posed the question in *The Last Days of Europe*—a fanciful scenario perhaps at the present moment. But tourism has already become one of the most important branches of the economy of many European countries, the main earner of foreign exchange with a steady, impressive growth rate. Such developments—certain regions or whole countries turning into a museum—are by no means unprecedented in history. Tim Blanning, a leading historian of early modern Europe, writes (in *The Pursuit of Glory*, 2007) that by the eighteenth century northerners were coming south, to Italy, "as if to a museum, their admiration for its past exceeded only by their contempt for its present." And he quotes an English visitor in 1778 (an officer in the Guards who also translated Voltaire) to the effect that Rome had once been "inhabited by a nation of heroes and patriots but was now in the hands of the most effeminate and most superstitious people in the universe."

The Process of History, the Prospects for the Future

The situation in which Europe finds itself may not be entirely Europe's fault. For many centuries Europe did play a leading role in world history, and no country or continent keeps such a role forever. A process of exhaustion sets in, leading to decline and sometimes to fall. Throughout history nations (and continents) have been rising and falling, and historians have been searching for explanations. Such reflections were abundant in ancient Rome. Among the Roman writers some blamed the change in climate—not enough rain in winter, not sufficient warmth in summer. In the eighteenth century, Edward Gibbon adduced a variety of reasons for the decline and fall of Rome—the loss of the old, traditional virtues, the love of pleasure, malice, ambitions, corruption, the impact of Christianity ("clergy successfully preached the doctrines of patience and pusillanimity"). Modern historians have adduced a number of other causes for the fall of Rome, such as a shrinking tax base that made it impossible for the central government to finance a sufficient military budget and the units needed to defend the empire.

Gibbon and his theories have become very popular in our time. Oswald Spengler, with his fascination for Italian fascism and other aberrations, has been less popular, but he also addressed decline—the decline of the West—which he saw as cyclical and inevitable. But elsewhere in *The Decline and Fall of the Roman Empire* Gibbon also makes an interesting observation: "There exists in human nature a strong propensity to depreciate the advantages and to magnify the evils of the present times." All the factors that led to the fall of Rome applied equally to Eastern Rome, and yet Byzantium continued to exist for another thousand years. So perhaps we are asking the less relevant question; perhaps it is more surprising that the Roman empire lasted as long as it did, not that it eventually collapsed.

Predictions about the impending demise of cultures and states are even more risky than predictions in general. There are many examples right from the beginning of historiography. Sallust is sometimes mentioned in this regard; he noted that all civilizations and empires grow old sooner or later and predicted a sad fate for his native Rome—probably in the near future, he said, in view of the laxity of manners, the loss of the old virtues, and the degeneracy of the ruling aristocracy. But his predictions were at the very least premature. Sallust died in 34 B.C., three years before the battle of Actium, which most historians now believe initiated the Golden Age of Rome's great empire, the flowering not only of arts and literature but an era of progress and prosperity and peace, an absence of war.

As the first millennium drew to a close there were horrible predictions as to the impending apocalypse, but the following two or three centuries were by no means worse than those preceding them. There are many other examples in the Middle Ages and modern times. France in the second half of the eighteenth century was thought by many visitors to be an enormous sink of iniquity and decadence, but it was followed by the French Revolution and Napoleon, who conquered almost all of Europe.

In 1870–71, following the lost war against Prussia, many books and pamphlets were published in Paris entitled *Finis Galliae,* or words to this effect, and there were good reasons to accept their prophecies: demographic decline, rise of alcoholism and other negative social trends, a mood of general pessimism, decadence in literature. France had not only fallen behind the other major European powers; it had no will left to compete. It was said France had no future. This mood lasted for about three decades and then, during the first years of the new century, the mood changed with a cult of youth, activism, sports, even militarism. The basic demographic facts had not changed, and there still was a lot of drinking, so there is no full accounting for this dramatic shift in the national mood. Perhaps it was just the emergence of a new generation bored with the pessimism of their elders. After World War I, French defeatism was caused largely by the terrible bloodletting of that war.

In recent decades, Europe has not suffered similar shocks. So why has it more or less abdicated as far as world politics is concerned? Why is it unwilling to accept Spengler's dictum that opting out of world politics provides no protection against its consequences? Europe, having been accustomed to giving orders during the imperial era, now has to request and even implore in its relations with other countries. Its governments have to be careful about whom they receive as guests, to whom they accord small favors, so as not to provoke the ire of China or the Muslim world. One thinks also of the British military personnel who were so much in a hurry to sell their story to the media about being taking captive by the Iranians, of the Dutch troops watching the Srebrenica massacre, of the German prime minister who without a cooling off period went to work for Valdimir Putin's Russia, of the French politicians with one foot in prison. Jugurtha, king of the Numidians, who knew the Romans well, having fought with them, described Rome as "urbem venalem et mature perituram, si emptorem invenerit"—a city for sale and doomed to quick destruction if ever it should find a buyer. This, broadly speaking, has been the impression concerning the West held by Osama bin Laden and other Islamists.

Why has Europe abdicated, and what are the prospects for a reversal of the process? What causes the loss of self-confidence? Is it, perhaps, as some have argued, the collective mood of academics who invariably blame their own government whenever conflicts arise? But this attitude is less pronounced in Europe than in the United States. Like all generalizations it is somewhat exaggerated, and the political importance of academics should not be overrated. Is it, as Spengler thought, an inevitable consequence of the process of aging—an old peoples' desire for a quiet life, unperturbed by anything that may interfere with their tranquillity and enjoyment? Is it the material well-being of a comfortable, postheroic society that strengthens the desire to be left alone, not to be entangled in the disputes of the world, to suppress all warning signs that might disturb the peace of mind?

Sometimes we can know causes, but often we do not. Generally speaking, the intensity of the *Wille zur Macht*, the will to power that preoccupied Friedrich Nietzsche, is not what it used to be. The world has become too large and world affairs too diffuse and complicated. World domination no longer seems very attractive. The United States has suffered great setbacks. China, Russia, and India want to be regional superpowers but no more. While communism is dead, Putinism is alive but does not aim at world revolution, only great power status.

Some spokesmen of the Asian-African century have insisted on the irresistible shift of global power from West to East. They are right, of course, inasmuch as the end of Western domination is concerned and the spectacular rise of Asian economic power. It is also true that their political power is increasing even though the heralds of Asian triumphalism tend to underrate the internal conflicts of these countries and the tensions between them. They also believe in the coming (if not the arrival) of an Asian high culture, of China and India taking over the flame of civilization from an exhausted Europe to become the standard-bearers of freedom, liberty, and democracy—albeit not as the West interpreted and practiced them. But these are, for the time being at least, engaging fantasies.

In view of so many wrong prophecies in the past, why give more confidence to present-day predictions, whether demographic or concerning the future of countries or continents? Was it not said by some of the experts that man would never be able to fly to the moon or that no more than five computers would ever be needed? The brief answer is that while there are never absolute certainties, not all prophecies have been wrong. Even some of Malthus's have been right (or almost right), even some of Spengler's. Our observations on the future of Europe rest not only on developments that may or may not take place but also on developments that have already happened.

The brief answer is that, in contrast to Spengler, who was convinced that he was able to look farther ahead than all the others, we do not know. There have been, as recorded all through this chapter, cases of sudden reversal and recovery.

Whether such a reversal is possible in Europe in present conditions, or whether the trends that have been described have progressed too far, no one can say for certain. As the critics of *The Last Days of Europe* who charged me with excessive pessimism might express it, hope is the thing left to us in a bad time, or to quote Apocryphs, What is past I know, but what is to come I know not.

Postface

Among the many proverbs we learned in first-year Latin, there was one according to which one should always act prudently and consider the end. In other words, Look before you leap. It is excellent advice in both private and public life, but, the historian will interject, it is not foolproof, because there is no real end. Actions, however prudent and farsighted, may have unintended and unwanted consequences.

To put it in a different way: even seemingly obvious lessons in both private and public life are not a key to success because each situation is different. It does not mean that commonsense and experience count for nothing. If there are no certainties there still are probabilities, and everyone is not (or should not be) his own historian or political scientist. The few guidelines we have cannot be ignored with impunity. Unfortunately, the work of the historian is made even more difficult because quite often what lessons there are cannot be bequeathed by teaching; people learn from suffering setback and disaster more effectively than from lectures or books.

One of the prominent themes in the 2008 U.S. election campaign was the call to stop being afraid, to regard the policy of fear one of the main dangers confronting us. Sterling advice, and it was given by Franklin Roosevelt in his First Inaugural Address. Roosevelt went even further and said, "The only thing we have to fear is fear itself."

Such advice has been applicable, for instance (if not taken too literally), to the behavior of stock exchanges from the days of the South Sea Bubble to the present age. In 1720, a British company's fraudulent, very exaggerated claims about its holdings and prospects in the South Sea Islands caused a major breakdown of the London stock exchange. When Sir Isaac Newton was asked about his predictions with regard to shares, he replied, "I can calculate the motions of heavenly bodies, but not the madness of people." Such comments could be appropriate even in our age—the utter lack of caution on the part of experts and the panicking once things started to go wrong. Among the Nobel Prize winners in the economic field in recent years there have been psychologists; perhaps there should have been a few psychiatrists as well. Of course, it is not only fear that we have to fear in the economy because, the hysteria quite apart, there are essential problems and things that are wrong with the economy, but it is certainly true that exaggerated fear has always had a negative impact.

But what about fear (or unease or suspicion) in world affairs? If only we could be less influenced by the policy of fear, say the apostles of hope. Perhaps I have moved in the wrong circles in recent years, but I have not come across such all-pervasive paralyzing fears. True, I have not come across much wild optimism either. The prevailing attitude seems to have been indifference, the feeling that whatever will be, will be.

I mentioned in the first chapter of this political education the optimistic tenor of the editorials all over the world when the twentieth century was rung in. This optimism can, of course, be traced back to a much earlier period. The humanism of the Renaissance comes to mind, with Desiderius Erasmus fervently believing in human flourishing, in tolerance, and in leaving earth a better place for those coming after. Or Ulrich von Hutten with his paean: "O Century! Science gains ground, spirits wax strong, barbarism is exorcised; it is a joy to live." Hutten advised barbarism to take a rope, leaving it open whether for hanging itself or for preparing for expulsion. "Die Luft der Freiheit weht," he proclaimed—"The air of freedom blows." Much later this became the motto of Stanford University.

A near-perfect example is the discourse, *On the Historical Progress of the Human Mind* (1750) given in Latin as customary, by Anne-Robert-Jacques Turgot. He became famous in later years as an economist, indeed as one of the founders of the study of economics: "Manners became more gentle, the human mind becomes more enlightened, isolated nations draw nearer to each other's commerce and politics connect all parts of the world, and the whole mass of the human race, alternating between calm and agitation, good and bad conditions, marching always, though slowly towards greater perfection."

It is interesting that Turgot, albeit an economist, did not mention economic progress among the reasons for his optimism. Today we are told that all over the world a rising tide lifts the mood, with GNP growth as the reason for greater personal contentment. But what may be true with regard to China and India does not apply to Europe and North America or, to be more precise, applies in reverse: increasing doubts prevail whether our children will be better off than the generation of their parents, and there are increasing fears of old age and poverty as the result of economic (and social) decline. There is rising discontent as the very wealthy have been doing exceedingly well whereas the middle class has been shrinking and declining. Rising inequality between rich and poor has been a growing problem in West and East. It is leading to political polarization and may even cause a return to the traditional class struggle, for the rising tide has been quite uneven. All this refers to China, the Middle East, and India as much as to

Europe and North America; it is interesting to what extent the economic progress achieved by China and India in recent years has blinded many outside observers to the great political and social problems these countries are bound to face in the future. *Enrichissez-vous* seems to be the slogan as it was in the nineteenth century, and politicians in West and East are in unseeming haste not to be left behind in this race—new Balzacs may appear in the near future to analyze and depict these passions.

There has been a striking expansion of the list of billionaires published annually by *Forbes Magazine*. The billionaires, too, suffered in the financial crisis of 2008, but inequality has not lessened. The trend with regard to greater democracy, freedom, and justice has been unmistakably negative, whereas only fifteen years ago worldwide democratization seemed to have triumphed. With the dawn of the new century the wave has turned; more and more countries are now considered "threatened democracies," and some in which prospects seemed quite good only recently can no longer be considered democracies however liberally defined. To blame corruption and an incompetent political leadership for this trend is to single out only one factor among several and probably not even the most important. All public opinion polls in Russia, in the Middle East, and in other parts have shown that greater democratization and political freedom figure high in the demands of a small minority but are regarded with indifference and even suspicion and hostility by the majority. Western political values are not necessarily those of other parts of the world, at least not at the present time. In America and Europe, too, there has been retreat, also among intellectuals, from the ideals of the Enlightenment. For some considerable time now the West has been facing a period of cultural exhaustion, a loss of self-confidence, in which all kind of strange flowers have blossomed and found their admirers. The growing discrepancy between superrich and poor is almost certainly bound to lead to growing political and social tensions in West and East, and it will add fuel to the antidemocratic impulses. Why this should have happened can be endlessly discussed, but in this field like in some others there are no conclusive answers.

Does this imply that we passed a historical turning point and that from now on it will all be downhill? For all one knows, fresh impulses may appear at some future date for reasons that cannot be foreseen or specified, making humankind move toward greater perfection such as envisaged by the sixteenth-century humanists, Turgot and his contemporaries.

As a very young man in Germany I read a new book by the great Dutch historian Johan Huizinga entitled *In the Shadow of Tomorrow* (1935). For reasons unknown it had been overlooked or not understood by Nazi censorship, was passed and enjoyed considerable popularity. Huizinga was deeply pessimistic about the days to come, an age of barbarism, humbug, and madness. He thought the world was facing an unprecedented cultural crisis; the state of popular thinking was full of decay and danger. We had more knowledge than ever before, he wrote, but infinitely less judgment. The critical spirit was vanishing, and the world was experiencing a massive (as one would now say) dumbing down.

Huizinga wrote during the heyday of rising Nazism, fascism, and Stalinism, and his pessimism was quite justified. World War II bore out much of what he had feared, but it was followed by a period of political and economic recovery. It is less certain whether it was followed by a lasting age of spiritual and cultural recovery. Moral and cultural relativism are as popular as ever, and the belief in timeless values weaker than ever.

At the present time it is difficult to see the impulses for a revival and for a renewal of the belief in human progress. Which takes me back to the starting point, namely that our lifetime, with all its achievement, did not coincide with the period of greatest happiness and contentment in modern history. The outlook is not brilliant either, and I see no reason to modify what little advice I have for my descendants not to nurture exaggerated hopes as far as the foreseeable future is concerned. I suspect they have reached this conclusion quite independently, without the benefit of my advice.

WORKS BY WALTER LAQUEUR

The following books and essays by Walter Laqueur form a record of his political education. Some of the discussions in this book are drawn from the publications listed here.

Europe and Germany

Young Germany: A History of the German Youth Movement. With an introduction by R.H.S. Crossman. New York: Basic Books, 1962.

Europe since Hitler. London: Weidenfeld & Nicolson, 1970. Published in the United States as *The Rebirth of Europe.* New York: Holt, Rinehart and Winston, 1970. Rev. ed., *Europe since Hitler: The Rebirth of Europe.* New York: Penguin, 1982. Also published as *Europe in Our Time, 1945–1992.* New York: Viking, 1992.

Out of the Ruins of Europe. New York: Library Press, 1971.

Weimar: A Cultural History, 1918–1933. New York: Putnam, 1974.

Fascism: A Reader's Guide: Analyses, Interpretations, Bibliography (ed.). London: Wildwood House, 1976.

"Europe: The Specter of Finlandization." *Commentary* 64 (December 1977): 37–41.

"Cowboys for the Kaiser." Book review of Karl May, *In the Desert, Winnetou,* and *Ardistan and Djinnistan. New York Times,* January 29, 1978.

"Letter to the Editor." *Commentary* 66 (October 1978).

A Continent Astray: Europe, 1970–1978. New York: Oxford University Press, 1979.

Political Psychology of Appeasement: Finlandization and Other Unpopular Essays. New Brunswick, N.J.: Transaction Books, 1980.

America, Europe, and the Soviet Union: Selected Essays. New Brunswick, N.J.: Transaction Books, 1983.

Germany Today: A Personal Report. Boston: Little, Brown, 1985.

Breaking the Silence: The German Who Exposed the Final Solution (with Richard Breitman). New York: Simon and Schuster, 1986.

"A Postscript on Finlandization." *Commentary* 95 (January 1993).

"Fin-de-siècle: Once More with Feeling." *Journal of Contemporary History* 31, no. 1 (January 1996): 5–47.

Fin de Siècle and Other Essays on Europe and America. New Brunswick, N.J.: Transaction Publishers, 1996.

Fascism: Past, Present, Future. New York: Oxford University Press, 1996.

The Last Days of Europe: Epitaph for an Old Continent. New York: Thomas Dunne Books/ St. Martin's Press, 2007.

The Soviet Union and Russia

Russia and Germany: A Century of Conflict. Boston: Little, Brown, 1965.

The State of Soviet Studies (ed., with Leopold Labedz). Cambridge, Mass.: M.I.T. Press, 1965.

The Fate of the Revolution: Interpretations of Soviet History. London: Weidenfeld & Nicolson, 1967.

"Confessions of a Self-Made Sovietologist." *Society* 26 (September 1989): 5–9.

The Long Road to Freedom: Russia and Glasnost. New York: C. Scribner's, 1989.

Soviet Union 2000: Reform or Revolution (with John Erickson). New York: St. Martin's Press, 1990.

Stalin: The Glasnost Revelations. London: Unwin Hyman, 1990.

Soviet Realities: Culture and Politics from Stalin to Gorbachev. New Brunswick, N.J.: Transaction Books, 1990.

Black Hundred: The Rise of the Extreme Right in Russia. New York: Harper Collins, 1993.

The Dream That Failed: Reflections on the Soviet Union. New York: Oxford University Press, 1994.

"Anti-Communism Abroad: A Memoir of the Congress for Cultural Freedom." *Partisan Review* 63, no. 2 (1996).

Jewish History, Israel, and the Middle East

Communism and Nationalism in the Middle East. London: Routledge & Kegan Paul, 1956.

The Middle East in Transition: Studies in Contemporary History (ed.). London: Routledge & Paul, 1958.

The Soviet Union and the Middle East. New York: Praeger, 1959.

"Israel, the Arabs, and World Opinion." *Commentary* 44 (August 1967): 49–59.

The Road to War, 1967: The Origins of the Arab-Israeli Conflict. London: Weidenfeld & Nicolson, 1968. Published in the United States as *The Road to Jerusalem: The Origins of the Arab-Israeli Conflict, 1967*. New York: Macmillan, 1968.

The Struggle for the Middle East: The Soviet Union and the Middle East, 1958–1970. Harmondsworth: Penguin, 1972.

A History of Zionism. London: Weidenfeld and Nicolson, 1972.

The Terrible Secret: An Investigation into the Suppression of Information about Hitler's "Final Solution." Boston: Little, Brown, 1980.

The Holocaust Encyclopedia (ed., with Judith Tydor Baumel). New Haven: Yale University Press, 2001.

Generation Exodus: The Fate of Young Jewish Refugees from Nazi Germany. Hanover, N.H.: University Press of New England, for Brandeis University Press, 2001.

The Changing Face of Antisemitism: From Ancient Times to the Present Day. New York: Oxford University Press, 2006.

Dying for Jerusalem: The Past, Present, and Future of the Holiest City. Naperville, Ill.: Sourcebooks, 2006.

Disraelia: A Counterfactual History, 1848–2000. Middle East Papers, April 1, 2008. Middle East Papers, occasional studies published by Middle East Strategy at Harvard University, is distributed exclusively as an e-publication: http://blogs.law.harvard.edu/mesh/papers.

Political Violence and Intelligence

Guerrilla: A Historical and Critical Study. Boston: Little, Brown, 1976.
Terrorism. London: Weidenfeld and Nicolson, 1977.
The Guerrilla Reader: A Historical Anthology (ed.). New York: New American Library, 1977.
The Terrorism Reader: A Historical Anthology (ed.). New York: New American Library, 1978.
A World of Secrets: The Uses and Limits of Intelligence. New York: Basic Books, 1985. Reprinted as *The Uses and Limits of Intelligence*, with a new introduction by the author. New Brunswick, N.J.: Transaction Publishers, 1993.
The Age of Terrorism. Boston: Little, Brown, 1987.
"Save Public Diplomacy: Broadcasting America's Message Matters." *Foreign Affairs* 73 (September/October 1994): 19–24.
The New Terrorism: Fanaticism and the Arms of Mass Destruction. New York: Oxford University Press, 1999.
No End to War: Terrorism in the Twenty-First Century. New York: Continuum, 2003.
"The Terrorism to Come." *Policy Review* 126 (August/September 2004).

Autobiography and Fictional Accounts

The Missing Years: A Novel. Boston: Little, Brown, 1980.
Farewell to Europe: A Novel. Boston: Little, Brown, 1981.
Thursday's Child Has Far to Go: A Memoir of the Journeying Years. New York: Charles Scribner's Sons, 1992.

Journals (founded and edited)

Survey (Soviet Survey)
Journal of Contemporary History
Washington Quarterly
Washington Papers

INDEX